THE **POLYVAGAL THEORY** IN THERAPY

A NORTON PROFESSIONAL BOOK

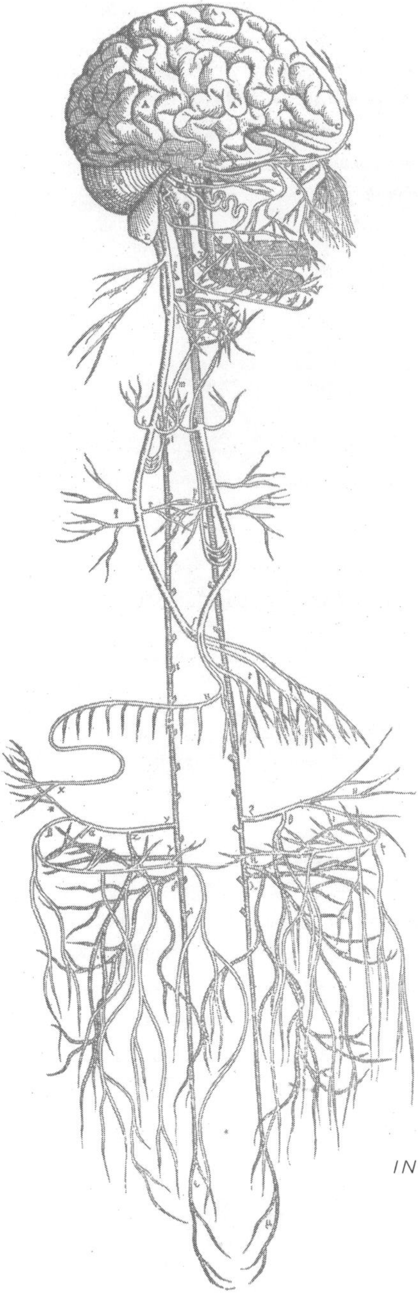

POLYVAGAL THEORY
IN THERAPY

ENGAGING THE RHYTHM OF REGULATION

DEB DANA

FOREWORD BY
STEPHEN W. PORGES

W. W. NORTON & COMPANY
INDEPENDENT PUBLISHERS SINCE 1923
NEW YORK | LONDON

Printed in the United States of America
First Edition

Manufacturing by Lake Book Manufacturing
Book design by Molly Heron
Production manager: Christine Critelli

Library of Congress Cataloging-in-Publication Data

Names: Dana, Deb, author.
Title: The polyvagal theory in therapy: engaging the rhythm of regulation / Deb Dana; foreword by Stephen W. Porges.
Description: First edition. | New York: W.W. Norton & Company, [2018] | Series: A Norton professional book | Includes bibliographical references and index.
Identifiers: LCCN 2017051973 | ISBN 9780393712377 (hardcover)
Subjects: LCSH: Autonomic nervous system. | Psychic trauma—Treatment. | Affective neuroscience.
Classification: LCC QP368 .D36 2018 | DDC 612.8/9—dc23 LC record available at https://lccn.loc.gov/2017051973

W. W. Norton & Company, Inc., 500 Fifth Avenue, New York, N.Y. 10110
www.wwnorton.com

W. W. Norton & Company Ltd., 15 Carlisle Street, London W1D 3BS

12 13 14 15 16 17 18 19

To Steve with gratitude for inviting me to join him on this great adventure, to my Polyvagal family who reminds me I'm not alone, and to Bob who fills my heart with joy every day.

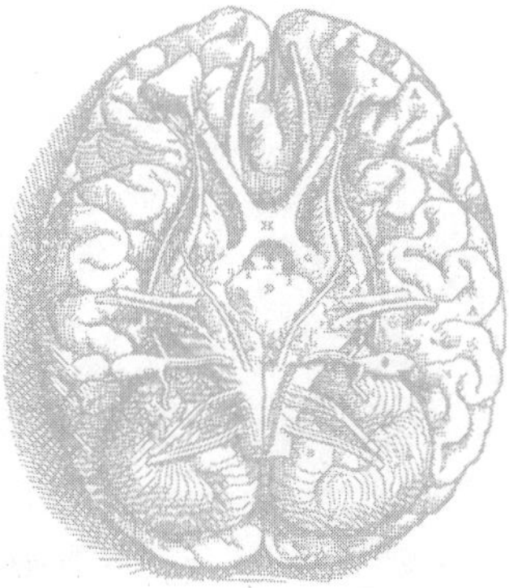

CONTENTS

FOREWORD

By Stephen W. Porges

Since Polyvagal Theory emerged in 1994, I have been on a personal journey expanding the clinical applications of the theory. The journey has moved Polyvagal concepts and constructs from the constraints of the laboratory to the clinic where therapists apply innovative interventions to enhance and optimize human experiences. Initially, the explanatory power of the theory provided therapists with a language to help their clients reframe reactions to traumatic events. With the theory, clients were able to understand the adaptive functions of their reactions. As insightful and compassionate therapists conveyed the elements of the theory to their clients, survivors of trauma began to reframe their experiences and their personal narratives shifted to feeling heroic and not victimized. The theory had its foundation in laboratory science, moved into applied research to decipher the neurobiological mechanisms of psychiatric disorders, and now through the insights of Deb Dana and other therapists is informing clinical treatment.

The journey from laboratory to clinic started on October 8, 1994 in Atlanta, when Polyvagal Theory was unveiled to the scientific community in my presidential address to the Society for Psychophysiological Research. A few months later the theory was disseminated as a publication in the society's journal, *Psychophysiology* (Porges, 1995). The article was titled "Orienting in a Defensive World: Mammalian Modifications of Our Evolutionary Heritage. A Polyvagal Theory." The title, crafted to cryptically encode several features of the theory, was intended to emphasize that mammals had evolved in a hostile environment in which survival was dependent on their ability to down regulate states of defense with states of safety and trust, states that supported cooperative behavior and health.

In 1994 I was totally unaware that clinicians would embrace the theory. I did not anticipate its importance in understanding trauma-related experiences. Being a scientist, and not a clinician, my interests were focused on understanding how the autonomic nervous system influenced mental, behavioral, and physiological processes. My clinical interests were limited to obstetrics and neonatology with a focus on monitoring health risk during delivery and the first days of life. Consistent with the demands and rewards of being an academic researcher, my interests were directed at mechanisms. In my most optimistic dreams of application, I thought my work might evolve into novel assessments of autonomic function. In the early 1990's I was not interested in emotion, social behavior, and the importance of social interactions on health and the regulation of the autonomic nervous system; I seldom thought of my research leading to strategies of intervention.

After the publication of the Polyvagal Theory, I became curious about the features of individuals with several psychiatric diagnoses. I noticed that research was reliably demonstrating depressed cardiac vagal tone (i.e., respiratory sinus arrhythmia and other measures of heart rate variability) and atypical vagal regulation of the heart in response to challenges. I also noticed that many psychiatric disorders seem to share symptoms that could be explained as a depressed or dysfunctional Social Engagement System with features expressed in auditory hypersensitivities, auditory processing difficulties, flat facial affect, poor gaze, and a lack of prosody. This curiosity led to an expanded research program in which I conducted studies evaluating clinical groups (e.g., autism, selective mutism, HIV, PTSD, Fragile X syndrome, borderline personality disorder, women with abuse histories, children who stutter, preterm infants). In these studies Polyvagal Theory was used to explain the findings and confirm that many psychiatric disorders were manifest in a dysfunction of the 'ventral' vagal complex, which included lower cardiac vagal tone and the associated depressed function of the striated muscles of the face and head resulting in flat facial affect and lack of prosody.

In 2011 the studies investigating clinical populations were summarized in a book published by Norton, *The Polyvagal Theory: Neurophysiological Foundations of Emotions, Attachment, Communication, and Self-Regulation.* The publication enabled Polyvagal Theory to become accessible to clinicians; the theory was no longer limited to the digital libraries linked to universities and research institutes. The publication of the book stimulated great interest within the clinical community and especially with traumatologists. I had not anticipated that the main impact of the theory would be to provide plausible neurophysiological explanations for experiences described by individuals who had experienced trauma. For these individuals, the theory provided an understanding of how, after experiencing life threat, their neural reactions were retuned towards a defensive bias and they lost the resilience to return to a state of safety.

This prompted invitations to talk at clinically oriented meetings and to conduct workshops on Polyvagal Theory for clinicians. During the past few years, there has been an expanding awareness of Polyvagal Theory across several clinical areas. This welcoming by the clinical community identified limitations in my knowledge. Although I could talk to clinicians and deconstruct their presentations of clinical cases into constructs described by the theory, I was *not* a clinician. I was limited in how I related the theory to clinical diagnosis, treatment, and outcome.

During this period, I met Deb Dana. Deb is a talented therapist with astute insights into trauma and a desire to integrate Polyvagal Theory into clinical treatment. For Deb, Polyvagal Theory provided a language of the body that paralleled her feelings and intuitive connectedness with her clients. The theory provided a syntax to label her and her client's experiences, which were substantiated by documented neural mechanisms. Functionally, the theory became a lens or a perspective in how she supported her clients and how she reacted to her clients. The theory transformed the client's narrative from a documentary to a pragmatic quest for safety with an implicit bodily drive to survive. As the theory infused her clinical model, she began to develop a methodology to train other therapists. The product of this transition is the current book. In *Polyvagal Theory in Therapy*, Deb Dana brilliantly transforms a neurobiologically based theory into clinical practice and Polyvagal Theory comes alive.

References

Porges, S. W. (1995). Orienting in a defensive world: Mammalian modifications of our evolutionary heritage. A Polyvagal Theory. *Psychophysiology, 32*(4), 301–318.

Porges, S. W. (2011). *Norton Series on Interpersonal Neurobiology. The Polyvagal Theory: Neurophysiological foundations of emotions, attachment, communication, and self-regulation.* New York, NY: Norton.

ACKNOWLEDGMENTS

Embarking on this journey, I discovered that in order to write I needed to step out of the flow of my ordinary life. And so, my husband and I moved to an ancient stone cottage in Sainte-Marie-du-Mont, France for a month. It was there I found my writing rhythm, moving in harmony with the ringing of the bells from the cathedral across the street that have marked the passage of time since the 11th century. The bells became a mantra for me as the words came, pages filled, and the first part of the book took shape. The rest of the book was written in Kennebunkport, Maine in my house near the sea at the edge of the woods. The trees and the ocean offered their steady presence, guiding me back into regulation when the challenge of finding the right words felt overwhelming.

Although writing is a solitary experience, in the process of writing this book I never felt alone. My family, friends, and colleagues listened patiently as my understanding of how to bring Polyvagal Theory into everyday application evolved. Their unfailing belief in my work, and in my ability to share it through my writing, made this book possible. Many years ago Linda Graham recognized my dream of writing about my work and gave me a pin with the words "Future Author" which still sits on my desk. Throughout the months of writing, Linda was a trusted guide generously sharing her wisdom as a successful author. I turned to Tina Zorger, my training companion for over a decade and my invaluable assistant in the Rhythm of Regulation training series, when I needed a sounding board. She celebrated my successes and asked the important questions that challenged me to look deeper. Deb Grant partnered with me in creating the Polyvagal PlayLab giving me a place to play with the theory and a stepping off point for creating the Rhythm of Regulation series which is at the heart of this book. I owe a special thanks to the therapists in my first three Rhythm of Regulation trainings who were so willing to be my test pilots and take on the challenges of discovering their own autonomic stories and experimenting with a new way of clinical practice. I am deeply grateful to my clients. This book would not have come to life without their courage to dive into uncharted waters with me and explore together how to look through the lens of the autonomic nervous system.

My life changed when I read Stephen Porges's book, *The Polyvagal Theory*. Suddenly the world made sense to me in a new way. My life changed again when I met Steve. He is a special human being who embodies the qualities of brilliance and kindness, a rare combination and one to be treasured. Steve welcomed me into his world and supported me in bringing his work into clinical application. His invitation to live life from a Polyvagal perspective is woven into every chapter.

And as always, I want to acknowledge with great love, my husband Bob who believed in me and supported me every step of the way. His delight when I finished a section and his unwavering presence when I came to a standstill made it possible to write this book. He reminded me that the words were there and reassured me that I would find them.

This book would not have become a reality without Caroline Pincus, a wonderful book midwife who encouraged me to bring this book into the world, and Deborah Malmud, my incredible editor at Norton who said yes to my question about the possibility of writing *The Polyvagal Theory in Therapy* and then guided me every step of the way. Working with her team at Norton was a joy.

My days have been graced by the countless people who came into my life while I was on my writer's journey. To each of you I offer a deep bow of gratitude…

INTRODUCTION

When I teach Polyvagal Theory to colleagues and clients, I tell them they are learning about the science of safety—the science of feeling safe enough to fall in love with life and take the risks of living. Polyvagal Theory provides a physiological and psychological understanding of how and why clients move through a continual cycle of mobilization, disconnection, and engagement. Through the lens of Polyvagal Theory, we see the role of the autonomic nervous system as it shapes clients' experiences of safety and affects their ability for connection.

The autonomic nervous system responds to the challenges of daily life by telling us not *what* we are or *who* we are but *how* we are. The autonomic nervous system manages risk and creates patterns of connection by changing our physiological state. These shifts are slight for many people, and, in the moments when large state changes happen, their system is resilient enough to help them return to a regulated state. Trauma interrupts the process of building the autonomic circuitry of safe connection and sidetracks the development of regulation and resilience. Clients with trauma histories often experience more intense, extreme autonomic responses, which affects their ability to regulate and feel safe in relationships. Polyvagal Theory helps therapists understand that the behaviors of their clients are autonomic actions in service of survival—adaptive responses ingrained in a survival story that is entered into automatically.

Trauma compromises our ability to engage with others by replacing patterns of connection with patterns of protection. If unresolved, these early adaptive survival responses become habitual autonomic patterns. Therapy through a polyvagal lens, supports clients in repatterning the ways their autonomic nervous systems operate when the drive to survive competes with the longing to connect with others.

This book is designed to help you bring Polyvagal Theory into your therapy practice. It provides a comprehensive approach to intervention by presenting ways to map autonomic response and shape the autonomic nervous system for safety. With this book, you will learn Polyvagal Theory and use worksheets and experiential exercises to apply that knowledge to the nuts and bolts of practice.

Section I, "Befriending the Nervous System," introduces the science of connection and creates basic fluency in the language of Polyvagal Theory. These chapters present the essential elements of Polyvagal Theory, building a solid foundation of knowledge and setting the stage for work with the clinical applications presented in the remainder of the book.

Section II, "Mapping the Nervous System," focuses on learning to recognize patterns of response. The worksheets presented in these chapters create the ability to predictably identify individual placement along the autonomic hierarchy.

Section III, "Navigating the Nervous System," builds on the newly gained expertise in identifying autonomic states and adds the next steps in the process: learning to track response patterns, recognize triggers, and identify regulating resources. A variety of "attending" practices are presented to support a new way of attuning to patterns of action, disconnection, and engagement.

Section IV, "Shaping the Nervous System," explores the use

of passive and active pathways to tone the autonomic nervous system and reshape it toward increased flexibility of response. These chapters offer ways to engage the regulating capacities of the ventral vagal system through both in-the-moment interventions and practices that begin to shift the system toward finding safety in connection.

Through the ideas presented in this book, you will discover how using Polyvagal Theory in therapy will increase the effectiveness of your clinical work with trauma survivors. In this process, not only will your therapy practice change, but also your way of seeing and being in the world will change. My personal experience, and my experience teaching Polyvagal Theory to therapists and clients, is that there is a “before-and-after” quality to learning this theory. Once you understand the role of the autonomic nervous system in shaping our lives, you can never again not see the world through that lens.

THE POLYVAGAL THEORY IN THERAPY

SECTION I

BEFRIENDING THE NERVOUS SYSTEM

The greatest thing then, in all education, is to make our nervous system our ally as opposed to our enemy.

—WILLIAM JAMES

If you do a Google search for "Polyvagal Theory," more than 500,000 results pop up, and if you search for "Stephen Porges," more than 150,000 results appear. Polyvagal Theory has made a remarkable journey from a relatively unknown and controversial theory to its wide acceptance today in the field of psychotherapy.

Polyvagal Theory traces its origins to 1969 and Dr. Porges's early work with heart rate variability and his "vision that monitoring physiological state would be a helpful guide to the therapist during the clinical interaction" (Porges, 2011a, p. 2). As Dr. Porges wrote, at that time he "looked forward to new discoveries applying these technologies to clinical populations. I had no intention of developing a theory" (p. 5). Polyvagal Theory was born out of the question how one nerve—the vagus nerve—and its tone, which Dr. Porges was measuring, could be both a marker of resilience and a risk factor for newborns. Through solving this puzzle, now known as the *vagal paradox*, Dr. Porges created the Polyvagal Theory.

Three organizing principles are at the heart of Polyvagal Theory.

— **Hierarchy:** The autonomic nervous system responds to sensations in the body and signals from the environment through three pathways of response. These pathways work in a specified order and respond to challenges in predictable ways. The three pathways (and their patterns of response), in evolutionary order from oldest to newest, are the dorsal vagus (immobilization), the sympathetic nervous system (mobilization), and the ventral vagus (social engagement and connection).

— **Neuroception:** This is the term coined by Dr. Porges to describe the ways our autonomic nervous system responds to cues of safety, danger, and life-threat from within our bodies, in the world around us, and in our connections to others. Different from perception, this is "detection without awareness" (Porges, n.d.), a subcortical experience happening far below the realm of conscious thought.

— **Co-regulation:** Polyvagal Theory identifies co-regulation as a biological imperative: a need that must be met to sustain life. It is through reciprocal regulation of our autonomic states that we feel safe to move into connection and create trusting relationships.

We can think of the autonomic nervous system as the foundation upon which our lived experience is built. This biological resource (Kok et al., 2013) is the neural platform that is beneath every experience. How we move through the world—

turning toward, backing away, sometimes connecting and other times isolating—is guided by the autonomic nervous system. Supported by co-regulating relationships, we become resilient. In relationships awash in experiences of misattunement, we become masters of survival. In each of our relationships, the autonomic nervous system is "learning" about the world and being toned toward habits of connection or protection.

Hopefulness lies in knowing that while early experiences shape the nervous system, ongoing experiences can reshape it. Just as the brain is continually changing in response to experiences and the environment, our autonomic nervous system is likewise engaged and can be intentionally influenced. As individual nervous systems reach out for contact and co-regulation, incidents of resonance and misattunement are experienced as moments of connection or moments of protection. The signals conveyed, the cues of safety or danger sent from one autonomic nervous system to another, invite regulation or increase reactivity. In work with couples, it is easy to observe the increased reactivity that occurs when a disagreement quickly escalates and cues of danger communicated between the two nervous systems trigger each partner's need for protection. In contrast, the attunement of the therapist–client relationship relays signals of safety and an autonomic invitation for connection.

Humans are driven to want to understand the "why" of behaviors. We attribute motivation and intent and assign blame. Society judges trauma survivors by their actions in times of crisis. We still too often blame the victim if they didn't fight or try to escape but instead collapsed into submission. We make a judgment about what someone did that leads to a belief about who they are. Trauma survivors themselves often think "It's my fault" and have a harsh inner critic who mirrors society's response. In our daily interactions with family, friends, colleagues, and even the casual exchanges with strangers that define our days, we evaluate others by the ways they engage with us.

Polyvagal Theory gives therapists a neurophysiological framework to consider the reasons why people act in the ways they do. Through a polyvagal lens, we understand that actions are automatic and adaptive, generated by the autonomic nervous system well below the level of conscious awareness. This is not the brain making a cognitive choice. These are autonomic energies moving in patterns of protection. And with this new awareness, the door opens to compassion.

A working principle of the autonomic nervous system is "every response is an action in service of survival." No matter how incongruous an action may look from the outside, from an autonomic perspective it is always an adaptive survival response. The autonomic nervous system doesn't make a judgment about good and bad; it simply acts to manage risk and seek safety. Helping clients appreciate the protective intent of their autonomic responses begins to reduce the shame and self-blame that trauma survivors so often feel. When offered the lens of Polyvagal Theory, clients become curious about the cues of safety and danger their nervous systems are sensing and begin to understand their responses as courageous survival responses that can be held with compassion.

Trauma-trained therapists are taught that a foundation of effective work is understanding "perception is more important than reality." Personal perception, not the actual facts of an experience, creates posttraumatic consequences. Polyvagal Theory demonstrates that even before the brain makes meaning of an incident, the autonomic nervous system has assessed the environment and initiated an adaptive survival response. Neuroception precedes perception. Story follows state. Through a polyvagal framework, the important question "What happened?" is explored not to document the details of an event but to learn about the autonomic response. The clues to a client's present-time suffering can be found in their autonomic response history.

The goal of therapy is to engage the resources of the ventral vagus to recruit the circuits that support the prosocial behaviors of the Social Engagement System (Porges, 2009a, 2015a). The Social Engagement System is our "face-heart" connection, created from the linking of the ventral vagus (heart) and the striated muscles in our face and head that control how we look (facial expressions), how we listen (auditory), and how we speak (vocalization) (Porges, 2017a). In our interactions it is through the Social Engagement System that we send and search for cues of safety. In both the therapy setting and the therapy session, creating the conditions for a physiological state that supports an active Social Engagement System is a necessary element. "If we are not safe, we are chronically in a state of evaluation and defensiveness" (Porges, 2011b, p. 14). It is a ventral vagal state and a neuroception of safety that bring the possibility for connection, curiosity, and change. A polyvagal approach to therapy follows the four R's:

- Recognize the autonomic state.
- Respect the adaptive survival response.
- Regulate or co-regulate into a ventral vagal state.
- Re-story.

The following "beginner's guide" is offered as a reader-friendly guide for therapists and an easy way to introduce clients to Polyvagal Theory.

A BEGINNER'S GUIDE TO POLYVAGAL THEORY

We come into the world wired to connect. With our first breath, we embark on a lifelong quest to feel safe in our bodies, in our environments, and in our relationships with others. The autonomic nervous system is our personal surveillance system, always on guard, asking the question "Is this safe?" Its goal is to protect us by sensing safety and risk, listening moment by moment to what is happening in and around our bodies and in the connections we have to others.

This listening happens far below awareness and far away from our conscious control. Dr. Porges, understanding that this is not awareness that comes with perception, coined the term *neuroception* to describe the way our autonomic nervous system scans for cues of safety, danger, and life-threat without involving the thinking parts of our brain. Because we humans are meaning-making beings, what begins as the wordless experiencing of neuroception drives the creation of a story that shapes our daily living.

The Autonomic Nervous System

The autonomic nervous system is made up of two main branches, the sympathetic and the parasympathetic, and responds to signals and sensations via three pathways, each with a characteristic pattern of response. Through each of these pathways, we react "in service of survival."

The sympathetic branch is found in the middle part of the spinal cord and represents the pathway that prepares us for action. It responds to cues of danger and triggers the release of adrenaline, which fuels the fight-or-flight response.

In the parasympathetic branch, Polyvagal Theory focuses on two pathways traveling within a nerve called the vagus. *Vagus,* meaning "wanderer," is aptly named. From the brain stem at the base of the skull, the vagus travels in two directions: downward through the lungs, heart, diaphragm, and stomach and upward to connect with nerves in the neck, throat, eyes, and ears.

The vagus is divided into two parts: the ventral vagal pathway and the dorsal vagal pathway. The ventral vagal pathway responds to cues of safety and supports feelings of being safely engaged and socially connected. In contrast, the dorsal vagal pathway responds to cues of extreme danger. It takes us out of connection, out of awareness, and into a protective state of collapse. When we feel frozen, numb, or "not here," the dorsal vagus has taken control.

Dr. Porges identified a hierarchy of response built into our autonomic nervous system and anchored in the evolutionary development of our species. The origin of the dorsal vagal pathway of the parasympathetic branch and its immobilization response lies with our ancient vertebrate ancestors and is the oldest pathway. The sympathetic branch and its pattern of mobilization, was next to develop. The most recent addition, the ventral vagal pathway of the parasympathetic branch brings patterns of social engagement that are unique to mammals.

When we are firmly grounded in our ventral vagal pathway, we feel safe and connected, calm and social. A sense (neuroception) of danger can trigger us out of this state and backwards on the evolutionary timeline into the sympathetic branch. Here we are mobilized to respond and take action. Taking action can help us return to the safe and social state. It is when we feel as though we are trapped and can't escape the danger that the dorsal vagal pathway pulls us all the way back to our evolutionary beginnings. In this state we are immobilized. We shut down to survive. From here, it is a long way back to feeling safe and social and a painful path to follow.

The Autonomic Ladder

Let's translate our basic knowledge of the autonomic nervous system into everyday understanding by imagining the autonomic nervous system as a ladder. How do our experiences change as we move up and down the ladder?

The Top of the Ladder

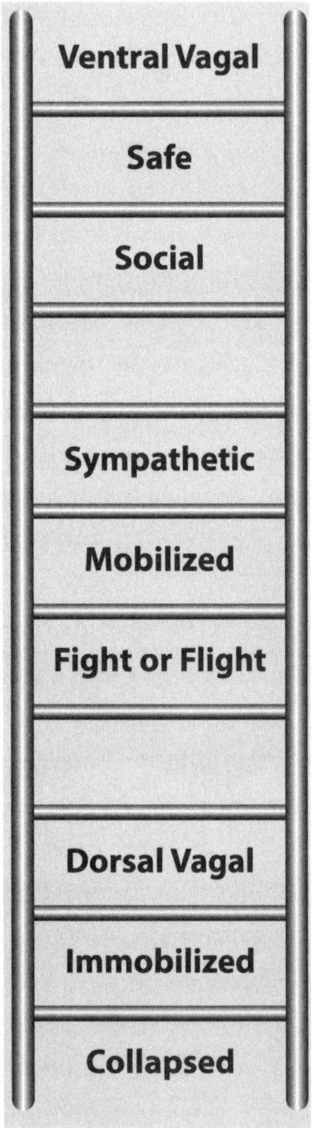

What would it feel like to be safe and warm? Arms strong but gentle. Snuggled close, joined by tears and laughter. Free to share, to stay, to leave . . .

Safety and connection are guided by the evolutionarily newest part of the autonomic nervous system. Our social engagement system is active in the ventral vagal pathway of the parasympathetic branch. In this state, our heart rate is regulated, our breath is full, we take in the faces of friends, and we can tune in to conversations and tune out distracting noises. We see the "big picture" and connect to the world and the people in it. I might describe myself as happy, active, interested and the world as safe, fun, and peaceful. From this ventral vagal place at the top of the autonomic ladder, I am connected to my experiences and can reach out to others. Some of the daily living experiences of this state include being organized, following through with plans, taking care of myself, taking time to play, doing things with others, feeling productive at work, and having a general feeling of regulation and a sense of management. Health benefits include a healthy heart, regulated blood pressure, a healthy immune system decreasing my vulnerability to illness, good digestion, quality sleep, and an overall sense of well-being.

Moving Down the Ladder

Fear is whispering to me and I feel the power of its message. Move, take action, escape. No one can be trusted. No place is safe . . .

The sympathetic branch of the autonomic nervous system activates when we feel a stirring of unease—when something triggers a neuroception of danger. We go into action. Fight or flight happens here. In this state, our heart rate speeds up, our breath is short and shallow, we scan our environment looking for danger—we are "on the move." I might describe myself as anxious or angry and feel the rush of adrenaline that makes it hard for me to be still. I am listening for sounds of danger and don't hear the sounds of friendly voices. The world may feel dangerous, chaotic, and unfriendly. From this place of sympathetic mobilization—a step down the autonomic ladder and backward on the evolutionary timeline I may believe, "The world is a dangerous place and I need to protect myself from harm." Some of the daily living problems can be anxiety, panic attacks, anger, inability to focus or follow through, and distress in relationships. Health consequences can include heart disease; high blood pressure; high cholesterol; sleep problems; weight gain; memory impairment; headache; chronic neck, shoulder, and back tension; stomach problems; and increased vulnerability to illness.

The Bottom of the Ladder

I'm far away in a dark and forbidding place. I make no sound. I am small and silent and barely breathing. Alone where no one will ever find me . . .

Our oldest pathway of response, the dorsal vagal pathway of the parasympathetic branch, is the path of last resort. When all else fails, when we are trapped and action taking doesn't work, the "primitive vagus" takes us into shutdown, collapse, and dissociation. Here at the very bottom of the autonomic ladder, I am alone with my despair and escape into not knowing, not feeling, almost a sense of not being. I might describe myself as hopeless, abandoned, foggy, too tired to think or act and the world as empty, dead, and dark. From this earliest place on the evolutionary timeline, where my mind and body have moved into conservation mode, I may believe, "I am lost and no one will ever find me." Some of the daily living problems can be dissociation, problems with memory, depression, isolation, and no energy for the tasks of daily living. Health consequences of this state can include chronic fatigue, fibromyalgia, stomach problems, low blood pressure, type 2 diabetes, and weight gain.

Daily Movements on the Ladder

Now that we've explored each of the places on the autonomic ladder, let's consider how we move up and down. Our preferred place is at the top of the ladder. The ventral vagal state is hopeful and resourceful. We can live, love, and laugh by ourselves and with others. This is not a place where everything is wonderful or a place without problems. But it is a place where we have the ability to acknowledge distress and explore options, to reach out for support and develop organized responses. We move down the ladder into action when we are triggered into a sense of unease—of impending danger. We hope that our action taking here will give us enough space to take a breath and climb back up the ladder to the place of safety and connection. It is when we fall all the way down to the bottom rungs that the safety and hope at the top of the ladder feel unreachable.

What might a real-life example of moving up and down the autonomic ladder look like? Consider the following two scenarios.

I am driving to work in the morning listening to the radio and enjoying the beginning of the day (top of the ladder) when a siren sounds behind me (quick move down the ladder). I feel my heart race and immediately worry that I've done something wrong (staying in my spot down the ladder). I pull over and the police car rushes by me. I pull back out and resume my drive to work and feel my heart begin to return to its normal speed (moving up the ladder). By the time I get to work, I have forgotten about the incident and am ready for my day (back at the top of the ladder).

I am having dinner with friends enjoying the conversation and the fun of being out with people I like (top of the ladder). The conversation turns to vacations, and I start comparing my situation to my friends' situations. I begin to feel angry that I can't afford a vacation, that my job doesn't pay enough, that I have so many unpaid bills I'll never be able to take a vacation (moving down the ladder). I sit back and watch as my friends continue to talk about trips and travel planning. I disconnect from the conversation and begin to feel invisible as the talk goes on around me (shutting down and moving to the bottom of the ladder). The evening ends with my friends not noticing my silence and with me feeling like a misfit in the group (stuck at the bottom of the ladder). I go home and crawl into bed (the only place I know now is the bottom of the ladder). The next morning, I wake up and don't want to get up or go to work (still at the bottom of the ladder). I worry I'll get fired if I don't show up and drag myself out of bed (a bit of energy and beginning of movement up the ladder). I am late to work. My boss comments on my lateness, and I have a hard time holding in an angry response (continuing to move up the ladder with more mobilized energy). I decide I've had enough of this job and will seriously look for a new one (still moving up the ladder). I begin to consider the skills I can bring to a new

> job and that with the right job I will be able to pay my bills and maybe even take a vacation. I have lunch with a coworker, and we talk about our jobs and dreams for the future (back at the top of the ladder).

Systems Working Together

We experience well-being when the three parts of our autonomic nervous system work together. To understand this integration, we leave the imagery of the ladder and imagine instead a home.

The dorsal vagal system runs the "basic utilities" of the home. This system works continually in the background keeping our basic body systems online and in order. When there is a glitch in the system, we pay attention. When all is running smoothly, the body's functions work automatically. Without the influence of the ventral vagal system, the basic utilities run the empty house, but "no one is home." Or, if we are home, the environment is one that brings no comfort. Everything is turned down to the lowest possible setting—enough to keep the air circulating and the pipes from freezing. The environment is just habitable enough to sustain life.

The sympathetic branch can be thought of as the home security system maintaining a range of responses and armed to react to any emergencies. This alarm system is designed to trigger an immediate response and then return to standby. Without the influence of the ventral vagal system, the alarm system receives a steady stream of emergency notifications and continues to sound the alarm.

The ventral vagal system allows us to soak in, and savor, this home we are inhabiting. We can enjoy it as a place to rest and renew by ourselves and as a place to join with friends and family. We feel the "basic utilities" running in the background. The rhythms of our heart and breath are regulated. We trust that the "monitoring system" is on standby. The integration of systems allows us to be compassionate, curious about the world we live in, and emotionally and physically connected to the people around us.

WHERE DO WE GO NEXT?

With this initial understanding of the role and responses of the autonomic nervous system in service of our safety and survival, we can begin to befriend the autonomic nervous system and map our personal response patterns. The befriending skills lead to attending practices. Our mapping leads naturally to tracking. With the awareness of tracking, we can begin to intentionally tune and tone our autonomic nervous system. We can successfully navigate our quest for safety and connection.

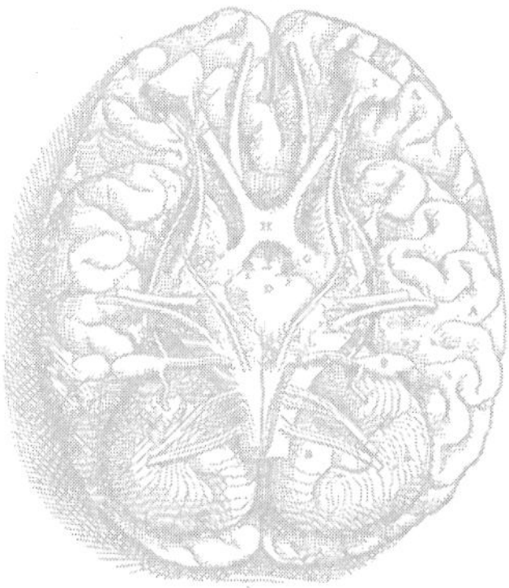

CHAPTER 1

SAFETY, DANGER, AND LIFE-THREAT: ADAPTIVE RESPONSE PATTERNS

We are more alike my friends than we are unalike.

—MAYA ANGELOU

The autonomic nervous system is a common denominator in the human family. We all share the same biobehavioral platform. The job of the autonomic nervous system is to ensure we survive in moments of danger and thrive in times of safety. Survival requires threat detection and the activation of a survival response. Thriving demands the opposite—the inhibition of a survival response so that social engagement can happen. Without the capacity for activation, inhibition, and flexibility of response, we suffer.

If we think of trauma as Robert Macy (president of the International Trauma Center) defined it, "an overwhelming demand placed upon the physiological human system," then we immediately consider the autonomic nervous system. Whether an isolated traumatic incident or recurring traumatic events, trauma and the autonomic nervous system are linked. Without ongoing opportunities for people to be anchored in systems of safety and to appropriately exercise the neural circuits of activation and inhibition, the ability of their autonomic nervous systems to engage, disengage, and reengage efficiently is impaired.

Within the framework of interpersonal neurobiology (Siegel, 2010), mental health diagnoses can be viewed as related to either a hyperaroused or hypoaroused state, and through a polyvagal perspective this makes sense. Without the ability to inhibit defense responses, the nervous system is in a continual state of activated mobilization (hyperaroused) or immobilization (hypoaroused) survival strategies. While a client's longing is for autonomic regulation, reaching the embodied state of safety necessary for regulation is often out of reach. Clients are dismayed at their dysregulation and their inability to either individually or interactively regulate. The result of this ongoing dysregulation is felt in physical illnesses, distressed relationships, altered cognitive capacities, and an ongoing search for safety and relief from the intensity of inhabiting a system so out of balance. Pharmacology targets the autonomic nervous system in an attempt to either calm overactive parts or excite underactive parts and move the system back toward regulation. Psychotherapy works similarly, albeit without the use of drugs, instead engaging the natural capacities of the nervous system. Therapy provides safe opportunities to experiment with co-regulation, to add skills for individual regulation, and to practice exercising the neural circuits of social engagement.

Humans carry an autonomic legacy: echoes of older pathways still present in our physiology today. Hardwired into our modern autonomic nervous system are features of risk and safety we have in common with other vertebrates (Porges, 2011a). Our primitive dorsal vagal circuit, 500 million years old, protects through immobilization, shutting down body systems to conserve energy, similar to the way that animals feign death in response to life-threat ("playing possum"). The sympathetic nervous system, next to evolve 400 million years ago, creates the possibility of survival through movement and the ability to actively engage or avoid (fight or flight). The newest system is our uniquely mammalian ventral vagal circuit, which evolved 200 million years ago and gives us the capacity to co-regulate (social engagement).

The Evolutionary Timeline

→	→	→
parasympathetic	*sympathetic nervous system*	*parasympathetic*
dorsal vagus		ventral vagus
life-threat	danger	safety
immobilization	mobilization	social engagement

The sympathetic nervous system originates in spinal nerves (nerves that arise from the spinal cord) and is our system of mobilization. Sympathetic nerves are located in the middle of the back in the thoracic and lumbar regions of the spinal cord. To get a sense of this, try moving your hands around to your back, one hand gently reaching from your neck down and the other from your waist up. The space between your hands is approximately where the neurons of your sympathetic nervous system start before extending out to reach their target organs (e.g., eyes, heart, lungs, stomach, and bladder).

Through two mobilization systems, the sympathetic adrenal medullary (SAM) system and the hypothalamic–pituitary–adrenal (HPA) axis, the sympathetic nervous system prepares our body for action. The SAM system is activated quickly, bringing a burst of adrenaline for a fast response to a stressor. The startle response happens within 100 milliseconds! SAM activation brings a short-term, rapid response followed by a return to regulation. The HPA axis takes over when this quick, adrenaline-fueled surge of energy doesn't resolve the distress. The HPA axis releases cortisol, commonly called the stress hormone. This release takes longer and is slower to take effect, requiring minutes rather than seconds. Using SAM and the HPA axis the sympathetic nervous system can stimulate individual actions (pupil dilation, sweating), progressively increase reactions (breathing and heart rates), or mobilize a massive full-body response (fight or flight).

The parasympathetic nervous system originates in cranial nerves (nerves that emerge directly from the brain). We have 12 pairs of cranial nerves, and the vagus nerve (cranial nerve X), the longest of the cranial nerves, is the main component of the parasympathetic nervous system. Through the actions of the vagus nerve, the parasympathetic nervous system is both our system of immobilization and our system of connection. The vagus is in fact not a single nerve but rather a bundle of nerve fibers woven together inside a sheath. A helpful image is an electrical wire that contains a number of wires inside its outer covering. *Vagus* comes from the Latin word *vagary* meaning "wanderer," and this nerve is truly a vagabond. The vagus travels downward from the brain stem to the heart and stomach and upward to the face through its connection with other cranial nerves. Because of this architecture, the vagus has been called a "conduit of connection." This wonderful wandering nerve is a mixed nerve communicating bidirectionally between the body and the brain. Eighty percent of its fibers are sensory (afferent), sending information from the body to the brain, and 20% are motor (efferent), sending action information back from the brain to the body. To trace the vagal pathway, place a hand on your cheek and a hand over your heart. Then move one hand to your abdomen. Experiment with moving your hands between these three positions and imagine the vagal fibers connecting these physical locations.

The vagus nerve is divided into two distinct pathways (thus the term *polyvagal*), the dorsal vagus and the ventral vagus, with the division occurring at the diaphragm. While both are branches of the same cranial nerve, the dorsal vagus and the ventral vagus are architecturally and functionally different. The dorsal and ventral aspects of the vagus originate in neighboring parts of the medulla oblongata (the part of the brain stem that connects to the spinal cord). The dorsal vagus, the oldest part of the autonomic nervous system, arises from the dorsal nucleus of the vagus. The ventral vagus, the newest part of the autonomic nervous system, originates in the nucleus ambiguus. Because the nucleus ambiguus is located in front of the dorsal nucleus of the vagus, it was given the label "ventral." The dorsal and ventral vagal fibers exit the brain stem together and travel their individual routes above and below the diaphragm. If you sense into your body and imagine your lungs and your abdomen, the diaphragm is the muscle that separates these two body regions. From the diaphragm downward (subdiaphragmatic) is the territory of the dorsal vagus, while from the diaphragm upward (supradiaphragmatic) is the realm of the ventral vagus. The fibers of the dorsal vagus are mostly unmyelinated, while the fibers of the ventral vagus are primarily myelinated. Myelin is a fatty substance that covers nerve fibers, insulating them so that information can be transmitted efficiently and quickly. Myelination of the ventral vagus, the process of covering fibers in myelin, begins in pregnancy during the last trimester and continues over the course of the first year of life (Porges, 2015a). The dorsal vagus affects organs beneath the diaphragm, especially those regulating digestion, while the ventral vagus, working above the diaphragm, influences heart rate and breathing rate and integrates with facial nerves to form the Social Engagement System. Out of these biological differences, the two extremes of autonomic response are activated. The dorsal vagus takes us out of connection into immobilization, and the ventral vagus moves us into social engagement and co-regulation.

Through these three unique pathways (ventral vagus, sympathetic nervous system, dorsal vagus), we react "in service of survival." Each autonomic state brings a characteristic range of responses through its own pattern of protection or connection. When the dorsal vagus comes to the rescue, there is not enough energy to run the system: The system is drained, and the client is numbed. In a sympathetic nervous system response, there is too much energy in the system, and the client is flooded. In a ventral vagal state, the system is regulated, open to connection, and the client is ready to engage. In Polyvagal Theory the three states of the autonomic response hierarchy are named (from newest to oldest) socially engaged, mobilized, and immobilized, or safe, danger, and life-threat. As clients become familiar with their personal response hierarchy, invite them to create their own labels. Many of my clients name their states safe, scared, and shut down. One client uses connected, stormy, and lost to identify her states. And another client, in what feels intensely evocative of the experience, named his states devoted, driven, and devoid.

To follow the autonomic hierarchy, envision your stomach and its digestive processes as the ancient dorsal vagus, move up to the middle of your back as the next layer in the evolution of the system with the sympathetic nervous system and its spinal nerves, and then move to your heart and face and the newest part of the autonomic nervous system, the ventral vagus.

A CLOSER LOOK AT THE AUTONOMIC HIERARCHY

Earliest Roots

The dorsal vagus, sometimes called the "primitive vagus", is the oldest part of the autonomic nervous system and one branch of the parasympathetic nervous system. In its nonreactive role, the dorsal vagal pathway is important in regulating digestion. As an ancient survival mechanism, the dorsal vagal response is one of conservation of energy through collapse and shutdown. The dorsal vagal response is analgesic, protecting from both physical and psychological pain. In the moment of a traumatic event, the dorsal vagus can come to the rescue through dissociation. A neurological outcome of this dorsal vagal response is reduced flow and oxygenation of blood to the brain, which then translates into changes in cognitive function and experiences of dissociation (Porges, 2013). Long after the event has ended, this adaptive survival response is often seen in our work with trauma survivors when dorsal vagal "leaving" becomes a posttraumatic pattern in the search for safety. One client described to me the power of her dorsal vagal response, telling me that she can't hear my words, my tone of voice, or make sense of what I'm saying. She often can't see my face at all.

The dorsal vagal pathway responds to signals of extreme danger. This is the "path of last resort" using stillness as a survival response, conserving energy to take us out of connection, out of awareness, and into a protective state of collapse. When we feel frozen, numb, or "not here," the dorsal vagus has taken control. The phrase "scared to death" fits the dorsal vagal experience. Just as it is for our early ancestor the tortoise, the autonomic message to a sense of life threat is, "Pull in your head. Be still. Hide."

Keeping in mind the role of the dorsal vagus in the function of systems beneath the diaphragm, we would expect that subdiaphragmatic trauma, including abuse, sexual trauma, medical procedures, illness, and injury, could trigger a dorsal vagal response. In the extreme, this causes fainting (vaso-vagal syncope), but the dorsal vagal response includes a continuum of experiences. Health issues might be seen through impaired immune function, a chronic lack of energy, and digestive issues and psychological consequences might present as dissociation, depression, or withdrawal from social connection.

Consider the following client expressions of dorsal vagal response you might encounter in a session: gazing out the window or into space; vacant eyes; flat, unresponsive face; collapsed posture; loss of speech; and "stilled" without ease. When a client moves into the shutdown state of the dorsal vagal pathway, there is a sense of absence that prompts the question, "Where did you go?" The therapist can feel the amorphous sense of reaching out and not finding anything solid to connect with. The client experience I have heard over and over is the sense of being alone, lost, and unreachable. Here is where despair lives.

Protected by Movement

The sympathetic nervous system, second on the evolutionary timeline, brings the ability to mobilize. In its homeostatic role, this system complements the parasympathetic system, working in concert with the ventral vagus to regulate heart and breathing rates and with the dorsal vagus to support digestion.

With the advent of the sympathetic nervous system, stillness is no longer our only survival response. The sympathetic nervous system prepares us to take action with the options of fight or flight, using movement to protect. This system is linked to action of the major limbs, and the feeling in this state is of being on the move. With the protective mobilization of the sympathetic nervous system, we move away from co-regulation. In the search for safety, we are cut off from others. In our evolutionary history, being alone and not a part of a group was dangerous, and the mobilization response of the sympathetic nervous system brings with it that sense of isolation and danger.

With a move into sympathetic response, there is a corresponding change in our hearing. The muscles of the middle ear control the ability to focus on human voice. When in a ventral vagal state, these muscles work to regulate frequencies and support listening to, and for, voices. When the sympathetic nervous system takes over, the middle ear regulation shifts away from listening for human voice toward listening for low-frequency sounds of predators or high-frequency sounds of distress. The system is now tuned to sounds of danger and not to the sounds of connection.

In addition to the effect on hearing, the ability to read facial cues is affected. In a sympathetically triggered state, we misread cues. Neutral faces appear angry. Neutral is experienced as dangerous (Porges, 2006). A client shared with me her experience of being sympathetically triggered and looking at faces, not being able to see a smile or decide if the person was friendly or dangerous. Consider this autonomic response in your interactions with clients. If your face is neutral, you may be seen as angry or even dangerous.

When moments of sympathetic activation are frequent and ongoing, the sympathetic nervous system stays on high alert. The release of cortisol makes it hard to sit still. Heart rate speeds up, breath is short and shallow, and we scan the environment looking for danger. Unable to resolve the cues of danger, the sympathetic nervous system becomes chronically active.

In a session with a client, you might notice the following responses to sympathetic nervous system activation: fidgeting; some part of their body is always in motion; they are unsettled, continually looking around the room; a stiff posture; and a sense of disorganization. When a client is in a "sympathetic storm," the options of fight or flight are both present. You may sense your client moving at you or moving away from you. The fight response often brings confrontation that can feel intense and antagonistic. Fight can be felt as your client's energy begins to fill the room. Their body posture becomes more rigid and their tone of voice challenging. Flight can be felt in the chaotic unfolding of the session. Flight can be seen in a body that can't come to rest, with constant changing of position, and can be heard when your client says, "I don't want to be here today. I shouldn't have come. I need to leave NOW." In the sympathetically charged states of fight and flight, danger lurks everywhere, and coming into connection is too big a risk. The world is an unfriendly place, and mistrust fuels the system.

Safe and Social

Connectedness is a biological imperative (Porges, 2015a), and at the top of the autonomic hierarchy is the ventral vagal pathway that supports feelings of safety and connection. The ventral vagus (sometimes called the "smart vagus" or "social vagus") provides the neurobiological foundation for health, growth, and restoration. When the ventral vagus is active, our attention is toward connection. We seek opportunities for co-regulation. The ability to soothe and be soothed, to talk and listen, to offer and receive, to fluidly move in and out of connection is centered in this newest part of the autonomic nervous system. Reciprocity, the mutual ebb and flow that defines nourishing relationships, is a function of the ventral vagus. As a result of its myelinated pathways, the ventral vagus provides rapid and organized responses (Porges, 1997). In a ventral vagal state, we have access to a range of responses including calm, happy, meditative, engaged, attentive, active, interested, excited, passionate, alert, ready, relaxed, savoring, and joyful.

The vagus has been called the "compassion nerve." As Dacher Keltner of the Greater Good Science Center explains, through the actions of the ventral vagus we are wired to care. The ventral vagal state supports compassionate connections. It is this state that slows our heart rate, softens our eyes, brings a kind tone to our voice, and moves us to reach out to others. This same ventral vagal energy supports self-compassion: the act of reaching in to be with our own suffering with kindness. Compassion practices, through the activation of the ventral vagus, bring health benefits including reduction in stress and enhanced immune function (Keltner, 2012). There is a beautiful Aztec word *apapacho* that means "to embrace or caress with the soul." The ventral vagal state of safety and connection brings with it the potential to offer and receive *apapacho*. Ventral vagal activity is good for each of us and good for the world!

When clients are in a ventral vagal state of regulation, there is a feeling of connection in the room. The session has a rhythm. Even though the work may be difficult, there is a sense of groundedness. Ventral vagal energy brings curiosity and a willingness to experiment. The edges of regulation can be stretched a bit here. There is a sense of possibility. New options are recognized as the old story no longer matches this state of ventral vagal safety. Clients may be surprised by the unfamiliarity of this state. In the ventral vagal state, hope arises and change happens.

In a ventral vagal state, our Social Engagement System is alive. The Social Engagement System is an evolutionary development that occurred when the pathways to the face and head were linked with the ventral vagus in the brain stem. The integration of five cranial nerves (cranial nerves V, VII, IX, X, XI) meant eyes, ears, voice, and head now worked in concert with the heart. The Social Engagement System not only signals, but also searches for, cues of safety. This "safety circuit" is present from birth and regulates behaviors along a continuum from social engagement to surveillance. We send cues of safety and invitations to come into connection through the signals of tone of voice, facial expression, the tilt of the head. We communicate, one nervous system to another, that it is safe to approach and come into relationship. As a surveillance system, when the cues perceived through another's face, voice, and gestures are ones of safety, the Social Engagement System affirms the possibility of connection. When the cues are ones of danger, we move into watchfulness. Through the Social Engagement System, we sense whether others are safe to approach and signal that we are friend not foe.

THE VAGAL BRAKE

Although we may think that the heart beats steadily, in fact a healthy heart does not beat like a metronome in an even, unchanging pattern. The ventral vagus influences our heart rate, slowing it during exhalation and allowing it to speed up during inhalation. The change in heartbeat, the rhythm of the heart during spontaneous breathing, is called respiratory sinus arrhythmia (RSA). Vagal tone, measured through RSA, indicates not only physiological well-being but also social and psychological well-being (Kok & Fredrickson, 2010).

The vagal brake is an important concept in Polyvagal Theory. One responsibility of the ventral vagus is to suppress heart rate to around 72 beats per minute through its influence on the heart's pacemaker, the sino-atrial node. Without this action, the heart would beat dangerously fast. Polyvagal Theory describes this as a "vagal brake" (Porges, 2009b; Porges & Furman, 2011). Think of the brakes on a bicycle. As you release the brakes your speed increases, and as you apply the brakes you slow down. The vagal brake functions in a similar way, releasing to allow us to quickly energize and reengaging to bring a return to calm. Through its actions on the heart, the vagal brake offers flexibility to our system.

The experiences of alertness and danger originate in different parts of the autonomic system. When the vagal brake is relaxed but not fully released, the ventral vagal system regulates the call to action, allowing more sympathetic energy into the system while inhibiting the release of cortisol and adrenaline. Danger, in contrast, brings with it a full release of the vagal brake, and, with that, the sympathetic nervous system takes over, discharging cortisol and adrenaline and triggering the fight-or-flight response.

We depend on the vagal brake's capacity to relax and reengage as we navigate the demands of a normal day. The actions of the vagal brake are an efficient way to quickly increase and decrease heart rate and change the autonomic tone while maintaining ventral vagal control. A vagal brake that is working well brings a sense of ease to these transitions. This ability for rapid regulation and smooth transitions is affected by traumatic experience. Think about clients who are trauma survivors through the frame of the vagal brake. The loss of the vagal brake and yielding of control first to the sympathetic nervous system and then to the dorsal vagal system takes its toll. A client who is quick to dysregulate and be pulled into a survival response often missed the co-regulating experiences in childhood needed to effectively exercise their vagal brake. Trauma survivors without those necessary experiences generally find small moments of distress to be too great of a challenge to their vagal braking capacities. In therapy, pendulation (intentionally moving between activation and calm) and titration (using tempo and parsing of experience to monitor and manage response) techniques are examples of experimenting with the safe release and reengagement of the vagal brake (Payne, Levine, & Crane-Godreau, 2015).

The vagal brake is designed to release and reengage as a way of responding to challenges while still maintaining ventral vagal regulation. Once the autonomic challenge is met, the vagal brake recovers, reengages and returns the system to balance. This is a commonly experienced pattern throughout the course of a day as we energize to meet the demands of the multiple and often conflicting needs dictated by work and family schedules.

When the ventral vagal system cannot meet the needs for safety, the vagal brake releases, allowing the sympathetic nervous system to come into full activation. An example of this is when, despite your efforts to titrate the work, a client gets pulled into a piece of their trauma story and re-experiences that moment. In a fight response, a client is entangled with the story, doing battle with it. They may experience the rush of adrenaline, and feel intense emotions, showing them in movements punctuated by sharp gestures. In a flight response, a client may be frantic to get away from the memory. Their speech is often rushed and pressured, and they may express an urgent need to stop the work or end the session. In each of these experiences, if your client feels you meeting them in their distress with your ventral vagal state sending cues of safety, their autonomic nervous system can sense the offer of co-regulation, helping their vagal brake to reengage, and can come back into regulation.

If the intensity of your client's experience overwhelms their ability to take in your offer of co-regulation and cues of safety, then the dorsal vagal system takes over, sending them into shutdown. This is the client who is no longer present with you, who has moved out of reach. To come back into connection, their autonomic nervous system needs to feel your ventral vagal presence, take in cues of safety, and climb back up the autonomic hierarchy through sympathetic activation to reach ventral vagal regulation. Your client needs to feel a gentle call to action for their sympathetic nervous system to begin to bring a return of energy (e.g., brief eye contact, engaging in small movements, return of speech). Too great a sympathetic surge will overload the system and trigger a return of dorsal vagal collapse. As you and your client notice the beginning of return of energy to the system, help them identify it as a safe response that is bringing their system back online. Then pause there together for a moment to honor the release from collapse before continuing through sympathetic mobilization into ventral vagal connection.

HOMEOSTASIS

Just as both the left and right hemispheres of the brain bring balance to our experience, all three parts of our autonomic nervous system cooperate to develop an embodied sense of well-being. The ventral vagus controls the face-heart connection. The sympathetic nervous system supports healthy breathing cycles and heart rhythms and plays a role in regulating body temperature, while the dorsal vagus promotes healthy digestion. With the regulating energy of the ventral vagus, and the sympathetic and dorsal vagal branches adding their nonreactive actions, a sense of homeostasis, or what Peter Levine calls dynamic equilibrium, is achieved.

If a baby is born at 30 weeks of gestation or earlier, the protective part of the vagus, the ventral vagus, has not yet fully developed and myelinated. Without a fully functional ventral vagal system, the baby is dependent on dorsal vagal "conservation" and sympathetic "activation" to regulate states. The many machines, wires, and tubes in a neonatal intensive care unit are doing some of the work of the ventral vagus while the baby's autonomic nervous system continues to develop.

Without a ventral vagal system that is able to meet the demands of the day with flexibility, people of all ages are pulled into "conservation" and "activation" to face the challenges of regulation. An autonomic nervous system that is missing the regulating influence of the ventral vagus brings health challenges, creates distress in relationships, and shapes a daily experience of suffering.

ATTENDING TO THE HIERARCHY

The autonomic nervous system guides our daily experiences. We first try to navigate using our ventral vagal system. We use strategies of social engagement and social communication in an attempt to co-regulate. We are social beings needing reliable, reciprocal relationships in our daily living experiences for both physical and emotional well-being (Hawkley & Cacioppo, 2010; Seppala, Rossomando, & Doty, 2013). It is when we are unsuccessful in using connection and communication to partner with others that our autonomic nervous system moves out of the safety of the ventral vagal state and engages the sympathetic nervous system's fight-or-flight response. The sympathetically triggered state brings strategies of confrontation or avoidance in an attempt to resolve the danger and return to the safety of ventral vagal regulation.

This cycle of reaction and return to regulation between these two autonomic states is not an uncommon experience during the course of a day. It is when the mobilization tactics of the sympathetic nervous system are not successful that we move the final step back on the evolutionary timeline into dorsal vagal collapse. Here we are disconnected from ourselves, from others, and from our internal and external resources. In the dorsal vagal immobilization response we wait, feeling lost and unable to find our way back into connection.

To recover from dorsal vagal shutdown requires moving forward along the evolutionary timeline through the energy of the sympathetic nervous system in order to reach ventral vagal regulation. Without sufficient resources (internal abilities, environmental safety, social support), a pattern of immobilization–mobilization–immobilization is replayed in a painful autonomic loop. The intense longing to reach the safety of ventral vagal connection is unmet and accompanied by feelings of hopelessness. When the system begins to find its way out of dorsal vagal collapse, there is the likelihood that "moments of messiness" will arise from the energy of the sympathetic nervous system. When these adaptive survival strategies don't result in a sense of connection, either to self or other, the exhaustion of the unremitting mobilized response turns back into a necessary conservation of energy through collapse. To safely navigate out of collapse through action and keep moving up the autonomic hierarchy into social engagement, we need to feel a real or imagined "hand on our back."

Autonomic patterns are built over time. The autonomic nervous system is shaped through experience. In response to experiences of connection and challenge, we develop a personal neural profile with habitual patterns of reaction. Recognizing these responses and seeing the patterns of activation is the first step in polyvagal-informed practices. Some clients move quickly into states of mobilization. Even small moments of misattunement are "too big a neural challenge," and their autonomic nervous system enacts a survival response. A client with this pattern told me, "My partner asked if I'd gotten everything done and I immediately felt my anger coming. I thought if he can't just trust that I'm doing it right then he can do it all himself. I'm done! Later my friend told me his question was a 'normal' one, even one that showed he cared, but I can't ever seem to see things that way." Other clients move almost imperceptibly through mobilization into collapse, their autonomic nervous system taking refuge in disconnection. A client with this response shared with me, "I don't know how to do the simple things in life everyone else does so easily because my childhood was spent making sure I survived the night. There was no room for learning the things normal people learn. Now I am not equipped to live in the everyday world. As soon as I begin to feel like a misfit, I collapse."

EXERCISE
Ask Your Nervous System

The following three questions and common responses invite a beginning look at the three states of autonomic activation. Read the statements, and consider how your autonomic nervous system would respond.

- **My dorsal vagal system takes hold when I**
  am without options; feel trapped in the situation; feel unimportant; am criticized; feel as if I don't matter; feel as if I don't belong.

- **My sympathetic nervous system kicks in when I**
  am pressed for time; am ignored; am confused; am pushed to make a choice or take a side; am around conflict; feel responsible for too many people and too many things.

- **My ventral vagal system comes alive when I**
  think about people who are important to me; am out in nature; give myself permission to make my own choices; listen to music; enjoy quiet time with my dog; stand under the stars; have my feet in the sea; am building Legos with my son; share a cup of tea with a friend.

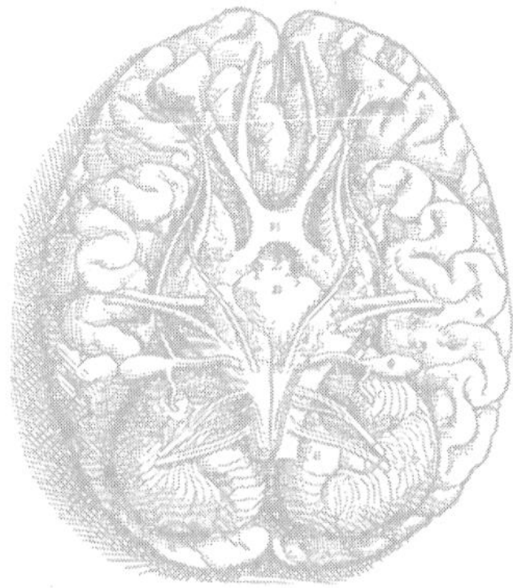

CHAPTER 2

AUTONOMIC SURVEILLANCE: NEUROCEPTION

There is a voice that doesn't use words. Listen.

—RUMI

We live a story that originates in our autonomic state, is sent through autonomic pathways from the body to the brain, and is then translated by the brain into the beliefs that guide our daily living. The mind narrates what the nervous system knows. Story follows state.

Polyvagal Theory makes an important distinction between perception, which involves a degree of awareness, and neuroception, which is reflexive with cues triggering shifts in autonomic state without an awareness of the influence of the cues. Neuroception results in the gut feelings, the heart-informed feelings, the implicit feelings that move us along the continuum between safety and survival response. Neuroception might be thought of as "somatic signals that influence decision making and behavioral responses without explicit awareness of the provoking cues" (Klarer et al., 2014, p. 7067). Through the process of neuroception, the autonomic nervous system assesses risk and takes action. From a neuroception of unsafety, there is a move toward sympathetic mobilization or dorsal vagal collapse. From a neuroception of safety, the sympathetic and dorsal vagal systems are inhibited, the ventral vagal system is in control, and the social engagement system is active and online.

Neuroception is a wordless experience. It is the response of the autonomic nervous system not only to cues in the world around us but also to cues from within our bodies (Porges, 2004). Information from the viscera (heart, lungs, intestines) and cues from the place we are in and from the people and things around us are all important components of neuroception. Before the brain understands and makes meaning of an experience, the autonomic nervous system, via the process of neuroception, has assessed the situation and initiated a response.

Some features of neuroception are wired into our nervous system—adaptive strategies carried forward through evolution (Porges, 2009b)—and are a shared human experience. The response to sound (vibration and frequency) is an example of this. Music, a way we intentionally connect to sound, is composed using themes that predictably provoke certain physiological states. Other ways neuroception is triggered are idiosyncratic, created in response to our personal traumatic and nourishing life experiences. Neuroception shifts our state, colors our experiences, and creates an autonomic response. We are often unaware of the stimulus but are very aware of the somatic response. A client tracking her autonomic responses sent me this message: "So, I'm at the store right now, looking at stamps for scrapbooking. Suddenly my heart starts pounding and I'm feeling flushed. No one is around and I'm not noticing anything obvious as a trigger. It's gone as fast as it came . . . strange."

Neuroception shapes the state, and then the state shapes the response. From a neuroception of safety, the qualities of the ventral vagus and the Social Engagement System are available. We can connect, communicate, and co-regulate with ease. The actions of the sympathetic and dorsal vagal systems are constrained. From a neuroception of unsafety, however, our abilities are limited to the mobilizing fight-or-flight energies of the sympathetic nervous system or the immobilizing collapse, shutdown, and dissociation flavors of the dorsal vagal system. To expect a person to access the qualities of social engagement when they are caught in a neuroception of danger or life-threat is futile. The ventral vagal pathways are biologically unavailable.

What might be the anatomy of this autonomic surveillance system? Possibilities include the temporal cortex, the periaqueductal gray (PAG), and the insula (Porges, 2009b, 2011a). The temporal cortex (think temples to get a general location) responds to familiar faces, voices, and hand movements with the query, "Is this person safe and trustworthy?" The temporal cortex communicates with the amygdala in evaluating movement and intention. The PAG is an ancient brain structure found at the top of the brain stem that communicates with the sympathetic nervous system and the dorsal vagal complex to regulate confrontational behaviors, escape behaviors, and immobilizing behaviors. The insula, buried deep in the cerebral cortex in the fold that separates the temporal lobe from the frontal lobe, is involved in interoception (the sense of our internal physiology), or bringing visceral feedback into awareness (Craig, 2009a). It is likely these three systems are involved in the process of neuroception.

Our response to neuroception can be private or public. We may feel the shifts internally in the beating of our heart, our digestive processes, sensations in our throat, or in a behavioral impulse felt but not brought to action. Or the shifts may be visible to the world in our facial expressions, tone of voice, gestures, and posture. Although we all share the same continuum of safety to danger to life-threat, movement along the continuum is an individual experience. Because the autonomic nervous system is a relational system that has been shaped by experience, it makes sense that clients will each have their own response patterns, experiencing both large-scale reactions with an intensity that moves them between safety and unsafety and nuanced responses that bring more subtle changes. When working efficiently, neuroception enables a match between risk and autonomic state (Porges, 2009a). When we receive cues of danger we react, and when we receive cues of safety we relax. But for many clients, neuroception brings a misattunement: They cannot reliably inhibit their defense systems in safe environments or activate their defense systems when needed in risky environments. Without an understanding of neuroception, this mismatch is perplexing and can lead to attempts to convince clients that their response is either unnecessary or inappropriate. By learning to track the nuances of neuroception and to honor the ways the autonomic nervous system listens and acts in service of safety and survival, therapists bring a different level of understanding to their clients' actions and experiences.

A client's neuroception is continually monitoring the therapeutic environment and the therapeutic relationship. The therapist's intention is to provide a safe place and to be a safe person for their client and yet, there are moments when a client does not receive that message, and neuroception instead activates a mismatch between their autonomic experience and the therapist's intention. Something familiar in the environment or in the therapeutic connection, some part of an old embodied story, comes to life and takes over. In this moment, is it safe in this environment? In and around my body? Is my therapist a restorative resource or a threat? These are the questions being answered by neuroception.

There is both an active and a passive pathway to safety and regulation (Porges, 2017b). The active pathway deliberately engages the ventral vagal safety circuit. The passive pathway operates outside of conscious awareness through neuroception. Through the passive pathway, the autonomic nervous system receives a steady stream of information addressing the question, "Is it safe to engage with this person in this moment in this place?" As neuroception answers this question, the autonomic nervous system acts to ensure survival, shifting autonomic states to limit or support social connection.

AUTONOMIC EXPECTATIONS

Polyvagal Theory introduces the concept of biological rudeness (Porges, 2017a); the experience of misattunement that happens when social connection is interrupted and neuroception changes from safety to danger. Moments of biological rudeness happen frequently in our personal lives and in our professional worlds. Some have become commonplace, such as those associated with the ubiquitous use of cell phones (Hyde, 2013). A colleague told me about an experience she had with a friend: "We were making plans and she turned away to look at her cell phone. I immediately felt like I didn't matter. It wasn't safe any longer. I wanted to disappear. All that just because she looked at her cell phone." No matter how common the moments are, our neurobiology still feels the autonomic rupture. Even the moments we describe as understandable bring an autonomic response because "understanding" is the territory of the brain and not the nervous system.

Polyvagal Theory describes a process of neural expectations and the accompanying process of a violation of these expectations (Porges, 2017a). We experience an autonomic reaction when an anticipated response doesn't happen. If the expectations are for reciprocal connections and those expectations are violated, the result is biological rudeness and a neuroception of unsafety. But what happens when the neural expectations that have been shaped by trauma are violated? What happens when a client's autonomic expectation is not how their therapist responds? In this case, the "violation" is a positive experience, a necessary disconfirming experience that interrupts habitual neuroceptive responses. These small moments are important events in the therapy process. Repeatedly violating neural expectations in this way within the therapist–client dyad influences a client's autonomic assumptions. As a client's nervous system begins to anticipate in different ways, the old story will no longer fit and a new story can be explored.

NEUROCEPTION SEARCHES FOR CUES

Our eyes send, and search for, signals of safety. The area around the outside of the eyes that wrinkles into crow's-feet is where our search for cues of safety begins. We can feel the power of the eyes to send cues of safety or danger and experience the neuroceptive response by experimenting with a variety of ways to focus. This simple exercise is a quick way to gain awareness of neuroception and of the associated state changes that occur with subtle shifts in eye contact. Try this with a colleague: Start with a stare (strong, focused, with a flavor of glaring). Then, shift to a look (neutral without conveying much information) and finally a soft gaze (warm and inviting). During each period of eye contact, notice what signals your neuroception is sending. Is your social engagement system alive or are your defenses engaged? Where are you on the autonomic hierarchy: ventral vagal, sympathetic, or dorsal vagal? Ask your colleague what messages their neuroception is sending them as they receive each of the three kinds of eye contact.

How is a genuine smile different from a social one? In a

genuine smile, often known as a Duchenne smile (named for the 19th-century French physician Guillaume Duchenne, who studied the physiology of facial expression), the eyes close a bit, the cheeks move upward, and there are wrinkles around the eyes. A genuine smile broadcasts a neuroception of safety to the autonomic nervous system of anyone in proximity, sending an invitation to approach. The muscle that moves the cheeks (the zygomatic major) and the muscle that wrinkles the eyes into crow's-feet (the orbicularis oculi) bring the face alive. In a social smile, the movement of the upper face is missing, the eyes don't wrinkle, and rather than communicating welcome, the neuroceptive message is one of warning.

Eons ago, when mammals joined the world that previously had been dominated by reptiles, the middle ear bones detached from the jawbone, and the nerves of the ventral vagus integrated with the nerves that regulated the middle ear muscles (Porges, 2015a). This important evolutionary event tied the ability to process sound to autonomic state. We are hardwired to be soothed by certain frequencies. Low-frequency sounds and vibrations send a neuroception of life-threat and initiate a vigilance for predators and a sensitivity to dorsal vagal immobilization, while high-frequency sounds and vibrations launch a neuroception of danger and a sympathetic nervous system mobilization response (Porges, 2010).

Sound is one of the strongest triggers of a neuroception of safety. The autonomic nervous system recognizes features of prosody—the music of the voice. It is not the words themselves, but the patterns of rhythm and sound along with the frequency, duration, and intensity of speaking that reveals our intentions. The autonomic nervous system, via neuroception, is listening beneath the words for sounds of safety and friendship.

"We are more focused on managing those who threaten or hurt us, than on understanding what our nervous system needs to feel safe" (Porges, 2015a, p. 2). Two elements are needed to create a neuroception of safety: resolve the cues of danger, and bring in cues of safety. Resolving cues of danger is an important step certainly. Without that, neuroception will continue to activate defensive survival responses. However, an environment that does not include cues of safety may be an environment that is still missing the ingredients necessary to stimulate a neuroception of safety. What cues does the autonomic nervous system need to move out of a neuroception of danger and fully into a neuroception of safety that supports curiosity, creativity, connection, and compassion? Ongoing opportunities for co-regulation, reliable relationships based on reciprocity, and time spent with safe people engaging in shared activities are all important elements of an enlivened neuroception of safety.

EXPLORING THE A, B, C, D'S OF NEUROCEPTION

Autonomic response is always happening. Our autonomic nervous system listens in a continual evaluation of risk and responds in service of our survival. Beneath awareness, we are swept along in the flow of neuroception.

Bringing awareness to autonomic response adds the influence of perception to the experience of neuroception. With the addition of awareness, we move from a state of "being in" to "being with" and bring observer energy to interrupt ingrained response pathways. Without this interruption, the pull of old patterns keeps us moving down the autonomic hierarchy and away from the neuroception of safety. As we experience the influence of awareness, we can make an intentional turn toward self-compassion.

Connecting with self-compassion, we enter a place of befriending. We may stay here offering inward kindness and care that, in and of itself, can bring us back to the ventral vagal state that tells us we are safe. From this place of self-compassion, we can also be moved into curiosity, resulting in a natural desire to explore our habitual neuroceptive loops more deeply.

Deepening into curiosity and active inquiry brings us into possibility. Curiosity has been called the opening of our heart intuition. Here in the flow of a ventral vagal state, the options and outcomes are limitless. This is where regulating, resourcing, reciprocity, reconnection, repatterning, and re-storying can happen!

FINDING YOUR AUTONOMIC SENSE OF HOME

> *Our bodies know they belong; it is our minds that make our lives so homeless.*
>
> —JOHN O'DONOHUE

Neuroception sends us messages of safety: that we are where we belong, that we are home. Our minds may disagree with those messages and want something else to be true. We can try to talk ourselves in or out of something, but our autonomic nervous system, by way of neuroception, has the last word. For me, my roots have been planted in soil by the sea for generations. The ocean is a part of my rhythm. When I travel away from the seaside, my nervous system reminds me I'm not home. When I return to the water, an experience of ease fills me. Where is the place your autonomic nervous system tells you that it is safe and you are home?

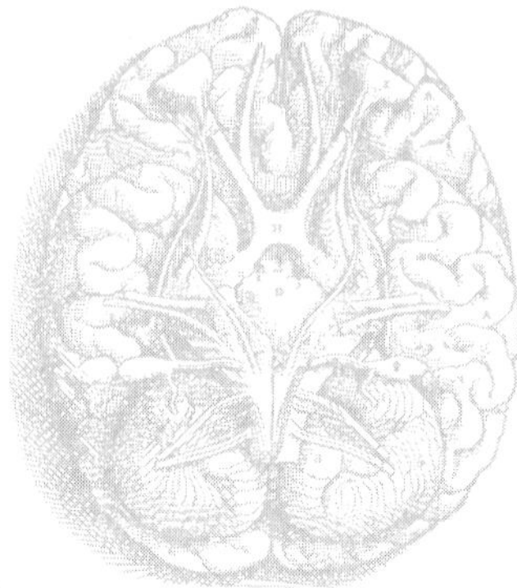

CHAPTER 3

WIRED TO CONNECT

The fittest may also be the gentlest, because survival often requires mutual help and cooperation.

—THEODOSIUS DOBZHANSKY

We are inherently social beings, and our nature is to interact and form relationships with others (Cacioppo & Cacioppo, 2014). From the first moments of life, when we instinctively turn toward our mother's face, to the end of life, we have an enduring need to be in attuned relationships with others. Polyvagal Theory describes autonomic safety as a "preamble to attachment" (Porges, 2012). Through co-regulation, a foundation of safety is created and attachment follows. Co-regulation creates a physiological platform of safety that supports a psychological story of security that then leads to social engagement. The autonomic nervous systems of two individuals find sanctuary in a co-created experience of connection.

The following sweet story a colleague shared with me beautifully illustrates the power of connection.

> My 2-year-old daughter, Iris, has recently started coloring with markers. She'll draw birds, fish, whales that all look like oblong circles with little faces but she knows what they are. One morning,

> she drew a whale and said to me, "The whale is sad." I asked her what she thought the whale needed to feel better, and she said, "She needs another whale to look at her." And then she asked me to draw another whale looking at her whale. I asked her how the sad whale was feeling now, and she said, "She's feeling better." I couldn't help but be amazed at our intuitive wisdom as human beings, knowing that we are wired to seek safety in the presence of another. Since then, Iris has drawn many animals that need another animal to look at them and we have talked in a 2-year-old way about how it helps us feel okay if we can see another person's loving face and how we can offer that sense of safety to others when they are feeling sad or lonely or hurt.

Co-regulation is at the heart of positive relationships: work alliances, enduring friendships, intimate partnerships. If we miss opportunities to co-regulate in childhood, we feel that loss in our adult relationships. Trauma, either in experiences of commission (acts of harm) or omission (absence of care), makes co-regulation dangerous and interrupts the development of our co-regulatory skills. Out of necessity, the autonomic nervous system is shaped to independently regulate. Clients will often say that they needed connection but there was no one in their life who was safe, so after a while they stopped looking. Through a polyvagal perspective, we know that although they stopped explicitly looking and found ways to navigate on their own, their autonomic nervous system never stopped needing, and longing for, co-regulation.

When opportunities for connection are missing, we carry the distress in our nervous system. Our loneliness brings us pain. Lonely people suffer from health and mental health problems including compromised immune function, heart disease, and depression (Cacioppo, 2011)—all issues related to autonomic function. While feeling lonely sometimes prompts us to reach out, loneliness also increases our watchfulness for threat (Hawkley & Cacioppo, 2010) with increased cortisol and activation of the sympathetic nervous system (Cacioppo, 2011). A lonely person feels not only unhappy but also unsafe. Loneliness triggers a neuroception of unsafety, activating our autonomic defense systems. Chronic loneliness sends a persistent message of danger, and our autonomic nervous system remains locked in survival mode.

Polyvagal Theory shows us that co-regulation is a requirement for feeling safe (Porges, 2012), that our physiology is regulated in connection to one another. Co-regulating connections invite a sense of belonging and feeling safely tethered in the world. We suffer when our biological need for connection is unmet, and our suffering leads to autonomic responses. This could be the sympathetic nervous system reaching out through mobilization (interrupting, arguing, fighting for attention) or the dorsal vagal system surrendering in a strategy of shutdown (silence, distancing, isolating). What are some of the autonomic survival strategies you see in your clients when they are feeling alone and out of attunement?

For many people, co-regulation is a missing experience in their lives. For clients with experiences of childhood trauma, not belonging is a common belief, and feeling alone is a familiar autonomic experience. The therapy hour may be the one time in their week when co-regulation is possible. Therapists have a responsibility to regulate their own autonomic state and bring a reliable flow of ventral vagal energy to the session. An essential part of the therapy process is reaching out and offering cues of safety to clients, inviting them into the safety of ventral vagal connection. When two autonomic nervous systems begin co-regulating in ventral vagal connection, they form a feedback loop that creates an upward spiral of increasing vagal tone (Kok & Fredrickson, 2010). For clients, these experiences begin to build new autonomic patterns, and the new patterns bring the beginnings of a new story.

RECIPROCITY IN RELATIONSHIPS

Reciprocity is an important regulator of the autonomic nervous system. In Latin, *reciprocus* means "returning the same way" or "alternating." "Reciprocity and the spontaneous reversal of the roles of giving and receiving are positive features of strong relationships. . . . Conversely, a lack of reciprocity often signals distressed and vulnerable relationships" (Porges & Carter, 2011, p. 55). Reciprocity is a connection between people that is created in the back-and-forth communication between two autonomic nervous systems. It is the experience of heartfelt listening and responding. We are nourished in experiences of reciprocity, feeling the ebb and flow, giving and receiving, attunement, and resonance. We feel in our bodies and in our stories the ways caring, and being cared for, bring well-being.

Reciprocity is a way to think about the dynamics of a relationship. Where on the continuum of reciprocal interactions does a relationship fall? We can use an individual interaction to look at reciprocity through measuring qualities of turn taking, talking and listening, the feeling of a "two-way street." But individual moments don't tell the full story of a relationship. Circumstances often disrupt the relational balance. One person has more needs in the moment, and the other shows up bringing regulating energy until there is a return to reciprocity. Caretaking is sweet when offered and received with equal intentions. As we look at reciprocity in a relationship over time, we ask: Is there an ongoing invitation into a flow of reciprocity? Does the relationship nourish a sense of connection? Is there symmetry in the relationship?

In most relationships, the balance temporarily leans, realigns, and then leans again. This intermittent inequality naturally deepens the relationship. In other relationships, the flow is more frequently out of balance, and a pattern emerges where one person's needs always seem to take preference over the other's. A relationship with a consistent lack of reciprocity feels draining. And sometimes, because of accident or illness, the disruption is ongoing, and the relational balance is permanently changed. The bidirectional flow of reciprocity is replaced by the one-way current of caregiving.

Remembered reciprocity uses the capacity of the body–mind to re-create an experience taking the memory of a moment of reciprocity and bringing it back to life. Therapists can help clients identify moments of connection and intentionally return to them. For clients who have few actual experiences of reciprocity, there is imagined reciprocity. Therapists can help these clients imagine an experience of reciprocity and bring it to life. Both remembered and imagined reciprocity practices engage the innate drive of the autonomic nervous system to connect and co-regulate. Remembering and imagining moments of reciprocity inhibits autonomic defense systems and activates the ventral vagal system and its move toward safety and connection. Because these are internal experiments, reciprocity exercises done in isolation (an oxymoron to be sure), they can be done whenever a client feels the autonomic sense of danger that comes with disconnection. For clients who don't have a reliable social support network, these practices offer a way to have an experience of connection when it is needed and when safe people are not available. Engaging in these practices begins to build a reciprocity resource.

In African Bantu, *ubuntu* means a person becomes a person only through other people. I am human because I belong. As a result of decades of studies, we know that being separated from social connection, isolated from other people, is a lifelong risk factor affecting both physical and emotional health. Social disconnection and social exclusion activate the same pain pathways as experiences of injury (Eisenberger, 2012). Our language speaks to this: our heart aches or breaks, our feelings are hurt, we're racked with pain. Over time, a lone and lonely autonomic nervous system moves into habitual patterns of adaptive defense, making the physiological state of safety unavailable. Our common human experience is to feel soothed in the presence of others and distressed when we are left behind (Eisenberger, Lieberman, & Williams, 2003). We live in a culture that encourages autonomy and independence, and yet we need to remember that we are wired to live in connection.

SECTION I **SUMMARY**

> *Hope is being able to see that there is light despite all of the darkness.*
>
> —DESMOND TUTU

Polyvagal Theory brings hope to therapists in their work with clients whose patterns of protection keep them imprisoned in experiences of disconnection. Through this "science of connection," the autonomic nervous system can be reshaped toward safety and connection. The Social Engagement System, down regulated in an adaptive survival response, is waiting to be awakened. The vagal brake is intact, and the "malfunction" is not one of structure but rather of safe opportunities to be exercised (Porges, 2003).

Autonomic regulation is a necessary ingredient for physical and psychological well-being. "The state of the autonomic nervous system is a component of nearly every function in which humans engage" (Williamson, Porges, Lamb, & Porges, 2015, p. 2). Trauma influences autonomic regulation, setting in motion a pattern of chronically active defense systems. The result is ongoing distress that alters a person's ability to create and sustain nourishing relationships, which often leads to a lack of social support. Then, in the absence of social support, the autonomic nervous system senses danger and moves further away from connection into protective response. This feedback loop creates the habitual response patterns so often found with clients. By bringing Polyvagal Theory into therapy, clients can be helped to recognize their persistent response patterns and understand the ways those patterns have been shaped by their environment.

We routinely move down and up the autonomic hierarchy. Over the course of a day, we travel that route frequently. With the many moving pieces of people and connections that make up our lives, there is often a chaotic mix of autonomic energies. The goal is to navigate the autonomic response hierarchy with flexibility.

Moving out of scarcity into abundance is a powerful change. From a polyvagal perspective, this means moving out of the survival responses of the sympathetic and dorsal vagal systems into a foundation of ventral vagal regulation. From that neural platform, we can weather the common, inevitable times when we are pulled into defense and still feel the solidity of the ventral vagal state of safety and the story of abundance.

Through Polyvagal Theory, we become familiar with the underlying processes that shape our daily living experiences. With a fundamental understanding of the basic elements of Polyvagal Theory, we can now turn our attention to exploring specific practices to repattern the nervous system. Therapy (intervention) that supports autonomic regulation, engages the social engagement system, and quiets protective responses should have a powerful impact (Williamson et al., 2015). Polyvagal Theory offers therapists a guide to reshape the nervous system and help clients move out of habitual patterns of protection into new patterns of connection.

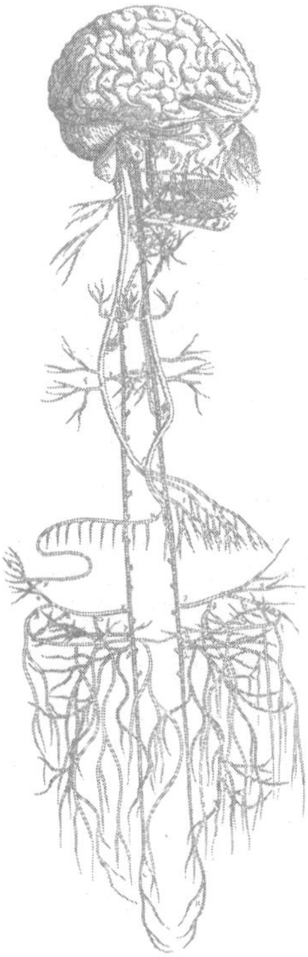

SECTION II

MAPPING THE NERVOUS SYSTEM

The good cartographer is both a scientist and an artist.

—ERWIN JOSEPHUS RAISZ

It is difficult to imagine a world without maps. People have been drawing maps for centuries. In 8,000 B.C. Babylon, maps of the sky and stars were being made. The sixth-century Greek philosopher Anaximander is often credited with creating the first map of the known world. Google Maps was launched in 2005, and now most of us don't venture out into the world without some device telling us the best route to our destination. Every culture uses maps (Blaut, Shea, Spencer, & Blades, 2003) and when we share a map, we can literally be "on the same page." We use maps when we're lost and need to find our way home. With an autonomic map, home is the safety of the ventral vagal state at the top of the autonomic hierarchy.

Clients are interested in their neurobiology—in understanding how the "vehicle they are driving through life" works. Adults and children are interested in learning about the three building blocks of the autonomic nervous system. The goal of autonomic mapping is for clients to illustrate their experience of the world from the three states of activation—safety, danger, and life-threat—by detailing body responses, beliefs, emotions, and behaviors. With map making, clients begin to recognize their individual profiles of engagement and activation, the first step toward creating a somatic sense of safety and stabilization.

Through the mapping process, therapists and clients create a shared understanding of the client's individual autonomic profile, making it a good fit for the initial phase of treatment. Mapping brings both left- and right-brain capacities together, first inviting an embodied sense of the autonomic state (right hemisphere bias) and then adding language to the experience (left hemisphere bias). The three maps of the mapping sequence become practical representations of a client's autonomic nervous system at work. These maps help guide clinical work. Because reshaping patterns of engagement is supported from a ventral vagal state and inhibited from states of sympathetic or dorsal vagal response, identifying a client's autonomic state is an important part of the therapy process.

Maps are powerful tools that help clients create a habit of knowing where they are on the autonomic hierarchy. Clients tell me that they hang their maps on the refrigerator or carry them in their wallets or pockets. With practice, clients begin to picture their maps in their minds and use these mental maps to routinely place themselves on their autonomic hierarchy. It's likely that children, even by age 4, can work with map-like models (Blaut et al., 2003), making autonomic mapping a useful tool in therapy with children and families. Creating an autonomic "family language" is helpful in managing the inevitable moments of messiness that occur in family work and at home in family systems. Couples can use their maps to explore the experiences of misattunement that so often bring them to therapy. Being able to see states of dysregulation on an autonomic map brings the understanding it's not that someone is unwilling to be present, but rather they are neurobiologically unable to be present. Maps also bring awareness to moments of autonomic intimacy; the sweetness of shared moments of ventral vagal attunement.

Mapping builds a habit of autonomic awareness. The basic mapping sequence is comprised of three maps: the Personal Profile Map, the Triggers and Glimmers Map, and the Regulating Resources Map.

Map 1, the Personal Profile Map, is the foundational map exploring the question, "Where am I?" With this map, clients identify their placement on the autonomic hierarchy. This map creates the basic skills necessary for recognizing autonomic states. With the Personal Profile Map, clients describe their somatic, thinking, feeling, and acting landmarks for each state.

Map 2 is the Triggers and Glimmers Map. This map helps clients begin to answer the essential question, "What brought me here?" Triggers are identified as sympathetic and dorsal vagal provocations, while glimmers are the moments the ventral vagal system lights up. It is important to recognize both, and in working with trauma survivors, therapists can get caught in the loop of focusing on dysregulation. Because the brain has a built-in negativity bias, it is necessary to bring attention to the micro-moments of safe connection or clients will move right past them and won't reap the benefits of those flashes of autonomic regulation.

Map 3, the Regulating Resources Map, is the final map in the sequence addressing the question, "How do I find my way to ventral vagal regulation?" We have the potential, and need, for both individual and interactive regulation and this map is designed to identify resources in both categories. In response to the ways life experiences have shaped their autonomic nervous systems, clients have a tendency to rely more on one than another. The Regulating Resources map brings attention to the presence and absence of individual and interactive resources and to the process of building new regulating pathways.

LIFE ON THE LADDER

> *From the moment you came into this world, a ladder was placed in front of you that you might transcend it.*
>
> —RUMI

The initial mapping sequence uses the ladder concept presented earlier in "A Beginner's Guide to Polyvagal Theory" (see p. 7). The ladder image invites a sense of safe transitions. Moving up and down a ladder does not require a leap across a gap but instead involves a steady progression from rung to rung. A ladder is always in contact with the ground, offering a way to safely reach higher places. In this case, the evolutionary roots of the dorsal vagus are the ground for our ladder, and the transition upward takes us through the energized sympathetic state into the ventral vagal state of social connection. Clients find it easy to answer the question, "Where are you on the ladder?" and also find it easy to track state shifts using the image of moving up and down the ladder. Ladder maps are simple to share with other people, creating a mutual understanding of autonomic states.

The use of a progression up and down a ladder is not meant to imply good or bad but rather is meant to represent the hier-

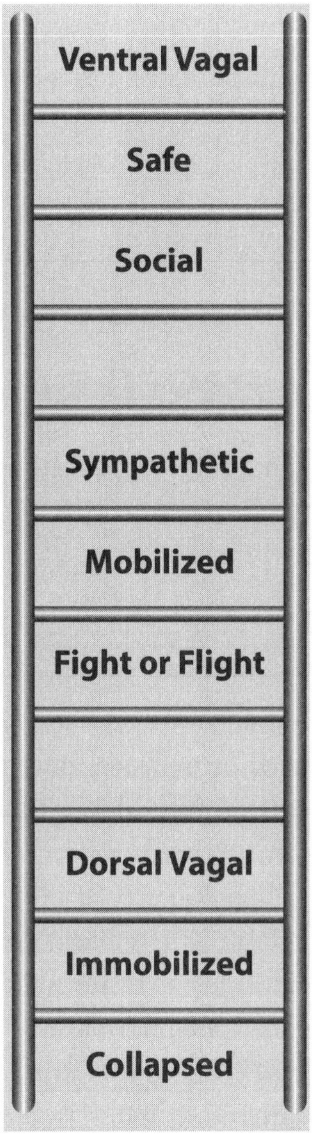

archy and the oversight of the ventral vagal state in maintaining homeostasis. Over the course of my clinical and teaching experiences, I have come across a handful of people who have a fear of heights and find the ladder image unsettling. One colleague creatively helped her client draw the top of the ladder wider than the base, which allowed the client to safely engage with the image. Another colleague turned the ladder image on its side, maintaining the sense of hierarchy using a progression of "back and forth" rather than "up and down."

On these maps, the ladder is divided into thirds. Each section represents an autonomic state (ventral vagal the top third, sympathetic the middle, and dorsal vagal the bottom third) and encompasses several rungs to illustrate that there is a range of responses within each state and a progression that happens when moving between states. The three maps use polyvagal terms to label the autonomic states: ventral vagal (safe, social); sympathetic (mobilized, fight, flight); dorsal vagal (immobilized, collapsed). It's also important for clients to have their own shorthand, their own ways of comfortably talking about their autonomic experiences, so each map section also includes a space for clients to create their own labels.

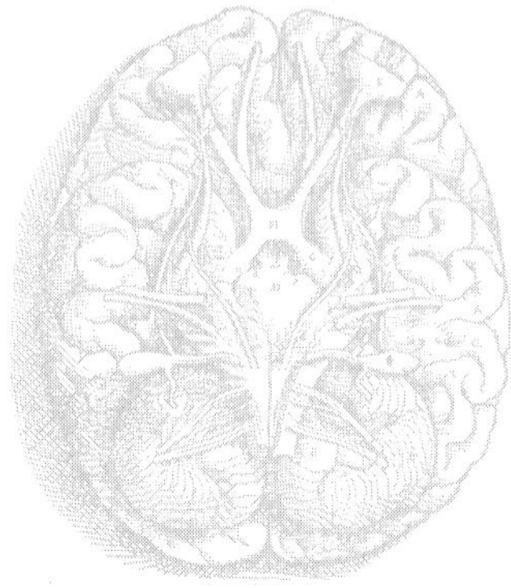

CHAPTER 4

THE PERSONAL PROFILE MAP

The Personal Profile Map offers clients a way to enter into autonomic awareness and bring perception to the wordless experience of neuroception. Once clients have created their map, it becomes an anchor they can return to with the orienting question, "Where am I on my map?"

The structure of this mapping experience is designed to maintain a "critical mass" of ventral vagal energy so clients can safely activate sympathetic and dorsal vagal states, be with each state but not hijacked by it, and intentionally shift between states. Therapists support their clients in safely moving between autonomic states by bringing their own ventral vagal energy to the process of co-regulation. Even though the client is the one making the map, it is a dyadic process. Because transitioning between states is difficult for many clients and can lead to extended periods of dysregulation, it's important for therapists to send autonomic cues of safety, creating a shared experience of befriending.

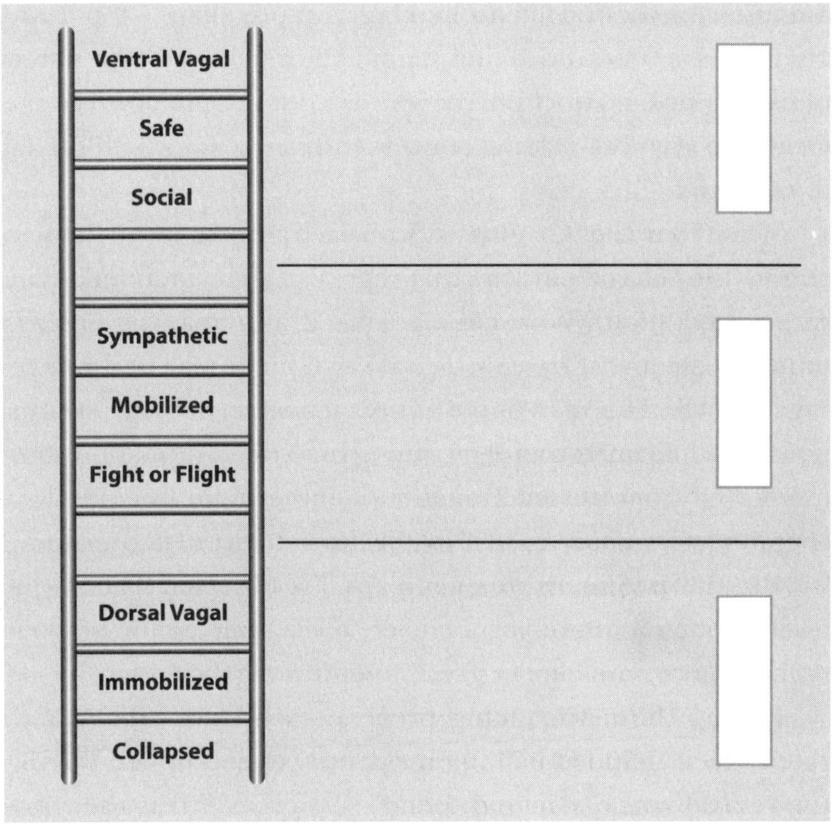

COMPLETING THE PERSONAL PROFILE MAP

Begin with a blank Personal Profile Map (template p. 217) and colored markers. The map can be drawn in pen or pencil, but my preference is to add color to the mapping process. Color is one of the first ways we learn to distinguish objects, and studies show colors evoke physiological arousal and psychological effects (Yoto, Katsuura, Iwanaga, & Shimomura, 2007). Working with markers takes adolescents and adults out of their ordinary habits, interrupting ingrained patterns of using pens, pencils, or typing. Offering colored markers brings clients' attention to the ways map making is more than a top-down cognitive exercise and invites them to move into a different way of experiencing. For children, who are not yet immersed in the grown-up ways of working, crayons and markers are still linked to creativity.

When your client begins work on each section, invite them to choose the colored markers that represent that autonomic state with the question, "What color are you drawn to as you prepare to map sympathetic danger, dorsal vagal life-threat, and ventral vagal safety?" This is an opportunity to practice making an autonomically informed choice by tuning in to the information communicated from the autonomic state rather than listening to a cognitive story about color. Notably, over the course of helping hundreds of people create their maps, I've observed that gray or black is often a dorsal vagal choice, red a sympathetic nervous system choice, and blue or green a ventral vagal choice.

During the map-making process, each state will be activated as it is mapped making it essential to end by completing the ventral vagal "safe and social" section as this is the autonomic state you want your clients to actively experience at the end of the exercise. Begin by completing the sympathetic section and then move to the dorsal vagal section. The shift from sympathetic to dorsal vagal is a move down the autonomic hierarchy and for most clients is a familiar pathway. After completing the dorsal vagal section, finish the map by filling in the ventral vagal section. The transition from dorsal vagal back into ventral vagal is more challenging and requires going through sympathetic mobilization. To support the return to ventral vagal regulation, you can guide your client with use of a breath to begin a return of energy (a sigh is often a sign of the system seeking regulation); offer cues the Social Engagement System watches for (warm tone of voice, eye gaze, perhaps leaning in a bit using proximity to signal connection); and name the sequence of leaving dorsal vagal collapse, mobilizing through the sympathetic nervous system, and coming into ventral vagal connection.

Mapping a state involves activating and then documenting the qualities of that state. When bringing sympathetic and dorsal vagal states to embodied aliveness for the purpose of mapping, help your client titrate the experience with just enough of a flavor, or taste, of the state for it to be accessible for mapping. For the ventral vagal state, invite your client to experience "filling from their core to their skin" creating a fully embodied and alive experience. Ask your client to sense their embodied experience (neuroception) and then bring that experience to awareness (cortical perception). Invite your client's attention to thoughts, feelings, body responses, and behaviors: "For each state, fill in the section by writing what it feels like, looks like, sounds like. What happens in your body? What do you do? What do you feel? What do you think and say?"

Once you get a feel for mapping, you'll find your own language to guide the process. As you routinely introduce your clients to mapping, you'll become comfortable offering words that invite the right amount of activation of each state. To give some examples to assist in that process, here are the introductions I often use for each phase.

Sympathetic nervous system: Remember a time when you felt the sense of sympathetic mobilizing energy moving through you. You might feel a sense of too much energy flooding your system, a sense of unease, perhaps even a sense of being overwhelmed. You might think one more thing will put me over the edge! And now let just enough of it into your mind and body to get a flavor of it, and then begin to map it.

Dorsal vagal: Think of a time when you felt the dorsal vagal sense of disconnect, a sense of collapse. There's not enough energy to run your system. If you were in a room full of people, it might feel as if there was a Plexiglas shield between you and them—you could see them but couldn't reach them. It might feel like depression. It's hard to find hope. Just let a tiny bit into your mind and body. Just enough to get a taste of it. And now begin to map it.

Ventral vagal: Think of a time when you felt the flow of ventral vagal energy. The sense that everything is okay, not wonderful or perfect but okay. The world is safe enough, and you can move through it with ease. Bring this moment to life and let it fill you . . . from your core to your skin. And when it's fully alive, begin to map that.

As your client fills in their map, have them notice how their sleep, relationship to food, and use of substances is affected in each section.

When your client finishes each section, ask them to complete the two sentences, "I am . . ." and "The world is . . ." These two sentences identify the core beliefs at work in each state, and, although not new realizations, clients often recognize them in new ways.

At the completion of the mapping exercise, ask your client to share each section with you following the same order in which the map was created: sympathetic to dorsal vagal ending in ventral vagal. Travel the map with your client. Get to know the body, behavior, and belief landmarks they have identified. In this process, you and your client can sense the shifts, noticing together difficulty or flexibility in moving between states. This is a time of ventral vagal connection as you remain curious and compassionate and actively engage your client in co-regulation.

Some clients struggle to find a moment of ventral vagal regulation. They may believe that ventral vagal energy is missing in their nervous system. One client told me she was convinced her vagus was broken! The present-moment attuned connection between you and your client can be the source of safe social engagement that brings the ventral vagal state alive for mapping. You might ask, "In this moment, between us, in this safe space, what is your autonomic nervous system telling you?" Connection with a pet is another way to find a moment of ventral vagal safety. A loving connection with an animal predictably brings a ventral vagal response. Research with dogs and their owners has shown that an elevated human heart rate is regulated when an owner is reunited with their dog (Beetz, Uvnäs-Moberg, Julius, & Kotrschal, 2012). Experiences in nature also bring the ventral vagal state alive. A person's relationship with nature has been shown to have important effects on well-being (Nisbet, Zelenski, & Murphy, 2011); time in the natural environment reduces stress (as measured in cortisol levels) and affects psychological health positively (Ewert, Klaunig, Wang, & Chang, 2016). When relationships have been a source of dysregulation, nature can be a pathway to finding a ventral vagal moment to map.

Using the Personal Profile map help your client consider which state they most often use to navigate daily living. An alarmed, hypervigilant sympathetic response or a dulled, nonreactive dorsal vagal response? For some clients, the border between ventral vagal and sympathetic responding is their familiar spot. Without sympathetic vigilance, they feel unsafe. For other clients, the flavor of dorsal vagal disconnection is their accustomed place. For many clients, the starting point is "dipping a toe" in ventral vagal energy and getting used to the state of safety that their nervous system has not had access to. A client's place on their autonomic ladder helps guide your session. In a sympathetic or dorsal vagal state their autonomic nervous system stays locked in a story of survival while a ventral vagal state brings connection and opens the system to the possibility of change. Once your client can map their autonomic states, together you can assess safety and risk from an autonomic perspective. Nearing the end of a session, the question "Where are you on your map?" is a reliable gauge for exploring what would be helpful for your client as they transition back into the world beyond the safety of the therapy session.

Sometimes clients act from a simple desire to do something, sometimes their actions are prompted by an unmet need, and knowing where they are on their map offers useful information. Take the question to engage or not to engage? Remembering that state drives story, a decision to engage might be a ventral vagal–inspired desire to be in connection with someone or might be a sympathetically driven need to not be alone. One brings a story of friendship and reciprocity, the other a story of the relentless search for connection. On the other side of that question, a decision to not engage might again be a ventral vagal experience of finding delight in an evening of reading and a story of self-care or a dorsal vagal experience of despair with an accompanying story of being a misfit.

In beginning therapy with new clients, it is helpful to complete the Personal Profile Map early in the therapy process. When introducing ongoing clients to Polyvagal Theory, the Personal Profile Map is a good starting point. Clients get to know themselves in different ways through map making. In the process of creating their Personal Profile Map, clients learn to turn toward their experiences without judgment and see their dysregulation as an attempt at protection and their need for connection as a common human need.

A colleague shared the following story of his mapping experience with a client.

I have been working with a fifth grade girl whose parents recently got divorced and wanted her to have someone to talk to. Recently, I walked her through Polyvagal Theory, and we mapped the three states of her autonomic nervous system. In our next session, I asked her if she'd been aware of her autonomic state during the past week. She said she was sitting in the cafeteria alone at one end of the table and her friends were at the other end. When she noticed she was alone, she asked herself if she was in dorsal vagal because she was by herself. She thought about her autonomic response and decided she was in ventral vagal and she was okay right where she was.

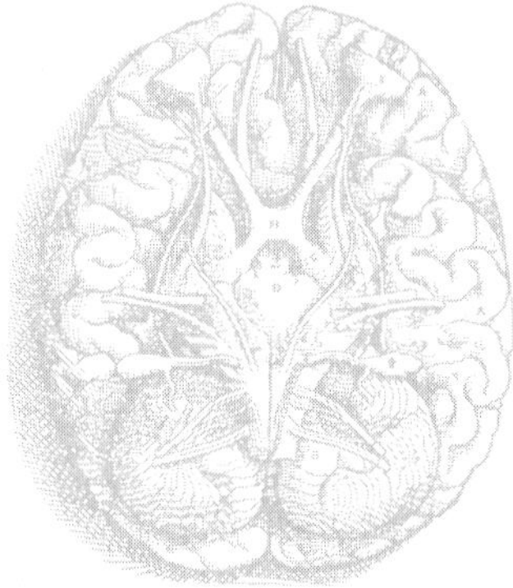

CHAPTER 5

THE TRIGGERS AND GLIMMERS MAP

Many of the systems embedded in our communities—schools and workplaces in particular—have been developed without regard for the role of the autonomic nervous system in guiding engagement and disengagement in everyday experience and as a result are insensitive to individual autonomic needs for safety. In social settings, a "one-size-fits-all" approach has become the norm. Behaviors identified as conforming are considered proper and are expected. In the struggle to fit in, we may feel the presence of cues of danger and the absence of cues of safety. When the autonomic survival response overrides the abilities of the Social Engagement System, engaging with others in co-regulation is impossible. Without an autonomic lens, people whose underlying state prevents them from fitting into the accepted model are judged as misfits and criticized from a belief that they could modify their behaviors if they wanted to. Insensitive systems reinforce autonomic dysregulation through blame that engenders shame. It becomes a story about *who* and not *how* or *why*.

The second mapping tool is the Triggers and Glimmers

Map. This map brings attention to moments of activation and moments of regulation. We identify *triggers* as cues of danger that activate sympathetic and dorsal vagal defense and *glimmers* as cues of safety arising from a ventral vagal state of health, growth, and restoration. Our survival depends on accurate recognition of both helpful and hurtful experiences. Remembering that it is not enough to remove cues of danger but that we must also sense cues of safety, this map-making exercise brings attention to a client's experiences in each of the three autonomic states.

This second map in the series is designed to help clients learn what activates specific state shifts and begin to consider that their autonomic experiences might be reliably anticipated. With a sense of predictability, clients no longer feel they are simply at the mercy of the Fates. This map helps makes sense of what our clients often think "just happens." When clients understand there are precipitating factors (causes) for each state, they can then begin to recognize their movement in and out of states (effects). Effects depend on causes (Rim, Hansen, & Trope, 2013), and exploring "why" brings a bit of observer energy that makes it easier to then look at the autonomic state.

TRIGGERS

Identification of triggers is a way to begin to move out of the self-critical story of "who I am" into curiosity about "how I respond." In this mapping exercise, triggers are identified and linked to an autonomic state. Triggers occur when the vagal brake is not able to relax, reengage, and maintain ventral vagal regulation. Triggers are a result of a neural challenge that is too big for the flexibility of the system. They bring a neuroception of danger or life-threat, and the autonomic nervous system activates a survival response. These cues of danger prompt either a sympathetic mobilization or a dorsal vagal shutdown.

GLIMMERS

The ventral vagal system guides our experience of glimmers. The neuroception of safety creates the possibility of relaxing into a moment of connection to self, to others, or to the environment. Cues of safety bring glimmers that are often sensed in micro-moments of ventral vagal activation. Glimmers can help calm a nervous system in survival mode and bring a return of autonomic regulation. The research of Kok and colleagues (2013) found that even though the experience of a positive emotion is brief, it can build enduring resources. Bringing attention to these small moments moves the system toward a tipping point, and multiple micro-moments may become significant enough to create an autonomic shift.

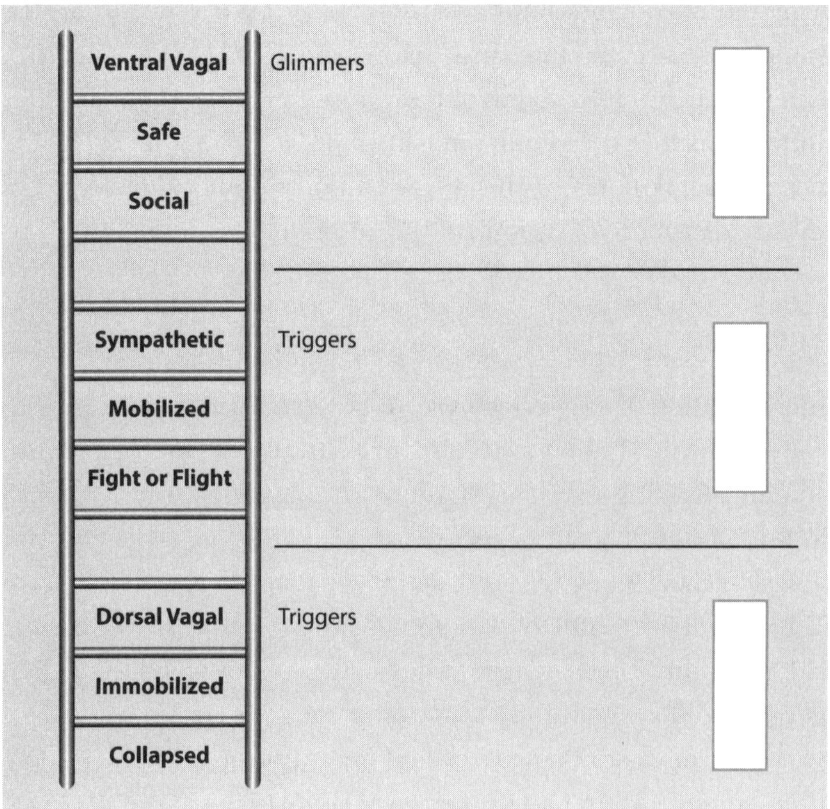

COMPLETING THE TRIGGERS AND GLIMMERS MAP

The Triggers and Glimmers Map (template p. 221) uses the same ladder template as the Personal Profile Map adding the "glimmers" label to the ventral vagal section and the "triggers" label to the sympathetic and dorsal vagal sections. This second map in the mapping sequence follows the Personal Profile Map, building on a client's beginning understanding of their experience in each of the three autonomic states. This map-making exercise brings clients' attention to what happens in their bodies, in the environment, and in relationships that sets autonomic state shifts in motion. Triggers and glimmers are the concrete events that move clients up and down the autonomic ladder. The question "What brings me here?" is the prompt that begins the exploration. Clients often first notice the "headlines" and then can be helped to name the "tangibles."

Dorsal Vagal Headline: feeling unwanted

- Tangibles: when my friends plan a date and don't ask me to join them; when my coworkers are having a conversation and don't notice me

Sympathetic Nervous System Headline: feeling disrespected

- Tangibles: when my friend turns away from me during a conversation; when my partner interrupts me

Ventral Vagal Headline: feeling seen

- Tangibles: when the store clerk looks at me and smiles; when my coworker asks me how my day is going

It is important to move from identifying the broad headlines to defining the specific events that create the headlines. Describing the specific factors that create entry into a state is necessary in order to understand how to predict, manage, or re-create state shifts.

Some clients like to have their Personal Profile Map to refer to. Others will simply use recent experiences as a guide in this second map-making process. As with the Personal Profile Map exercise, clients again are offered colored markers to use. Work with the triggers first. Because it is experiences of distress that bring our clients to therapy, the triggers are usually easily accessible. Ask your clients to identify which of the survival states (dorsal vagal or sympathetic) is easiest for them to name their triggers and start there. Map that state and then the other. Once sympathetic and dorsal vagal triggers have been mapped, move to exploration of glimmers. As your clients complete each section of the map, ask them to share that section with you. Keeping the focus on one state at a time helps clients become clear about what takes them into each state and see the distinctions between the states.

A client may struggle with any one of the states on this map because of their individual autonomic profile. If either sympathetic mobilization or dorsal vagal collapse is an unfamiliar state, identification of the associated triggers will be more difficult. Clients often find recognition of glimmers to be the most challenging part of this map-making exercise and feel encouraged when they discover that glimmers are in fact brought to life by specific incidents. Bringing attention to glimmers is not negating of the suffering our clients experience with triggers. Triggers and glimmers are one of the both/and experiences that therapy strives to foster. A strengths-based perspective reminds us that well-being is not simply the absence of problems but also the presence of strengths. We used to think of well-being as the absence of disease and disorder. More and more, we are recognizing that well-being goes beyond the lack of disease and just as importantly includes positive social and emotional functioning. From an autonomic perspective, Polyvagal Theory identifies the link between physiological and psychological well-being and identifies the need for both resolution of cues of danger and recognition and resourcing of cues of safety. In completing the Triggers and Glimmers Map, clients are supported in exploring their full autonomic experience.

The Triggers and Glimmers Map helps clients identify their sympathetic and dorsal vagal sensitivities and ventral vagal strengths from a stance of curiosity. Autonomic response is felt in how intense or nuanced moments of activation or ease feel, how long they last, and how often they appear. Considering the ratio of triggers to glimmers is another way to observe responses and note the impact on daily living. Change over time in each of these markers (frequency, intensity, duration, ratio) is a measure of movement along the autonomic continuum of sensitivity to resilience.

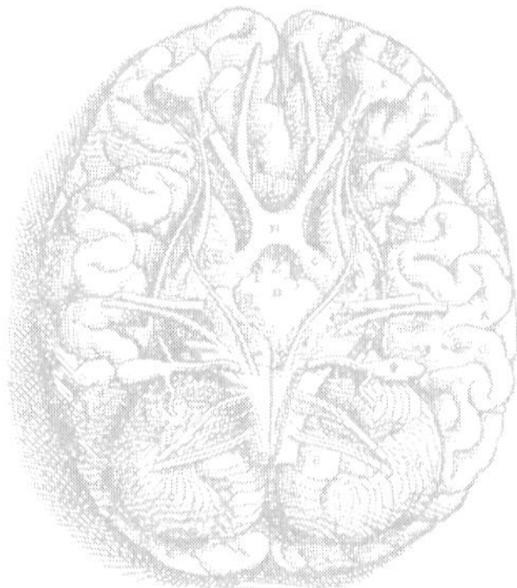

CHAPTER 6

THE REGULATING RESOURCES MAP

The Regulating Resources Map is the final map in the basic mapping sequence. Having mapped the experience of each autonomic state (Personal Profile Map) and identified the cues of danger and safety that prompt activation of each state (Triggers and Glimmers Map), clients work with this final map in the series to gain awareness of their patterns of regulation. The Regulating Resources Map is designed to help clients identify individual and interactive actions that move them out of dorsal vagal and sympathetic states and actions that maintain a ventral vagal state. In this map-making process, clients continue to get to know their autonomic profile as they discover both the presence and absence of individual and interactive resources in each autonomic state.

LEARNING ABOUT REGULATION

We come into the world with a need to co-regulate to survive. Babies and their mothers engage each other in reciprocal regulation, a baby naturally turning toward their mother and their mother responding, together co-creating a physiological and psychological state (Apicella et al., 2013). This interactive experience tones the baby's nervous system beginning the creation of their individual neural profile. When the expected and common moments of rupture happen, a regulated and attuned mother notices, makes a repair, and the baby experiences safety in the interactive regulation. An example of this is a mother who is playing with her baby and turns away to interact with her older child. The baby feels the loss of connection and signals distress (vocalizes, reaches out, cries). The mother recognizes her baby's dysregulation and returns her attention through her eye gaze and prosodic voice. Tronick and Reck (2009) demonstrated that moments of misattunement, or interactive mismatch, do not necessarily unfavorably impact attachment; rather, it is when ruptures happen and are not repaired that the baby begins to carry a negative expectation into future interactions. In the example above, if the mother doesn't recognize her baby's distress or if she responds with anger to her baby's demand for connection, the necessary repair does not happen. If a mother is chronically dysregulated, her ability to offer interactive regulation is affected, and her baby's autonomic nervous system moves into protective mode, no longer seeking the safety of co-regulation. For this baby, survival now depends on self-regulation.

The ability for self-regulation should optimally be built on the foundation of interactive regulation. A baby begins to learn to self-regulate from the interactive regulation in the attuned mother and baby dyad. This ability to self-regulate continues to develop throughout childhood supported by social engagement with autonomically regulated others. "The capacity to fully experience one's feelings, particularly when they are intense and/or painful, is greatly enhanced by being able to do so together with a supportive, empathic, and emotionally present other" (Fosha,

2001, p. 229). As the capacity for self-regulation increases, when reactions happen, regulation and recovery follows. When we are supported by a nervous system that can engage with both interactive and individual streams of regulation, safe and flexible navigation of the experiences of daily living is possible.

Research into social connection shows a downward trend in connection and a rise in isolation and loneliness (Seppala, Rossomando, & Doty, 2013). Without reliable people to interact with, we turn to our self-regulatory skills and the opportunity for interactive regulation and creating autonomic well-being through connection with others is lost. When we feel lonely, we also feel unsafe (Cacioppo & Cacioppo, 2014), and loneliness activates the survival systems of the autonomic nervous system.

Through the Social Engagement System, we use our eyes, our voice, and movement of our face and head to send and receive signals of safety and to reach out for and offer connection. When we use devices for communication, the important nonverbal elements conveyed in tone of voice, facial expression, and body language are often lost. As we rely more on online conversations to communicate, there are fewer opportunities to exercise our social engagement circuitry. Sherry Turkle, director of the MIT Initiative on Technology and Self, said: "Face-to-face conversation is the most human and humanizing thing we do" (2015, p. 3).

A history of misattuned caregiving and unrepaired relationship ruptures shapes the autonomic nervous system toward protection and away from connection. Social isolation and the perception of social disconnection can lead to a lack of interactive resources. Both experiences become a story of aloneness. A chronic neuroception of danger or life-threat that is triggered in response to being in connection with others makes using interactive resources difficult. With a nervous system that dysregulates when social engagement is offered, a client will likely initially find interactive regulation too great a neural challenge. For some clients, the first interactive regulation resource may simply be sitting in a place where people are present (mall, coffee shop, movie), and feeling the presence of others from a safe distance.

When exploring resources to move from a dorsal vagal or sympathetic response, it is important to remember the energy states involved in each. In dorsal vagal collapse, the autonomic nervous system has entered a state of "conservation" where there is not enough energy moving in the system to support regulation. To begin to recover, a gentle return of energy is needed. The resource can't bring too big of a shift in energy or it will feel dangerous and push the system further into disconnection. In a state of sympathetic mobilization, too much energy is flooding the system. To move from here, the resource has to bring a way to safely discharge energy.

Some actions may be a resource for each of the autonomic states when utilized with just a slight difference. Movement is an example of this. Humans are built to move. Movement was essential to survival (Owen et al., 2010) and is a fundamental resource for regulation. Through a polyvagal perspective, we understand that movement is a key feature of sympathetic activation, is missing in dorsal vagal collapse, and is a natural part of the ventral vagal state of connection. As a resource to shift the immobilization of the dorsal vagal state, movements can be small or can even simply be sensed (imagined rather than enacted, bringing the motor cortex alive). In the sympathetic state the intensity of movement needs to be shaped, and in the ventral vagal state movement can be savored. Using walking as an example, in dorsal vagal the movement might be small, slow-motion steps (or imagined steps); in sympathetic a fast-paced run; and in ventral vagal a refreshing, restorative walk or hike.

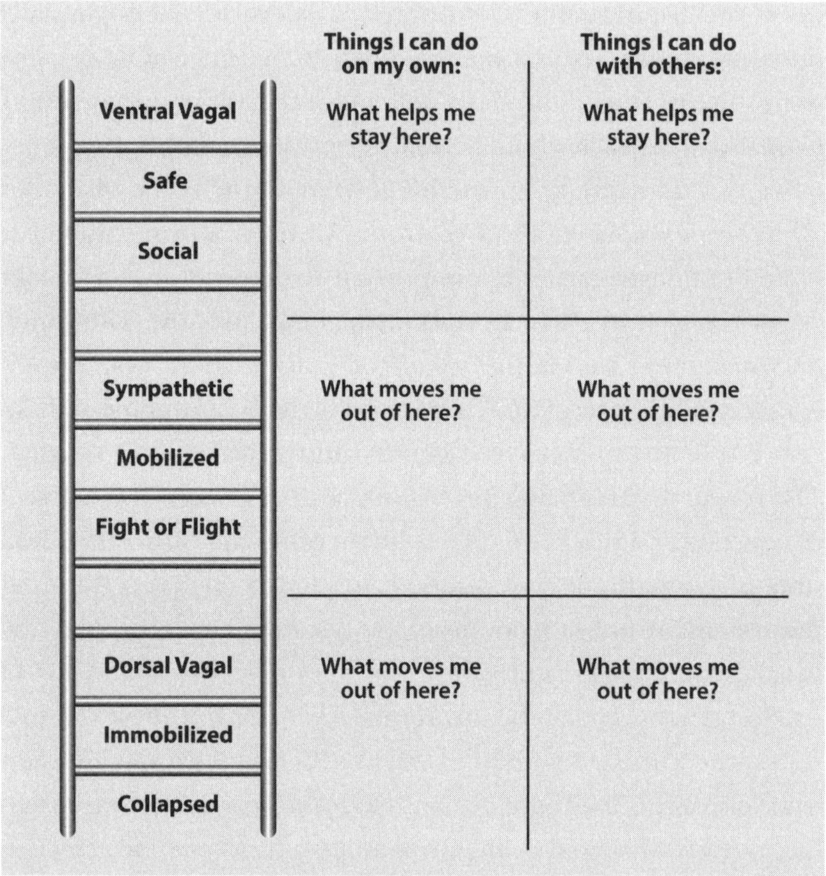

COMPLETING THE REGULATING RESOURCES MAP

The Regulating Resources Map (template p. 225) uses the same ladder template as the other maps in the series with the addition of a center line to divide the map into the two categories of regulation: interactive regulation (Things I can do with others) and self-regulation (Things I can do on my own). The sympathetic and dorsal vagal sections are labeled "What moves me out of here?" and the ventral vagal section is labeled "What helps me stay here?" As with the Triggers and Glimmers Map, it doesn't make a difference whether a client begins with the sympathetic or dorsal vagal section. Have your client start in the state that is most familiar to them and fill in their self and interactive resources for that state. Then do the same for the other survival state. Finish by filling in the ventral vagal section.

Like the other maps in this sequence, colored markers are used, but for this map invite your client to choose two colors for each state: one for individual resources and one for interactive resources. The picture this creates colorfully illustrates abundance and scarcity. With a clear picture of their present options, clients can begin to look at effectiveness and outcomes and explore where, and how, to add resources.

The Regulating Resources Map is a work in progress as your clients continue to create resources that lead them back into a ventral vagal state and exercise their vagal brake. The map becomes part of the therapy process with a focus on bringing balance to individual and interactive resources, creating resources where they are absent, and shaping resources toward actions that effectively bring a return to ventral vagal safety. This map is designed to draw your clients' awareness to the resources they already use and to the areas in which resources are scarce.

Clients are often surprised, and can be distressed, to see the variety of ways they engage in attempts to regulate. *Merriam-Webster's* defines a resource as "something to which one has recourse in difficulty" and "a possibility of relief or recovery." When your clients are autonomically dysregulated and experiencing an adaptive survival response, turning toward an action that brings the possibility of relief is powerful. While the resource might not be a response that is health giving, it is an attempt to resolve the pain of the present state of autonomic reaction. Food and substances are common examples of resources that your clients may turn to and may eventually want to change their relationship with. Understanding the autonomic need to ensure survival, clients can be helped to see their "resource responses" without shame.

Clients can also be surprised to notice an absence of resources for a particular state or a scarcity of resources in the individual or interactive category. It's important to remind clients that their autonomic nervous system has been toned by their past and is being retuned in the present. They will create new resources in the process of bringing balance to their system, using the information from their map to guide this process.

For your clients, just as important as identification of what moves them out of dorsal vagal or sympathetic dysregulation is identification of the resources that maintain their ventral vagal state of connection. If your clients struggle with this portion of the map, looking at previously identified glimmers can prompt recognition of regulating pathways. Because clients come to therapy in states of dysregulation, they may think they have no resources for this section of the map. Some clients will be relieved to find several resources, while others will be dismayed to see how few they have. Over the course of therapy, all of your clients will build numerous resources and find just the right amount of interactive and individual resources to fit their unique autonomic needs.

SECTION II **SUMMARY**

> *That which we persist in doing becomes easier to do, not that the nature of the thing has changed but that our power to do so has increased.*
>
> —RALPH WALDO EMERSON

The autonomic nervous system is our personal surveillance system, pursuing safety while remaining alert for danger. This system sends its information through our physiology, supporting engagement or creating disconnection while moving us toward or away from people, places, and things. Responses are translated into a story of "who and why" as we move further into the psychological story. We forget the opening lines: Once upon a time there was an autonomic response.

The initial mapping sequence outlined in the chapters of Section II provides a structure for your clients to identify the ways particular autonomic response patterns affect their experiences of daily living. A befriending process underlies the map making: The therapist guides their client in turning toward their autonomic experience and therapist and client together listen openheartedly and open-mindedly to the physiological underpinnings of their psychological stories. Through completing the three-map sequence, clients start to recognize autonomic states and the ways they are moved into and out of each state. They become expert state detectors. When clients become comfortable with their own mapping skills, they naturally begin to be curious about the autonomic states of the people around them. My clients often tell me they begin to see the world through the lens of the autonomic nervous system. The mapping process gives clients a way to use Polyvagal Theory to understand actions—their own and those of others.

These are dynamic maps, shifting as more ventral vagal regulation is realized. Clients will modify their maps as glimmers continue to emerge, triggers are resolved, and resources created. Once introduced, the framework of placement on the ladder is an effective tool to use throughout the therapy process. Many therapists keep a blank map available during the therapy session. The question "Where are you on your ladder?" or "Where is that experience on your map?" helps clients anchor their experiences. Between sessions, maps provide the structure for clients to continue to practice autonomic awareness, building skill through the small, regularly repeated experiences of mapping that are needed to shape the nervous system in new ways.

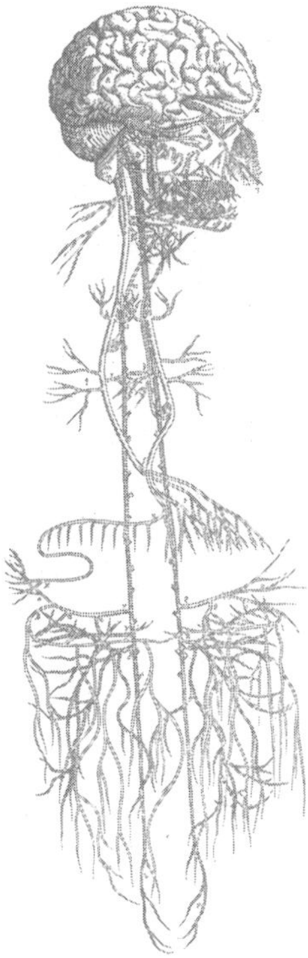

SECTION III

NAVIGATING THE NERVOUS SYSTEM

We ourselves must walk the path.

—BUDDHA

Section III continues the befriending process begun in Section II and introduces skills for attending. The ability of clients to navigate their nervous systems by first correctly placing themselves on the autonomic ladder and then tracking large and nuanced state shifts across time is a necessary foundation for making the course corrections that return the system to ventral vagal regulation.

Autonomic awareness is a part of our experience of self. Craig (2009a) talks about a sentient self, while Damasio (2005) describes a neural self. Body (autonomic) awareness is an integral part of self-awareness (Mehling et al., 2011) and shapes the sense of who we are. An impaired ability for autonomic awareness affects our human "being." With autonomic awareness, clients learn to listen to their embodied stories. Through befriending and attending skills, clients begin to bring curiosity to exploration of their daily experience, looking at how they interact or isolate, join or judge, move toward or away, speak or stay silent.

Through the practices presented in Section III, clients learn to attend to their autonomic state and to experience the state as separate from their familiar psychological story. The exercises are designed to support clients in moving into deeper understanding and honoring of their adaptive survival responses as they begin to reframe the meaning of their autonomic states of arousal.

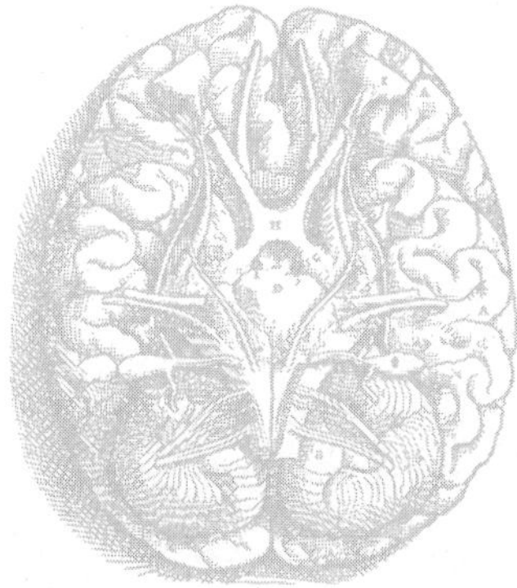

CHAPTER 7

COMPASSIONATE CONNECTION

The befriending process brings clients into connection with their autonomic stories with curiosity and without judgment. This chapter builds on the three maps of the basic mapping series helping clients explore the "art" of autonomic awareness through artwork, music, movement, and writing.

EXERCISE
Art Maps

I found I could say things with color and shapes that I couldn't say any other way—things I had no words for.

—GEORGIA O'KEEFFE

Creating art is a personal integrative experience—an experience of flow that increases functional connectivity in the brain and brings an increase in qualities of resilience (Bolwerk, Mack-Andrick, Lang, Dörfler, & Maihöfner, 2014). When we create an autonomic Art Map, we bring the right hemisphere and its love of imagery into action. And because the right hemisphere is less influenced by prediction, what emerges in an Art Map often brings new awareness. An example of this is the client who told me that when she created her Art Map, her ventral vagal space was filled with the color of sunshine, and she was surprised when she drew a little figure there in the sun. She hadn't realized she lived in that space too. Having seen over and over the power of creating Art Maps, I encourage you to invite all your clients to illustrate their autonomic nervous system.

Clients don't have to be artists to make an autonomic Art Map. They only need materials and a willingness to experiment—in this case paper, materials, and enough cues of safety in the room and in the therapeutic relationship to elicit a ventral vagal state of curiosity. Kids are naturally drawn to art paper and markers. With adults, using heavier weight, large-sized art paper avoids the implicit memories from childhood that newsprint can trigger, conveys a valuing of the process, and invites them to move beyond the confines of the world so often defined by 8.5-inch × 11-inch (printer size) paper.

Art Maps can illustrate one autonomic state or the three states of the autonomic hierarchy. Creating one state fosters an intimate connection to that autonomic experience, while illustrating the hierarchy brings awareness to the relationship between states. Art Maps come in an array of formats and sizes (collages on poster board using old magazine pictures, drawings with markers or crayons, painting, using objects from nature) dependent only on the materials available and a client's creativity. Once your client has decided on the style of the Art Map, encourage them to let their autonomic nervous system guide them. Creating an Art Map is a personal process, each map having its own shape, style, and story. The process and product are both important parts of making an Art Map. When your client's map is complete, ask them to take you into their creative process and tell you the story of their map. Art Maps can be created during a session or created between sessions and brought back to share. Many clients enjoy finding materials and making their maps at home. Clients who may feel an autonomic move into protection when thinking about making art while you are watching often find enough autonomic safety to create their map at home.

EXERCISE
Three Things: Show and Tell

Ask your client to choose an object to represent each of their three states of autonomic response. You can use a sand tray collection, a collection of objects in your office or ask your client to bring three things from home. If it feels comfortable, get out of your office and go for a walk with your client to look for three things. Invite your client to tune in to their autonomic responses to make the choice about what represents each state. Explore the process of choosing. What drew your client to that object? How did your client make the choice? What state was the most difficult? Easiest? Ask your client to tell the you story of each object. One of my favorite stories is from a client who told me: "For my dorsal vagal object I chose this china angel whose head is broken off. The head is somewhere in my house but I can't find it. This is how I feel—disembodied, lost. I know the rest of me is around somewhere but I can't seem to find myself." Invite your client to find a small object that represents their ventral vagal state to carry as a tangible reminder that the ventral vagal state exists and that they know it and can inhabit it, even if only for moments in time.

EXERCISE
Sand Tray: Taking Your Map into the Sand

The kinesthetic experience of working in the sand offers another way of seeing and sensing autonomic states. Sand trays offer your clients a way to visualize their autonomic response patterns through objects and metaphor and, through the story in the sand, are a way for you to enter a client's autonomic nervous system with them. Inviting a client to create their autonomic hierarchy in the sand is a way to take another look at the Personal Profile Map. Some clients use interesting objects to divide their tray in thirds, while other clients decide to simply let each state take up the space it needs. Because sand trays provide a necessary distance for clients to connect with what otherwise might bring too big of a neural challenge, their trays can be used in the beginning mapping phase to safely explore the full experience of each state. As your client creates each individual state in the sand, invite them to share the story of that scene with you.

Sand trays are also a valuable way to explore the Regulating Resources Map using objects to represent moving out of sympathetic or dorsal vagal dysregulation and nurturing a ventral vagal state. Once the initial tray has been created, invite your client to add objects and experiment with the shifts that happen as they introduce different resources. A sand tray construction of a ventral vagal state is a powerful way to explore the experience of a regulated nervous system. Have your client take a photo of their ventral vagal sand world. A photo of their tray brings back the memory of building it and brings the ventral vagal experience to life.

EXERCISE

Writing about Your Rhythm: The Story of a State

Writing, to me, is simply thinking through my fingers.

—ISAAC ASIMOV

Writing is often used as a way of making sense of things. It helps us organize experiences and often leads to a new perspective. The act of writing is a multilayered process that brings together several areas of the brain while calling on our visual, motor, and cognitive skills. Although writing is a top-down experience, the invitation to clients in these mapping exercises is to "let their state speak" and gather the information for their writing from connecting to their autonomic pathways. When your client completes a piece of writing, invite them to share it with you and then with other people in their social support network. Sharing brings the individual act of writing into an interactive act of resonance and reciprocity.

Writing about One State

Concentrating on one state invites your clients into a rich knowing of the state. For dysregulated states, the act of writing allows your client to see the state from a narrator role. Writing a reflection of an experience of sympathetic or dorsal vagal dysregulation supports a safe re-viewing of the experience. As your client writes, they bring perception to neuroception and consider what words accurately convey their autonomic experience. Writing a reflection of a moment of ventral vagal regulation is a way for your client to move into an intentional savoring of the experience. Ask your client to use all their senses in their writing as they bring the story of their state of safety and connection alive and celebrate it in words.

Writing about the Cycle of States

Writing about their rhythm of response brings clients into awareness of habitual patterns. This form of writing helps your client sense into the relationship between states. Have your client attend to how they move between states. Is there a stuck place? How do they get unstuck? Is there a flow? How do they feel that flow?

Although writing is not everyone's method of choice, for some clients the written word brings clarity. These clients see autonomic patterns and hear the story of their states through the process of writing.

EXERCISE
Musical Maps

Do you know that our soul is composed of harmony?

—LEONARDO DA VINCI

Music is all around us and accompanies us as we move through our daily lives. Its roots are ancient, with evidence of music making present in every known culture (Schäfer, Sedlmeier, Städtler, & Huron, 2013). Music is both a modulator and an activator of the autonomic nervous system. Reactions to music, including stimulation of emotion-processing parts of the brain and effect on levels of hormones, seems to be deeply embedded in the nervous system (Chanda & Levitin, 2013). Music can send sounds of safety or signal a call to survival. Muscles of the Social Engagement System (face, head, middle ear) are active in both listening to and producing music (Porges, 2010). Autonomically, a neuroception of unsafety occurs in response to low- and high-pitched frequencies, while frequencies of the human voice bring a neuroception of safety (Porges, 2010). Music moves us, not only putting bodies in motion but also stirring autonomic state shifts.

In his book titled *What to Listen for in Music,* the American composer Aaron Copland describes sensuous and expressive planes of listening. From the sensuous plane, we hear without thinking, without considering. Copland describes how we bathe in the sound and how the atmosphere of a room can be changed with one note (Copland, 1998). Through our neuroception we take in the music and an autonomic state is activated. In the expressive plane, we hear the mood of the music, and neuroception moves into perception, as we connect our own meaning to a song.

One client, whom I call my "musicologist," inspired me to use playlists. She taught me about the power of using music to safely explore memories of sympathetic and dorsal vagal states and to embrace those lived experiences. She showed me the power of song to deepen connection with ventral vagal regulation. From her experiences, I began to invite clients to create their own playlists and bring them to sessions to share. I also started to create a music sampling experience for clients and to explore with them what musical selections activate each of their autonomic states.

Music is meant to be shared and experienced with others. One approach to understanding music suggests that listening to music with others serves an evolutionary purpose of holding people together—caring for, and about, each other (Schäfer et al., 2013). The shared listening experience is powerful. Levitin (2016) reports that increased empathy, increased trust, and social bonding are outcomes of listening to music out loud together. Creating, sharing, listening, and experiencing playlists together with a client is a meaningful experience of reciprocity.

A playlist can focus on the ventral vagal state with songs that elicit responses along the continuum of safe and social including calm, excitement, passion, compassion, connection, play, celebration, joy, rest, and restoration. Invite your clients to make playlists that resource different aspects of the ventral vagal experience and begin to build a collection of songs that invoke their experiences of ventral vagal safety and connection.

Another playlist can bring a musical revisiting of dysregulated moments during which the listener and the instruments and voices are joined in shared experiencing. There is a "growing body of evidence for the 'paradoxical' effect of enjoyment of negative emotions in music" (Hall, Schubert, & Wilson, 2016, p.11). Your clients can sink into and even savor the suffering of sympathetic and dorsal vagal moments that otherwise are too intense and overwhelm their system. When the music matches their mood, the autonomic resonance makes it possible for them to safely touch their suffering.

Yet another playlist creates the experience of moving through the response cycle by including songs that evoke each state. Ask your clients to choose songs for each state and arrange them in an order that intersperses songs of safety among songs of dysregulation. The listening experience brings a steady flow of moving in and out of states, validating that state shifting is possible and that ventral vagal energy is a strong regulating influence.

Once your clients have created their playlists, connecting with their musical resource is simple. Music is portable and easily accessed, making it a readily available regulating resource. Using music to regulate or reinforce autonomic states doesn't take a lot of effort. Music is commonplace in everyday lives so turning to it for comfort is a natural response.

EXERCISE

Moving with Your Map

Movement never lies. It is a barometer telling the state of the soul's weather to all who can read it.

—MARTHA GRAHAM

Moving with Your Map exercises offer your clients a way to deepen into relationship with a single state or intentionally explore their experience of the autonomic hierarchy. These exercises are useful across the range of therapy environments: individual, couple, family, group. In each of the variations, clients are asked to create a movement to represent individual autonomic states. Most clients find they can safely engage in these exercises from a seated position using hand movements, and some will feel safe in standing and moving their full body.

Introduce the skills of movement mapping to your clients as a way for them to first connect to an individual state and express it in the form of motion and then to experiment with transitioning between states by linking one movement to the next. Movement can be used to help your clients get to know an activated state, to induce state shifts by intentionally creating movements, and highlight a ventral vagal state of safety to resource a glimmer experience. Ventral vagal movements are commonly shaped by gestures with a circular flow, sympathetic motions are often jagged and fast, while dorsal vagal motions are slow and labored.

Mirroring of movements has been shown to increase somatic and emotional understanding between people, enhance the feeling of connectedness, and increase empathy for the person whose movements are being mirrored (McGarry & Russo, 2011), and when you join your client in their movements, moving becomes an experience of autonomic resonance. Therapists often tell me that when they mirror a client's movements, they understand their client's autonomic experiences in a new way. Invite your client to find the movement that represents an autonomic state and then mirror their movement. If there are other participants in the session, have them join in the mirroring. Ask your client what it's like to have you and others moving with them. What is your own autonomic response? The response of other participants? When working with a couple, one partner told me that he hadn't understood his partner's description of her sympathetic state, but when he mirrored her movement, his autonomic nervous system understood what she had been trying to say.

To use movement to help your client experiment with transitioning between states, first make sure their ventral vagal movement is strong enough to bring a return to regulation. Test the strength by manipulating the ratio of time spent in each state. Begin by extending time with ventral vagal movements and abbreviating time with sympathetic and dorsal vagal movements. Change the ratio as your client gains confidence in the ability to use their ventral vagal movement. Feeling confidence in their ability to return to regulation is an experience that needs to be nourished. Active engagement with your client in the movement experience is an important co-regulating factor. For some clients, transitioning through the sequence of states is an unfamiliar or even unknown experience. They are used to being pulled into a state and not being able to find their way out. Your ventral vagal "anchor" and co-regulating actions bring safety to the experiment.

For all Moving with Your Map exercises, have your clients take turns leading and following. It is important to try out both roles. To lead involves inward listening and bringing that autonomic awareness to movement. Following brings attention to the ways other nervous systems represent states through movement. Leading and following creates awareness of the two sides of attunement. With children, you can frame the mirroring exercises as a game of autonomic follow-the-leader.

EXERCISE
Sculpting

When you slow down enough to sculpt, you discover all kinds of things you never noticed before.

—KAREN JOBE TEMPLETON

A sculpture is a work of art that invites observation from multiple angles and perspectives. Seeing the human form in a sculpture feels personal and familiar. Sculpting autonomic states, either in a dyadic practice or with art mannequins, enables your client to bring an internal state to external physical form and safely explore the story of their states.

The dyadic sculpting practice happens between the client in the role of sculptor and another person who takes on the part of the sculpture. To sculpt an autonomic state, ask your client to choose an autonomic state to work with and invite them to move between internal awareness and external action, listening to the state and then sculpting, repeating the process as their sculpture takes shape. Using talk or touch, your client "molds" the other person (you, their partner, family member, other group member) into the form of their chosen autonomic state. The sculpting process brings the sculptor and sculpture into a shared autonomic state.

The second way of sculpting is to use the articulated wooden mannequins available in art stores. Mannequins come in a variety of sizes. The small one is a satisfying size (5.5 inches) to hold and shape. The tactile sense of the mannequin in the hands invites an ongoing connection between internal experience and external representation. The larger size mannequin (8 or 12 inches) is good for shaping and displaying when the autonomic state and story is the focus of the session. Outside of sessions, mannequins offer a way for your clients to continue to attend to autonomic states and gain confidence in their autonomic mapping abilities.

Shaping a mannequin to match an autonomic state requires the ability to stop, notice, and create a pose that fits the feeling. With an articulated mannequin, your clients can play with shaping their mannequin to explore specific states. Stop at points of activation and points of regulation and ask your client to use their mannequin to "recognize and represent" their autonomic state. The recognize-and-represent practice can also be used at the beginning of a session to inform the direction of the work and at the end of a session to consider your client's autonomic state and what is needed to support their safe return to everyday activities. Mannequins are a valuable tool for experimenting with the transitions between states. In this kinetic form of sculpting, your clients can shape and reshape their mannequins to see and feel their movement between states. Changing the shape of the mannequin's poses is often felt simultaneously by your client in their own changing autonomic energies.

With couples and families, you can use a "shape-and-share" practice. This two-step practice can be used to illustrate states emerging in the therapy session or as a way to reflect on the autonomic dynamics of a prior experience that is the focus of the session. Invite each participant to shape their mannequin and then place the mannequins together. The sharing step is carried out first through wordless contemplation and then through adding voice to tell the autonomic story.

EXERCISE
Mapping in Space

Mapping in space gives your clients a safe way to get to know their autonomic states by physically moving in and out of them. This exercise encourages clients to actively engage and disengage with states and to gain skill in transitioning between states by moving around the therapy space. Because many clients are hijacked by an autonomic survival state and find themselves caught and unable to recover, this mapping exercise is a way for them to experience movement and counteract the sense of being stuck that so many clients report. In this practice, along with the commonly experienced states of sympathetic mobilization and dorsal vagal shutdown, the ventral vagal state that is unfamiliar to many clients is also actively explored. The sense of control clients identify as a result of moving around the space starts to translate into the capacity to transition between states in their daily life. Bringing active attention to these intentional shifts begins to wire in the belief that transitions are safe and regulation is possible.

To begin this exercise, have your client identify individual spaces around the room for each autonomic state and begin to move between them. In a large room, take advantage of the full expanse. If you don't have access to a large floor space, identify states using particular seats or different corners in your office. Lay out the states so that the autonomic hierarchy is evident. If the space is large enough, use a linear layout; in a smaller space, use a circular design.

Start by intentionally structuring the experience as one of motion where sympathetic and dorsal vagal spaces are experienced for brief periods, and the ventral vagal space is used to "rest and regulate." Work with your clients to move in and out of states to help them get a feel for state shifts, for the relationship between states, and for the presence of ventral vagal safety as a resource. Walk with your clients to offer them the experience (often a new experience) of not being alone in their dysregulated state. Hearing the words "I'm walking with you" along with the experience of having you by their side as they move around the map can bring your clients a sense of safety and support. Begin by navigating the experience through resonance and without words. Then bring the implicit autonomic experience to explicit awareness by narrating the new story.

Individual Exploration

Invite your clients to inhabit each space and narrate the story of the state. Let the story include somatic experience, feelings, behavioral impulses, thoughts, and memory. If dual awareness begins to decrease and the state begins to feel too big, bring in more ventral vagal energy by having your client move back into the identified ventral vagal space, using eye gaze to connect to the ventral vagal space, or by holding an imagined or actual rope or ribbon with one end anchored in the safety of the ventral vagal space. In the beginning, clients often report the sense of safety they feel with an actual ribbon tied to the ventral vagal space. Holding it and feeling the security in that physical connection allows them to walk into the dorsal and sympathetic spaces with enough confidence that they can get back to safety. (The Autonomic Navigation meditation, p. 208, is a good accompaniment to this exercise.)

Interactive Exploration

Co-regulation is an important autonomic experience and one that is often a missing or distressing experience for clients. This exercise is designed to identify autonomic patterns, experiment with regulating resources, and explore recovery from sympathetic and dorsal vagal states. To begin, ask your client to move into the space for either of the dysregulated states and take on that state in an attenuated form—just enough to swim in it and not drown in it.

- **Recognize:** Acknowledge your client's present autonomic state. Name it with them. Ask your client to describe their state to you.

- **Reach:** Begin to explore ways to move into connection with your client, watching for the beginnings of state shifts. Experiment with actions that support coming into safe proximity. Track with your client how their autonomic nervous system is experiencing your different offers of connection. What message is neuroception sending in the moment? What are the cues of safety? Experiment until you find the right kind, and the right amount, of contact.

- **Resonate:** Inhabit the autonomic space with your client. Let your ventral vagal energy surround your client. Rest there together.

- **Regulate:** Help your client begin to notice the ways your ventral vagal presence is affecting their state. Experiment with regulating actions to engage your client's Social Engagement System. When your client feels the beginnings of connection and a move toward regulation, start to physically move around the map together.

If the ventral vagal state is not part of your client's experience, experiment with ways to interrupt their habitual pattern and add an experience of the regulating ventral vagal state to their cycle. Use your Social Engagement System (voice, eye gaze, proximity) to offer a moment of co-regulation. If your client's history has not included enough opportunities to exercise the vagal brake, then both the initial return to ventral vagal regulation and the ability to maintain that state can be challenging. Without enough experiences for their vagal brake to relax and reengage, your client may manage to return to a ventral vagal state but struggle to stay there. The unfamiliarity of this state brings a neuroception of danger that then leads them back into sympathetic mobilization, creating a back-and-forth pattern of shifting between ventral vagal and sympathetic states. To begin to interrupt this pattern, bring attention to it, name it, track it, and play with moving between the states, resting a bit longer each time in ventral vagal. Look for just the right degree of challenge to stretch your client's experience of ventral vagal safety as they exercise their vagal brake.

Another common pattern is the loop between dorsal vagal and sympathetic states. In this pattern, as your client begins to recover from collapse, the mobilized state brings a sense of danger. The energy of the sympathetic system feels big, scary, and uncontrollable, triggering an autonomic survival response and a move back into collapse. Clients need active co-regulation to successfully find their way back into ventral vagal connection. Therapists often feel a sense of relief when a client's state of collapse and dorsal vagal despair begins to lift and energy starts to move again. The temptation when this happens is to think, "My client is okay, coming back to regulation, and I can relax now." Instead, this is the time to stay in close connection. When your client begins to move out of dorsal vagal immobilization, the stirring of energy often brings both relief and a corresponding feeling of fear. Continue to actively co-regulate and guide your client through sympathetic mobilization to the safety of ventral vagal regulation.

Families and Groups

With families and groups, there are multiple people moving around the identified autonomic spaces, offering a visual representation of relational patterns. Diverging reactions and chaotic responses can be both seen and sensed. Use freeze-frame moments to stop the action and invite participants to "recognize and report" their individual responses and then expand their view to take in the full map. Seeing the system in action brings increased awareness to all the participants in the system. In a freeze-frame moment, experiment with ways participants might move in or out of connection. Play with movement around the map intentionally asking participants to connect or separate while continuing to "recognize and report" the autonomic outcome of their movements.

You may choose to identify one person as the ventral vagal anchor and support this person in regulating the system. After a return to regulation, the process can be entered into again with a different person becoming the ventral vagal anchor. With families and groups, it is helpful for multiple people to explore being the anchor in the system.

Couples

With couples, it is important that each partner has the experience of being the anchor and of being anchored—both offering and receiving regulating acts. The acts of offering and receiving often come with their own autonomically embedded stories and trigger habitual response patterns. Support your clients in moving from neuroception to perception to narration from each side of their experience.

Therapist Learning

Try this practice with a colleague or group of colleagues: What is your autonomic response to a client's activated sympathetic nervous system or state of dorsal vagal collapse? How do you maintain ventral vagal regulation? How do you make contact and approach a client in a dysregulated state? Experiment with meeting your clients in each state.

Building autonomic awareness through creative arts experiences supports clients' ability to listen to the stories of their states. There are many pathways to awareness and clients will be drawn toward the ones that bring cues of safety and invite moving toward the experience. As they begin to get to know their autonomic states, clients become increasingly curious and want to know more. They are ready to explore and willing to try out new practices.

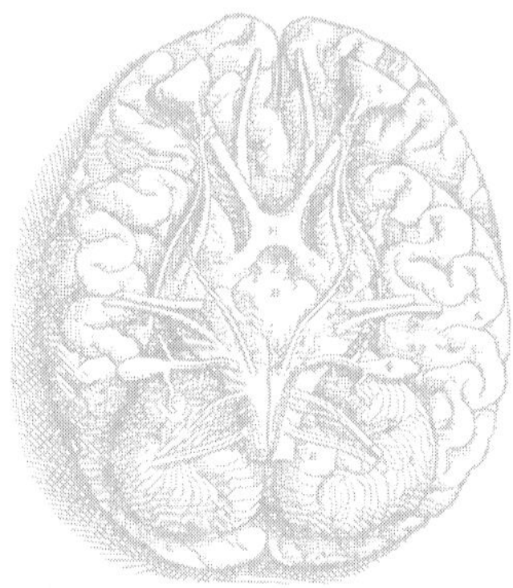

CHAPTER 8

SAFELY AWARE AND ABLE TO ATTEND

To pay attention. This is our endless and proper work.

—MARY OLIVER

Building on your clients' befriending skills, the exercises in this chapter move into the practice of attending to autonomic states. The energy of attending is one of "close and thoughtful attention" and "a general interest that leads to wanting to know more" (*Merriam-Webster's*). Just as befriending is an act of kindness, attending is similarly grounded in a ventral vagal state of compassion.

EXERCISE

Notice and Name: Becoming an Expert State Detector

When we notice our autonomic experience, we have the chance to engage with it, not simply be engaged by it. The process of reshaping the relationship to an experience of arousal, of seeing the activation differently, is called reappraisal. It begins a sequence of reengaging with the experience in a new way (Garland, Gaylord, & Park, 2009). Positive reappraisal can improve cardiovascular function and reduce attention to threat (Jamieson, Mendes, & Nock, 2012). Through a polyvagal lens, reappraisal is a way of increasing ventral vagal tone through an active vagal braking action. When we name a response and assign it to a category, we can change the perception of the response. For clients, being able to classify a response in one of the autonomic state categories begins to build their skill in recognizing states. Their ability to correctly and predictably identify autonomic states is a prerequisite to interrupting habitual response patterns. Because distinct autonomic states require different regulating responses, accurate state information is important for choosing the right intervention.

The first part of the Notice-and-Name practice, the act of noticing, requires your client to tune in to their autonomic nervous system, connect to their present-moment neuroception, and turn toward it, bringing it into active awareness. Noticing brings perception to the autonomic experience, and, with perception, your client can move into the naming part of the practice.

The notice-and-name skill is both difficult and important. Many clients routinely live in a disembodied state as an adaptive protective response, and their ability to tolerate body awareness is limited. Why inhabit the body when it is a source of pain and holds trauma memories? Yet if clients are disconnected from autonomic awareness, their state automatically becomes their story. When clients are able to predictably identify their autonomic state, their sense of being in the dark, caught in confusion is reduced. Knowing where they are on their map brings a sense of organization to their experiences. Stopping to notice and name interrupts the automaticity of a client's old story and begins to build the important capacity to separate state from story.

The four steps of the Notice-and-Name practice are as follows:

- Tune into your thoughts, feelings, and the way your body feels.

- Notice where you are on your autonomic map.
- Name the state.
- Bring curiosity. What is there to learn from your autonomic nervous system in this moment?

Stay with this practice until it becomes easy and automatic.

Teach your clients this practice and then use it in sessions, routinely stopping to notice and name. Write down the steps and send them home with your clients. Encourage them to use the skill often. With repetition, placement on the autonomic map becomes a habit.

Just as important as the capacity of our clients to notice and name is our own skill as therapists in placing ourselves on our autonomic maps. Without the ability to know our own autonomic state, we aren't able to recognize moments of dysregulation, return to regulation, and provide the safe, predictable ventral vagal presence that is an integral part of the therapy relationship.

EXERCISE
Four-Map Tracking

The Four-Map Tracking Worksheet (template p. 229) builds on the Notice-and-Name practice, offering another way for clients to develop skill in identifying and explicitly expressing their present-moment autonomic placement. This worksheet has four individual mapping sections designed to be filled in over a span of time. Clients first mark their placement on the autonomic ladder and then briefly describe their state through words or pictures. As a way to introduce this practice, use the worksheet to track the flow of a session; entering the session, stopping twice during the session, and again at the end of the session. Once your client is familiar with the process, this is a good worksheet to use between sessions. Some clients choose to schedule specific times to listen in while others decide to pause and track when they feel an autonomic pull. To bring attention to the autonomic path of a day, I often ask clients to do one map first thing in the morning, two during the day, and one at the end of the day.

EXERCISE
Soup of the Day

The Soup of the Day exercise is designed as a way for clients to reflect on their autonomic experiences at the end of the day. In creating their "soup," they identify an overall tone of the day and reflect on the individual experiences that are woven together to create that tone. This exercise draws on your client's ventral vagal energy to help them step back, observe, and bring active reflection to the autonomic pathways they traveled over the course of the day.

The Soup of the Day Worksheet (template p. 233) helps bring attention to experiences of safety and connection, moments of mastery that may be missed among the moments of messiness that accompany experiences of activated survival responses. The negativity bias may partially explain this tendency to overlook ventral vagal experiences: We preferentially attend to negative information and experiences over positive ones as an adaptive survival mechanism (Norris, Larsen, Crawford, & Cacioppo, 2011).

Imagine your autonomic tone is like a bowl of homemade soup, an ever changing soup of the day. The ingredients bring a variety of flavors, and the final product is distinctive. Our overall autonomic state (the soup) is flavored by the influence of ventral vagal, sympathetic, and dorsal vagal energies (the ingredients). Using the soup metaphor, some flavors are intense (sudden and extreme state shifts), and some bring milder hints of seasoning (the nuance of movement within a state).

This worksheet is a way for your clients to write the recipe for their "soup of the day." This can be done in two ways, either first naming the soup and then looking for the ingredients or finding the ingredients first and seeing what soup they produce. If a client has a strong sense of autonomic tone, they can begin with naming that and then bring curiosity to the medley of experiences that generated the tone. Alternatively, a client may clearly remember experiences from the day and choose to name those and see what the overall tone is. Using either process, it is important to look for not only the intense experiences but also the more mildly activating events. Have your clients look both for the experiences that are similar and may support a theme and the outlier experiences that add diverse energies. As your clients fill in their soup recipes, they will notice the ways moments of ventral vagal, sympathetic, and dorsal vagal activation create a unique overall tone depending on their frequency, duration, and intensity. Engaging in this process over time helps clients build a habit of autonomic reflection and name the blend of autonomic states that come together to create their daily soup.

A GOLDILOCKS GUIDE TO ATTENDING

> *There are three things which if one does not know, one cannot live long in the world: what is too much for one, what is too little for one, and what is just right for one.*
>
> —SWAHILI PROVERB

The Goldilocks effect, or Goldilocks principle, is a term adapted from the classic fairy tale in which Goldilocks experiments to find the "just right" porridge, chair, and bed. The Goldilocks principle characterizes the just right space between extremes. This rule is applied across many disciplines. For Earth scientists, the Goldilocks zone is the habitable zone that supports life on a planet (Sumner, 2016). Research in the field of infant learning shows that babies seek out situations with just the right amount of surprise or complexity including visual and auditory cues (Kidd, Piantadosi, & Aslin, 2012, 2014), and adult learners pay attention to experiences with the right level of complexity to trigger just the right amount of arousal (Yerkes & Dodson, 1908).

Looking at events through a polyvagal lens, we each have our own embodied Goldilocks continuum. Our autonomic nervous systems move between just right, too much, and not enough in both large-scale shifts and in micro-movements. What in one moment feels just right can in the next moment feel like too much or not enough.

Following Goldilocks's trial-and-error process, clients can track their autonomic responses and look for experiences that are autonomically just right. Too much and they move into sympathetic distress. Too little and they feel the isolation of dorsal vagal collapse. Therapists can help clients experiment with actions that bring the right amount of neural challenge until they find their own just right place.

EXERCISE

The Goldilocks Graph

The Goldilocks Graph (template p. 237) provides a way to bring attention to events and track movement along the just right, too much, not enough continuum. The graph follows the evolutionary hierarchy of our autonomic nervous system with "just right" representing the newest, ventral vagally inspired spot, "too much" coming online with the triggering of the sympathetic nervous system, and "not enough" being the place of dorsal vagal emptiness. The simplicity of the graph allows a quick check-in. Clients use the horizontal axis to move through time and the vertical axis to mark just right, too much, and not enough events with a few words. Your clients can review the events in their completed graph to look for experiences in each of the three Goldilocks states. They can use individual elements to identify the qualities that activate each autonomic experience.

EXERCISE
Time and Tone Graph

Our experience of time may be a result of the way emotions and visceral states are processed in our bodies in the insular cortex (Craig, 2009b). Attending to the autonomic state and the accompanying psychological story over a specific period of time is a way of tracking patterns of response with an eye toward identifying sequences of connection and protection.

The Time and Tone Graph (template p. 241) is similar to the Goldilocks Graph in that they both use a graphing structure to track autonomic state shifts. The horizontal axis is again used to move through time and the vertical axis represents the autonomic hierarchy. Where the Goldilocks Graph focuses on events and the qualities of each event that are resourcing or dysregulating, the Time and Tone Graph focuses on mapping states over a specified period of time and then connecting the points on the graph to create a visual representation of the autonomic path traveled. The image can be one of gentle curves, steep slopes, jagged or flattened lines. This visual is a powerful representation of the autonomic story and another way for clients to feel the influence of autonomic state shifts over time. The graph connects individual moments into a larger autonomic story, illustrating the autonomic shape of a day. Clients tell me that seeing their experiences strung together reduces the intensity of individual moments and gives them a larger perspective of the felt sense of their day.

The Time and Tone Graph offers a panoramic view of autonomic movement through time. It is a versatile graph that can be used to track any desired period of time. It can be used to track autonomic state shifts during a therapy session with the ending image representing the autonomic story of the session. As an end-of-the-day reflection process, this graph provides a way to see the overall autonomic flow of the day. Over the course of therapy, this graph will still show some steep lines and also more of the softer curves that characterize a more regulated life.

THE COMPARISON EXPERIENCE

Comparison is a universal experience (Fiske, 2010). We make sense of the world by making comparisons. It is a normal part of our daily experience. Comparing ourselves to others is an inherent part of being human; we know ourselves through comparison (Festinger, 1954). We tend to underestimate how much other people struggle with negative emotions and overestimate their positive ones, which leads to a sense that we are alone in our suffering (Jordan et al., 2011). Comparing activates autonomic state shifts, and with those shifts come stories of disconnection or connection.

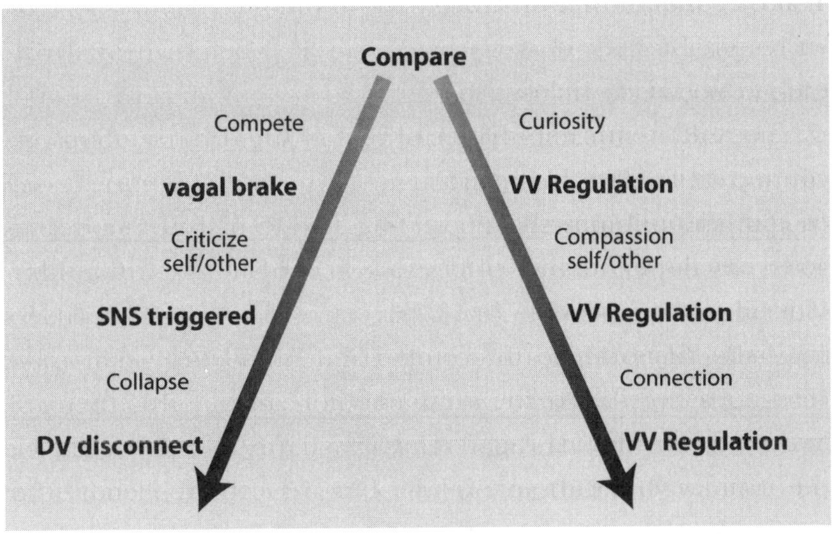

Through an autonomic lens, there are two pathways of response to the comparison experience. One takes clients back along the autonomic hierarchy away from safety. The other maintains a ventral vagal state and an active Social Engagement System. The right-hand side of the compare chart represents an active ventral vagal experience in which your client's neurobiology supports safety and social connection. The vagal brake releases and reengages, resourcing the client's ability for curiosity, communication, and cooperation. Reciprocity happens here. This is a pathway of connection.

The left-hand side represents the "comparing trap" (DeLong, 2011). When your client travels that pathway, their autonomic nervous system pulls them into an adaptive survival response as they engage in either a downward or an upward comparison. In a downward comparison, clients move into a "better than others" competitive stance. This comparison triggers the sympathetic nervous system. In an upward comparison, clients see themselves in the opposite way as "not measuring up." This begins a sequence that can include anger, feeling unfairly treated, embarrassment, helplessness, and shame (Fiske, 2010). Tracking this response through the autonomic nervous system, we see sympathetic nervous system mobilization that eventually ends in dorsal vagal collapse.

The autonomic experience of ventral vagal safety and social connection is one of cooperation, the sympathetic state is one of competition, and the dorsal vagal state of collapse occurs when any hope of either competing or cooperating disappears. If your client is able to bring perception to the process and interrupt the competitive comparison, then the vagal brake reengages, regulating the sympathetic response, and they can move into the ventral vagal–mediated pathway. From here, on the *right* (right-hand) side of the compare chart, a client can appreciate the ventral vagal benefits of cooperation and safety in connection. If instead, the experience is too big of a neural challenge for a client's vagal braking capacities, then they will continue to experience the competitive response. The sympathetic nervous system maintains the mobilized survival state until that is no longer a viable response, at which point the dorsal vagal collapse is triggered.

Understanding that both sides of the compare chart are common human responses normalizes the experiences. Clients are reassured to know that the experience of cooperation or competition, of embodying an active ventral vagal state or moving back along the autonomic hierarchy, is not necessarily a linear one. At many points along the way, they can create acts of interruption to move out of physiological dysregulation, resource ventral vagal regulation, and create a story of connection.

Using the compare chart, ask your clients to track their autonomic state, acknowledge the accompanying story, and experiment with acts of interruption that engage their vagal brake and move them into safety and the possibility of social connection. As your clients investigate an experience of comparing, questions to consider are as follows:

- Are you on the right-hand side?
- If yes, how do you deepen into that experience?
- If no, what are the ways you can reengage your vagal brake?
- At what points do the acts of interruption work? No longer work?

Working with the exercises in this chapter, your clients can explore how they navigate their personal autonomic pathways, first as they learn to track autonomic states and attune to moment-to-moment state shifts and then through the larger perspective of viewing autonomic movements across time. The landscape is seen in both the momentary responses that create the sense of a singular event and in the panoramic view that offers a broader picture of the autonomic story of self.

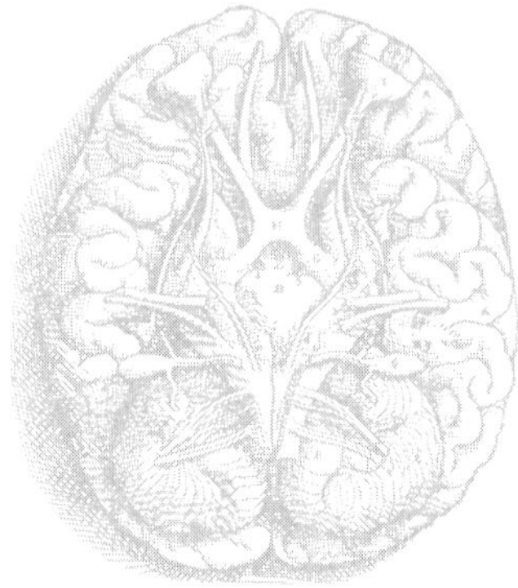

CHAPTER 9

CREATING SAFE SURROUNDINGS

Out of this nettle, danger, we pluck this flower, safety.

—WILLIAM SHAKESPEARE

As an embodied system, the autonomic nervous system uses internal physical experience to guide actions of engagement, mobilization, and disengagement. But the autonomic nervous system is also influenced by our social relationships and by our environment. The field of human social genomics has begun to identify the ways that subjective experiences of the physical and social environments influence the expression of genes (Slavich & Cole, 2013). Everyday experiences are autonomically received and read through the process of neuroception as safe, dangerous, or life-threatening. This initiates a regulating response, activating either an adaptive survival state or social engagement. Slavich and Cole propose that given the fact our cells are continually in a state of regeneration, "our physiological state on any given day can influence our molecular makeup for weeks and months into the future (2013, p. 3). The neuroception of safety or unsafety has a powerful effect on the ways we survive and thrive.

PASSIVE PATHWAYS: THE DANCE BENEATH CONSCIOUS AWARENESS

How do we learn to tune in to the passive pathways of neuroception and use that information to shape the therapy experience? Acting as a personal surveillance system, the autonomic nervous system is exquisitely attuned to conditions in the environment. Beneath conscious awareness, the passive pathway of neuroception engages in moment-to-moment monitoring of the therapeutic relationship and the therapy environment. Within the therapy relationship, these passive pathways receive a continuous stream of information sent from the therapist's Social Engagement System. If the signals are of safety, a client's autonomic nervous system calms, connects, and co-regulates, supporting active engagement in the therapy process. If, however, the therapist sends autonomic signals of unsafety or only intermittent signals of safety, a client's neuroception, sensing the need for protection, initiates a move away from connection, out of engagement, and into a survival response.

Within the therapy environment, the passive pathways of neuroception are tuned to features of the physical environment. When the environment elicits a neuroception of safety, ventral vagal regulation moves a client toward engagement in the therapy relationship and the therapy process. When the environment elicits a sense of danger or life-threat, neuroception sets in motion a survival response taking a client away from the therapy relationship and out of the therapy process.

Without these passive pathways receiving enough cues to activate a neuroception of safety, a client can't engage in the therapy process. Their autonomic nervous system is turned away from connection and focused on survival. Regulating the passive pathways of neuroception is the necessary first step in the therapy process.

Clinical training for therapists includes learning skills to create safety in the therapeutic relationship, to enter into resonance and empathic attunement, and to walk with clients through their traumatic experiences. Therapists use ventral vagal energies and features of the Social Engagement System to connect with clients. Cues of safety come from eyes and smiles. Prosody is powerful. Gestures offer an invitation to connection. Proximity is a regulator of the autonomic nervous system. These actions actively invite a client's autonomic nervous system into ventral vagal safety and co-regulation. Beneath awareness, a client's nervous system receives the cues, a neuroception of safety results, and the therapy relationship is established and strengthened.

Most therapists, however, are not well trained to attend to the ways the environment around their offices and in their clinical spaces affects a client's sense of safety. The therapy space tells a story; a story of who a therapist is and how the therapist practices. The "language of design" (Golembiewski, 2017) can be used to send cues of safety. How might autonomic awareness be used by therapists to build a co-regulating environment?

A Welcoming Environment

The physical environment in the office, in the waiting area, in the building, and even in the surrounding area, affects your client's physiology. Before a client reaches your office, their nervous system has taken in cues of safety and danger, and they have created a story to match their autonomic experience. While you can't always change the surrounding environment, you can create an interior environment that tells a story of welcome. Polyvagal Theory describes the sensitivity of the autonomic nervous system to features of safety and points out that encountering cues of safety fosters resilience (Porges, 2015a). Through attention to your office setting, you can nurture client resilience and shape your clients' autonomic responses toward safety and connection.

It is also meaningful to acknowledge that, as a therapist, your nervous system spends long stretches of time immersed in the cues of safety and danger present in your office environment. Research on home environments indicates that features of spaces affect what happens within those spaces and influence the thoughts and moods of the people inhabiting them (Graham, Gosling, & Travis, 2015). The office is a psychological and physiological home for you for many hours a day. It is important that the space you create and inhabit inspires your own ventral vagal regulation. An environment of autonomic well-being is essential not only to afford a space that creates cues of safety for your clients but also as a basic ingredient in your own self-care. A space that extends an autonomic welcome is a space that supports the difficult work of therapy for both you and your client.

The following categories (sound, temperature, and nature) are briefly explored to draw attention to how dimensions of a therapist's environment might be affecting clinical work. What changes are possible to maximize your sense of well-being and your clients' feelings of safety and connection while in session?

Through a polyvagal perspective, we understand that the autonomic nervous system responds to sound, certain frequencies activating ventral vagal safety and others signaling danger and a move into sympathetic or dorsal vagal survival responses. Low-frequency sounds bring a neuroception of danger with an autonomic reminder of long-ago predators. Your client's focus shifts from social connection to survival actions. High-frequency sounds take your clients out of connection into concern as their attention shifts to the source of the sound. Unpredictable sounds from outside the therapy office door can activate protective reactions. Sound machines with their constant hum, often necessary to ensure privacy, may bring autonomic activation. Sound is an area of interest in architectural design following research indicating the direct influence of acoustics on occupant productivity (Al horr et al., 2016). Acoustic comfort directly influences autonomic state, and the "occupant productivity" in this case is the therapist's and client's ability to successfully engage in the therapy process.

Because the autonomic nervous system is our thermoregulating system, what architects call "thermal comfort" is an important element of the therapy office. The autonomic nervous system continually adjusts to temperature changes in search of homeostasis. Outside of their thermal comfort zone, therapists and clients may be distracted from the work of therapy by the neuroception of danger that accompanies the sense of being too hot or too cold. And giving even more importance to the need for the right degree of warmth, the neurobiological systems that regulate physical warmth are shared with those that regulate social warmth (Inagaki & Eisenberger, 2013; Williams & Bargh, 2008). Beneath awareness, experiences of physical warmth and psychological warmth influence each other as they travel common pathways.

E. O. Wilson with his concept of "biophilia" describes an inborn affinity and an emotional affiliation to other living things (as cited in Krcmarova, 2009). His proposed need for humans to be in contact with nature to ensure healthy development is proving to be true. An environment with natural elements is restorative, while lack of natural elements creates discord, a mismatch that brings stress (Grinde & Patil, 2009). We have learned that viewing nature invites parasympathetic response. Being in a natural environment reduces sympathetic response, and exposure to natural elements decreases stress and increases well-being (Ewert, Klaunig, Wang, & Chang, 2016). Humans have a need to connect with nature and can benefit just from looking out the window onto a natural scene (Kahn, Severson, & Ruckert, 2009). Even experiencing technological nature (a plasma screen in a windowless room) is better than no nature (Kahn et al., 2009).

We have a preference for landscapes that include the elements of open spaces with trees, water, animal and bird life, and a path that invites the viewer to travel off into the distance (Dutton, 2010). Regarded as beautiful around the world, this is an experience of beauty across cultures (Dutton, 2010); a ventral vagal experience universally shared. Research into the use of nature scenes for restoration and resilience shows that autonomic regulation returns faster when viewing nature out a window or even seeing projected scenes (Brown, Barton, & Gladwell, 2013). Further research demonstrates that five minutes of viewing a nature scene prior to a stressor enhances autonomic recovery (Brown et al., 2013). Could images of nature in the office space or taking time to enjoy the view out the office window create a more resilient nervous system and add safety to the often difficult elements of therapy?

Out of survival needs, we likely have an evolutionary preference and reverence for water (White et al., 2010). Nichols and Cousteau in their book *Blue Mind* (2014) report on the ways water seems to reduce stress and enhance well-being. We have a preference for scenes with water and feel greater positive affect and restorativeness from scenes with water than from those without (White et al., 2010). Notably, it may be that the acoustics of water—hearing or even remembering the sounds of waves, rivers, and brooks moving—may also be restorative (White et al., 2010). Responding to the human need for nature in the therapy environment can send powerful cues of safety.

EXERCISE

The Path to Therapy: How the Autonomic Nervous System Finds Its Way

Dr. Heidelise Als, originator of the Newborn Individualized Developmental Care and Assessment Program (NIDCAP), talks about the "path to the infant"—the experience of the family of a premature baby from the moment they walk into the hospital to the time they reach their tiny baby in the neonatal intensive care unit. The autonomic nervous system plays a primary role in how this is experienced. Similarly, you can think about the path your clients take to your office. What is their autonomic experience on the path to therapy? What do their autonomic nervous systems "hear" as they make their way from the everyday world to the sacred space of therapy?

The best way for your client to explore the path to therapy is for you to make the walk together, tracking neuroception and associated state shifts moment to moment. If the actual walk isn't feasible, invite your client to imagine the walk and describe their moment-to-moment experience. This active tracking helps your clients identify the individual cues of safety and danger they confront and brings you into a shared awareness of the effect on their autonomic state. When perception is brought to neuroception, you and your client can explore actions to consciously influence their autonomic state. Regulating these passive pathways is a necessary pre-condition to working with the active pathways of therapeutic intervention.

During the Path to Therapy exercise, the goal is to identify cues of safety and danger:

- arriving at the building
- entering the building
- coming into the waiting area
- entering the office
- in the office

At each point, explore what might increase cues of safety and decrease cues of danger.

Remind your client that their physiological state translates into a psychological story. Explore the story created by neuroception at each point along the way. Then reverse the process, as a client's entering and exiting cues may be different.

Many clients experience autonomic dysregulation when approaching new places. Transitions from one place to another activate their adaptive survival responses. Beyond the experience of coming to therapy, the questions from the Path to Therapy exercise become useful for your clients as a way to track their cues of safety and danger when arriving, entering, and leaving other environments.

This is also an informative walk for you to take, tracking your own neuroceptive experience as you arrive at your workplace. Answering the question, "How does my autonomic nervous system enter the workday?" can lead to savoring glimmers or acknowledging distress. When you reach your office, have the passive pathways of neuroception created a ventral vagal-mediated, openhearted readiness to meet clients? Or have cues of danger prompted an autonomic move into protection? Continuing with the questions in the exercise, track your neuroception in your office and as you leave at the end of the day. At the end of a day, the ratio of cues of safety to cues of danger defines an autonomic nervous system that is either nourished or drained.

EXERCISE
Cue Sheets

Both recognizing and resolving cues of danger and identifying and inviting in cues of safety are necessary to move into the ventral vagal state of safety and connection that creates the physiological readiness to engage in therapy. To "light up" the safety circuit, cues of danger need to be alleviated, and your clients need to actively encounter cues of safety.

This exercise helps your clients deconstruct an interaction, identify the ways their autonomic states supported or restricted behaviors, and consider possibilities to engage differently in the future.

Cue Sheets (template p. 245) offer a way to use a specific experience to track passive pathways, increase awareness of cues of danger and cues of safety, and explore ways to decrease cues of danger and utilize cues of safety. Each sheet includes a space to write a brief description of an incident, space to identify the cues of both danger and safety, and space to explore opportunities for resolution and regulation. Begin by completing the worksheet in session with a client. Once your client is familiar with the process, they can track an event between sessions and bring in their completed Cue Sheet to review.

In the first section, a client briefly describes an experience, paying attention to both the concrete events and their autonomic responses. The next sections focus attention on the cues of danger and safety, looking at each through the environment, the body, and elements of the Social Engagement System. In filling out these sections, clients often find that cues of safety were in fact present but their autonomic state of protection prevented them from noticing. The last sections invite curiosity about ways to engage differently in the future. These final sections encourage clients to experiment with shaping the next interaction through manipulating environmental, embodied, and Social Engagement System cues.

In any building design, the foundation is the most important element. It is the ground upon which the structure rests. For humans, safety is the foundation. When the autonomic nervous system senses safety, the footings are deep and secure; when the system senses danger, the ground feels shaky. With nervous systems toned through experience, our trauma-survivor clients are sensitive to the most subtle shaking. Therapy is a process of building the new, deep, autonomically supported foundation of safety through attending to environmental, embodied, and relational cues.

SECTION III **SUMMARY**

Our habitual patterns are, of course, well established, seductive, and comforting.

—PEMA CHÖDRÖN

In its role as our personal surveillance system, the autonomic nervous system simultaneously attends to messages from inside the body while tracking elements of the external environment. With a full range of responses organized through evolution of the autonomic hierarchy, the autonomic nervous system is our built-in bodyguard on the lookout for danger and opportunities for connection. Beneath the level of conscious awareness, this system directs movement toward and away from people, places, and experiences.

The skills in Section III build clients' capacity for autonomic awareness and autonomic tracking. Clients learn to observe the flow of their autonomic states. They begin to recognize how their physiological state creates a psychological story and start to feel state and story as separate experiences. The multiple skills presented in this section offer slightly different tracking techniques to support your clients in developing a regular practice of attending. With routine befriending and attending habits, clients have access to a rich stream of autonomic information.

The abilities to befriend and attend bring clients into recognition of the ongoing flow of autonomic states. Befriending the nervous system requires self-compassion—often a challenging experience for clients. Self-criticism is more often the habitual response. As clients learn that their system works in accordance with the same survival actions that all humans share, they begin to make space for self-compassion. A client told me how she had always considered herself to be broken, but learning that her autonomic nervous system responds to experiences in universal ways has begun to help her feel less critical of who she is.

Attending to autonomic states calls for present-moment awareness, also a challenging experience for clients. When relationships have not been safely co-regulating and when experiences have not resourced the ventral vagal state of health, growth, and restoration, clients' adaptive survival responses take them out of present-moment awareness into a sense of danger accompanied by an insistent need to predict what will happen next or a sense of life-threat and a need to not exist in this moment. They may experience an alarmed, overreactive pattern or a dulled, nonreacting pattern, and these patterns can be linked in one way to environmental events and in another way to relational incidents. In attending to her autonomic responses, one of my clients discovered that when a tree fell outside her house she was undisturbed but when her friend cancelled a date she collapsed. Engaging with the skills of befriending and attending not only lays the foundation for the next phase of active regulation but also begins to influence the actions of nervous system.

Sections II and III create a foundation for clients to recognize the moment-to-moment actions of their autonomic nervous system. With these skills in place, therapy can move into autonomic regulation and reshaping. Using an understanding of the human autonomic nervous system and the ability to track their "life on the ladder," clients are ready to directly engage with their habitual patterns of response and begin to rewrite their autonomic stories.

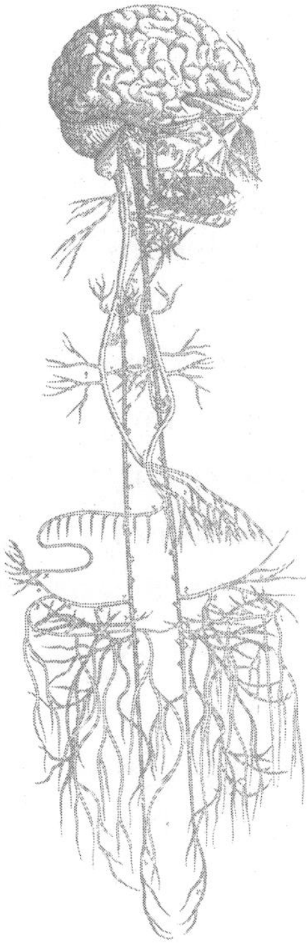

SECTION IV

SHAPING THE NERVOUS SYSTEM

One day you finally knew what you had to do, and began.

—MARY OLIVER

The autonomic nervous system is at the heart of our lived experience. When we say something is a shock to our system or we are moved by an experience, we are in fact speaking for our autonomic response. We see eye to eye, are all ears, face up to something, put our best foot forward, or put our finger on it. We stick our necks out and encourage friends to keep their chins up. We have cold feet and our blood boils. These figures of speech describe our autonomic experiences.

Our autonomic nervous systems are shaped by events. Experiences of neglect and experiences of nourishment affect autonomic tone. The moment we move between states, the point at which there is a shift from connection to protection, is affected by individual and environmental variables (Williamson, Porges, Lamb, & Porges, 2015). Our autonomic profiles fall along a continuum of sensitive and rigid to resilient and flexible. On one end, the nervous system is exquisitely tuned toward danger, and the drive to survive activates persistent patterns of protection. Low vagal tone leads to hypervigilance, heightened startle responses, interpretation of neutral cues as dangerous, and a failure to recognize cues of safety (Park & Thayer, 2014). On the other end, the urge is to safely connect and be in relationship, leading to patterns of social connection and flexible transitions in response to the demands of the present moment. And along the points in between the two ends of the autonomic continuum are the nuanced places that lean more toward protection or connection.

Autonomic response patterns create risk and resilience factors. Vagal tone regulates our responses to positive emotions and to stressors and affects our ability for social connection (Kogan et al., 2014), and higher vagal tone is related to adaptive responses to environmental demands (Park & Thayer, 2014). The reassuring, *heartwarming* news is that autonomic flexibility can be shaped over time.

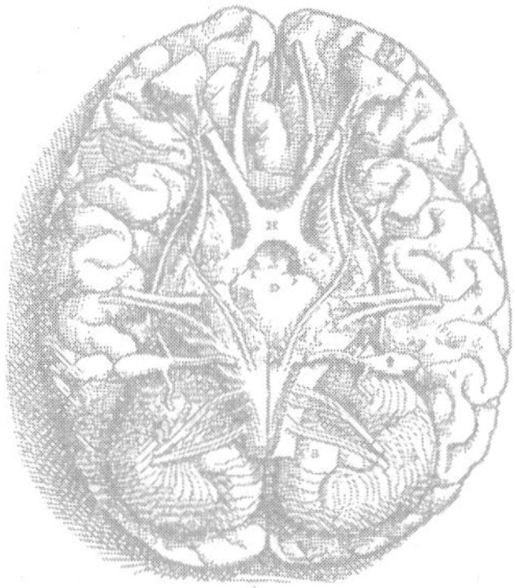

CHAPTER 10

THE AUTONOMIC NERVOUS SYSTEM AS A RELATIONAL SYSTEM

There is one word that can be the guide for your life—it is the word reciprocity.

—PEARL S. BUCK

The autonomic nervous system is a relational system toned in experience with others. A capacity for, and pull toward, reciprocity (the dyadic interaction necessary to reach shared goals) is present in typically developing infants at birth (Apicella et al., 2013). Throughout the course of our lifetime, we rely on connections with others to find meaning in our lives (Stillman et al., 2009).

The autonomic nervous system creates a platform of safety to serve these necessary connections. To do this, one nervous system enters into back-and-forth communication with another nervous system, creating a feedback loop. If the signals conveyed are cues of safety, reciprocity and resonance lead to connection. If the cues sent from one system to another are ones of danger, the outcome is dysregulation and protection through disconnection. As individual nervous systems connect or collide, reciprocity or rupture results.

Unintentional moments of disconnection happen when there is a violation of neural expectancies (Porges, 2017a). Whether micro-moments that register like a blip on a radar screen or lingering stretches of disengagement, the experience of biological rudeness is autonomically unsettling. When we start noticing these moments, we find they are routine events: a person glancing to check a cell phone, looking away, being distracted by a momentary internal thought. While not meant to disrupt the connection, the unintended consequence is an experience of rupture. A different experience of rupture stems from emotional misattunement and the loss of co-regulation. Similar to moments of biological rudeness, misattunement begins when one person's autonomic state shift triggers a corresponding shift from the other person. There is an autonomic response to sudden, unexpected cues of danger or the loss of autonomic cues of safety from the Social Engagement System. Unlike biological rudeness, which can be an experience of neuroception that doesn't come into full perception, this loss of reciprocity comes with a powerful psychological story and is felt more explicitly both on the provoking and receiving ends of the experience.

There is a natural, ongoing flow of rupture and repair in relationships. Tronick (1989) reported that in healthy caregiver and child relationships, mutual coordination happens about 30% of the time, with ruptures and active repair happening the rest of the time. Extending that into adult relationships, we would imagine that moments of biological rudeness and emotional misattunement happen frequently with family, friends, and colleagues. The goal is not to avoid these normal experiences but to create a habit of tracking the ruptures and making repairs. Reconnection after a rupture is sometimes awkward, often painful, and a practice we need to become skillful with because the end result is a return to the sweetness of connection.

We can move quickly from experiencing an autonomic rupture into a story of self-criticism or judgment of others. Without a foundation of reciprocity, a shared autonomic language, and trust in the other person's willingness and ability to be responsible for their own autonomic responses, cues of danger are overwhelming and ruptures go unrepaired. Reactivity rather than reflection is the result, leading to habitual protective response patterns. Reciprocity is a neural exercise requiring a relational give and take that involves the release and reengagement of the vagal brake. The energy of reciprocity is one of sending care back and forth, of shared intimacy, of balance in the relational exchange. Reciprocity is not equality, but it is also not a greater than or less than experience always flowing in one direction. Finding a balance in the reciprocity equation is necessary to satisfy our biological needs for connection. We suffer when the people we care about are unable to meet us in the middle. The sense of falling out of reciprocity into rupture brings with it a neuroception of danger. The experience is often described in its simplest terms as a sense of moving from friend to stranger. The repair brings a return to the safety of friendship.

THE SKILLS OF REPAIR

How can therapists help clients build the ability for reciprocity and repair? One of the ways is to experiment within the therapy relationship. Even in the most attuned therapy relationships, moments of biological rudeness and emotional misattunement are not isolated experiences, and research continues to demonstrate that ruptures between therapists and clients are common events (Muran & Safran, 2016; Safran, Muran, Samstag, & Stevens, 2001). Muran and Safran (2016) describe two types of rupture: withdrawal and confrontation. Autonomically this translates to activation of the dorsal vagal (withdrawal) and sympathetic (confrontation) systems. When a rupture in the therapy relationship occurs, look for the moment when the work became too big of an autonomic challenge, name it for your client, and take responsibility for the misattunement. Here is an example of this practice from my work with a client: "Let's stop for a moment. I felt like I asked you to go a bit too deep too quickly and your protective system did just what it is supposed to do, moving you out of connection with me. I'm sorry. Let me try this again and see if it feels safer."

Ruptures when repaired can be a catalyst for change and when unrepaired negatively affect the therapeutic alliance, often leading to clients leaving treatment (Safran et al., 2001). Trauma survivors characteristically have a history of relational ruptures, while repair experiences are uncommon and unfamiliar. The small, expected moments of rupture in the therapeutic alliance are opportunities to offer clients a disconfirming experience—an experience of repair. The rupture that occurs when a therapist makes a more significant misstep shakes the therapeutic alliance and often calls for repeated repair attempts. Therapists need to be dedicated to staying in the repair process until it is completed and to be persistent in returning to the question, "What does my client's nervous system need to come back into safety and trust?"

The therapist–client relationship is a good laboratory for exploring repairs. A foundation to safely experiment with rupture and repair includes the following:

Moments of reciprocity: The therapeutic alliance is built on therapist presence, resonance, and reciprocity. This ventral vagal–mediated process offers many moments of reciprocity that clients can be supported in noticing. For many clients, the feeling of reciprocity is unfamiliar, unexpected, and unpredictable. The therapy relationship is a perfect proving ground given that an outcome of therapeutic presence is that clients experience a relational neuroception of safety and an emergence of reciprocity (Geller & Porges, 2014). Once the ability to attend to, and trust in, moments of reciprocity has been established, clients can then be helped to notice the disruption of reciprocity—the experience of rupture.

Shared autonomic language: Working from a polyvagal perspective, therapists and clients share an autonomic language. Clients first learn to focus on the information relayed from their autonomic nervous system and then learn to speak for their experiences of connection and disconnection.

Trust in the willingness and ability to be responsible for autonomic states: Through a therapist's actions and use of the notice-and-name skills, a commitment to autonomic responsibility and regulation is demonstrated. Over time, a client's beliefs change as they wire in the new neural expectations that their therapist is predictably reciprocal and that ruptures are common, can be small and not life threatening, and most important can be repaired.

Once clients feel competent in these repair skills, they then can look for safe moments to expand their experiments outside of therapy into their personal relationships. It's important for clients to identify relationships along a continuum of ease to challenge and start by bringing this process into their relationships on the easeful end of that continuum. Relationships that have plenty of identifiable reciprocal moments can usually withstand naming of ruptures and support repair.

EXERCISE
The Reciprocity, Rupture, and Repair Process

The Reciprocity, Rupture, and Repair process is designed as a way to track reciprocity and build a habit of repair. In this process, clients learn to deconstruct an incident, understand it autonomically, and use their nervous system to guide the repair. Repeatedly engaging with this skill creates a habit of tracking autonomic connection, attending to disconnection, and practicing repair. The therapist actively helps their client track moments of rupture and together, therapist and client explore ways to create repair.

- **Track reciprocity:** Tracking reciprocity is dependent on the ability to be tuned in to the relationship and recognize moment-to-moment shifts. As clients learn to use autonomic state shifts to track reciprocity, questions to explore include: How does your autonomic state send the message that we have fallen out of reciprocity? What is the autonomic state shift? Is there an autonomic difference between when you create the rupture or are on the receiving end of the rupture?

- **Notice and name the rupture:** Once a rupture has been recognized, the next step is to help your client explicitly notice and name the experience. In everyday experiences, ruptures are often dismissed or disregarded. If unacknowledged and unnamed, they can't be repaired. In this step, the acknowledgment and naming is through the language of the autonomic nervous system. Rather than talking about the story of the rupture, making meaning and assigning blame, ruptures are described through changes in autonomic state and protective responses ("I noticed a shift toward disconnection"), identification of cues of danger ("I felt a sympathetic alarm in response to your voice"), and habitual response patterns ("When you moved a bit away from me, I felt myself mobilize to fight and then quickly collapse").

- **Find the right repair:** The repair requirement is for a return to ventral vagal safety and co-regulation. To bring about a successful repair, take time to explore what your client's autonomic needs are to feel fully repaired and reconnected. It often takes a few attempts to find the regulating words—the words that mend the tear. When there is a return of reciprocity, the repair is complete.

- **Come back into connection:** The last step of the process is to make an intentional, explicitly named return to relational connection. Identify the steps of the process and celebrate the outcome. Feel the autonomic return to a ventral vagal state and the activity of the Social Engagement System. Taking time to savor the experience of resolution and return to connection begins to create an autonomic expectation of safely navigating future ruptures.

Even small moments of misattunement will be autonomically registered and, if not recognized and repaired, will build into a more consequential experience of disconnection. With a successful repair experience, clients begin to gain confidence in their abilities to engage in repair. Successful repair experiences invite a commitment to building a habit of repair.

PATTERNS AND TEMPO

Harmony exists in difference no less than in likeness.

—MARGARET FULLER

Looking at autonomic patterns and tempo brings clarity to areas of alignment and misalignment in relationships not through narrative but through the lens of the autonomic nervous system. It is a rare relationship that matches in all areas, which leads to the question: Are there enough patterns of connection to feel satisfied, and do the tempos bring a sense of reciprocity and autonomic intimacy?

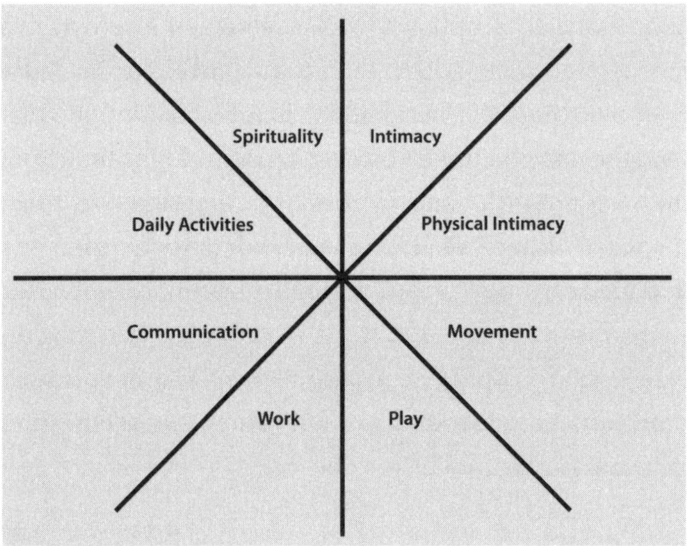

Patterns of connection can be tracked within the eight broad categories of daily activities, communication, work, play, movement, physical intimacy, intimacy, and spirituality. Do connections happen and if so how frequently? Is there a shared initiation of the actions or is one person always extending the invitation?

Within each connection there is a tempo. When the tempo

brings a sense of ventral vagal meeting, both people in the relationship are nourished. The tempo can also bring a sense of autonomic missing, the experience of two ships passing in the night; coexistence without connection. In this experience of being autonomically out of sync, we suffer.

Questions to consider when looking at reciprocity and autonomic intimacy include: Where are the resourcing tempos? Is there a disharmony that can be adjusted? Can the areas of imbalance be accepted and the relationship still feel attuned and in resonance? Are there enough moments of autonomic meeting to sustain overall ventral vagal connection? Are the tempos so dissimilar that reciprocity is unattainable?

Use the following exercise (template p. 253) to help your clients explore their autonomic experiences of a relationship.

EXERCISE
Exploring Patterns and Tempo

- Choose a relationship to focus on. Any relationship can be looked at through this process (partners, friends, family members, coworkers).

- Move through the eight broad categories and identify a general pattern of connection or disconnection for each.

- Review the areas of disconnection. Do you bring ventral vagal energy or are you in a state of protection? Are there enough cues of safety to support talking about your sense of autonomic disconnection? If not, is there a way to resolve the cues of danger that prevent this from happening?

- Return to the areas of connection and bring attention to the tempo within the pattern. Where along a continuum of draining to filling do you place the tempo? Is it a predictable tempo or does it change? As you bring your attention to the tempo, what information does your autonomic nervous system send you?

- Take a step back and consider the entirety of what you have identified. Is there enough overall reciprocity in this relationship to keep you invested in making it work? Are there places of misalignment that don't overwhelm your ventral vagal state, allowing you to accept the mismatch? Are there places that bring an adaptive survival response and need to be resolved for the relationship to feel sustainable? With the autonomic story in mind, what are your next steps?

Partnership Example

Daily activities: We have a great "designation of duties" plan. Works well.

Communication: We can have deep conversations, playful ones, and ones about the plan for the day. We don't talk at the same pace, though, and I have to remember to slow down.

Work: Our work schedules are opposite, so we only share a pattern on days off.

Play: We have fun together, enjoy the same amount of play, although often different kinds of play.

Movement: We tend to move at different speeds and are learning to try and meet in the middle.

Physical intimacy: One-sided initiating, not always satisfying.

Intimacy: An on again-off again experience because it still feels very vulnerable and not always safe sharing deep feelings.

Spirituality: We are similar in our nonreligious, nature-based beliefs, but he needs more connection to that than I do. I'll go if he asks but don't suggest it.

Human connections, necessary for survival, are nonetheless challenging, and moments of relationship messiness are common. In the therapeutic alliance, therapists and clients together cultivate awareness and shape a habit of attending to these moments. Exploring connection through the lens of an "autonomic goodness of fit" brings attention to the ways autonomic states initiate rupture and invite repair. Practicing first in the safety of the therapy session and then in everyday relationships, your clients become skillful with the challenges of navigating the ebb and flow of connection.

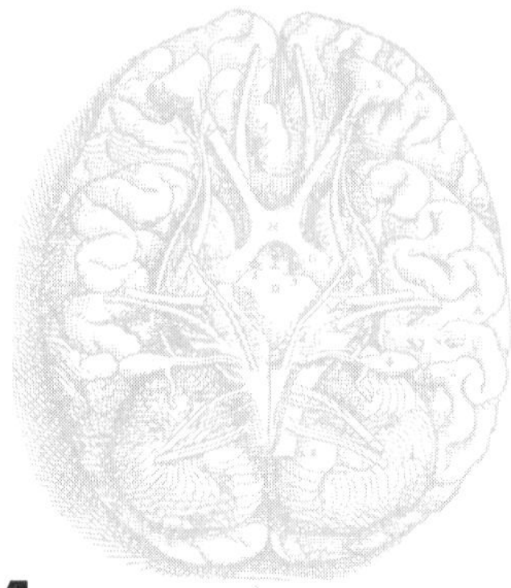

CHAPTER 11

TONING THE SYSTEM WITH BREATH AND SOUND

> *There is a way of breathing that's a shame and a suffocation and there's another way of expiring, a love breath, that lets you open infinitely.*
>
> —RUMI

In the 13th century, Rumi knew the power of breath. And with the development of Polyvagal Theory, Dr. Porges reminds us of that power. Breath is a direct pathway to the autonomic nervous system. The average respiration rate for adults is 12–18 breaths per minute (Mason et al., 2013). With 18 breaths per minute, an adult takes 25,902 breaths a day, 9,460,800 breaths a year, and at age 80 will have taken about 756,864,000 breaths in a lifetime. And in each of those breaths, there is an opportunity to shape the nervous system toward safety and connection.

CHANGING THE RHYTHM OF RESPIRATION

The autonomic nervous system regulates our breathing in response to moment-to-moment metabolic needs. We see this in action with a breath of fear and a sigh of relief. Breathing is automatic; we breathe without thinking. We can also breathe with intention, changing the tone of the autonomic nervous system. By simply bringing attention to the breath, respiration rate often slows, and breath deepens. The action of placing our hands on our chest, belly, or sides of the ribs brings a physical reminder of the breath cycle and often changes the respiration rate and rhythm. What happens when we take actions to consciously manipulate the rhythm of respiration? Through altering the type, rate, and ratio of breath, we engage the vagal pathways that influence the beating of the heart and the messages sent to the brain.

"Breathing is an efficient and easily accessible voluntary behavior to systematically reduce and increase the influence of the vagus on the heart" (Porges, 2017b, p. 13). Voluntary regulation of breathing practices influences psychological states and often improves symptoms of anxiety, depression, and post-traumatic response (Gerbarg & Brown, 2016; Jerath, Crawford, Barnes, & Harden, 2015). Generally, slower breathing, prolonged exhalation, and resistance breathing increase parasympathetic activity. Matching inhalation and exhalation maintains autonomic balance, while rapid breathing, irregular breathing, and sharp inhalation or exhalation increase sympathetic activity.

Moving from typical breathing to slow breathing (5–7 breaths per minute) creates a sizable shift in average respiratory rate and changes our physiology. Slow breathing increases vagal activation and parasympathetic tone, leading to better physical and psychological well-being (Mason et al., 2013). Emotions and respiration are linked, and slow, deep breathing can effectively inhibit distress (Jerath et al., 2015). Slowing and deepening the breath during moments of distress brings a return of ventral vagal control, and, as our autonomic state changes, so can our story.

For clients, beginning to attend to the breath often triggers cues of danger and activates their sympathetic or dorsal vagal systems. One client beautifully described to me that she knew she breathed but had never watched it before. When her breath pattern started to change, she felt there was now room for something else, and that scared her. People using deep, slow-breathing exercises for the first time often experience the protective response of sympathetic flight or fight, but over one to three months, with regular practice, autonomic activation shifts from sympathetic protection to parasympathetic safety (Chinagudi et al., 2014). Mason and colleagues found in a study of people new to yoga, that introducing slow breathing with equal inhalation and exhalation was the simplest way to use breath to experience positive autonomic shifts (2013). Using that finding, slow and balanced breathing may also be a good choice to safely and successfully introduce clients to breath practices.

Resistance breathing uses a slight contraction of the larynx and glottis to add resistance to the exhalation. Reducing airflow during exhalation brings an increase in vagal activity (Mason et al., 2013). *Ujjayi breath,* or the ocean breath, a commonly practiced form of resistance breathing, seems to occur naturally when toddlers are playing with blocks, when children are doing math problems, and when adults are exerting effort under stress (Fokkema as cited in Brown & Gerbarg, 2005). Take a moment and imagine working hard to figure something out, and listen to your breath. You will likely hear a sound in the back of your throat. Resistance breathing brings a sense of feeling calm, alert, and attentive.

Sighing

> *Sighs are the natural language of the heart.*
>
> —THOMAS SHADWELL

Sighs naturally occur several times an hour as part of healthy lung function (Li et al., 2016), and sighs are also associated with feelings of sadness, tiredness, relief, and even contentment. Sighs can be thought of as "resetters of regulation" in response to both physiological and psychological demands (Vlemincx, Van Diest, & Van der Bergh, 2012). From an activated sympathetic state, sighing returns the autonomic nervous system to parasympathetic balance (Vlemincx, Taelman, Van Diest, & Van der Bergh, 2010). Heaving a sigh of relief truly is a release of tension! I watch for my clients to sigh during a session and stop to name the way their autonomic nervous system is working to bring regulation. "Your nervous system knew just what was needed. Let's rest in that regulating sigh for a moment." Bringing attention to the innate wisdom of the autonomic nervous system encourages clients to begin to trust that their nervous system is working. Connecting to regulating sighs can be a first step for your clients toward believing that their bodies aren't damaged beyond repair.

Sighs spontaneously arise but can also be intentionally breathed to life, making the practice of sighing a regulating resource. When your clients notice they are beginning to move into sympathetic activation, they can bring a soothing sigh that often resolves the activation and leads to a sigh of relief. In a ventral vagal state, ask your clients to savor the state through a sigh of contentment. Sighs are normal breath experiences that are repeated many times in the course of a day, making them low-threat ways for your clients to begin to experiment with using breath as a resource. One warning: Because people typically assign a negative motive to sighing, when you teach your clients to use sighing as a resource make sure they tell the people around them about sighing's autonomic regulating effects.

EXERCISE
Two Breaths in Transition

This exercise is designed for clients to intentionally move between a "breath of fear" with its associated quick surge of sympathetic activation and a "sigh of relief" that brings them back into ventral vagal safety. The autonomic nervous system is designed to transition between these two states with a degree of flexibility. Many clients, however, are challenged with habitual autonomic response patterns shaped by early environments of threat that make the movement into sympathetic protection easy and regulation back into ventral vagal safety unreachable. As you guide your clients through this exercise, they can experience the release and reengagement of their vagal brake and the possibility of a safe transition.

- The breath of fear is initiated with a sense of startle accompanied by a quick, audible inhalation and often a brief holding of breath. One hand moves to the heart, and the shoulders tense upward. The face freezes with eyes opened wide. If standing, there is a move up onto the toes, and when either standing or sitting there is a sense of energy moving upward and of losing contact with the ground triggering a sense of being unanchored.

- The sigh of relief that follows begins with the release of breath in an audible, deep sigh characterized by a long, slow exhalation and some form of resistance to the breath either through contraction at the back of the throat or slightly pursed lips, often followed by a moment of apnea (temporary suspension of breath). The hand remains on the heart as the shoulders relax. There is a feeling of the face softening, especially around the eyes. If standing, there is a settling back onto the soles of the feet, and when either standing or sitting there is a sense of energy moving down to connect with the earth, bringing a sense of being safely grounded.

Explore your client's response with them, looking first at the experience of activation and the full or partial return to regulation and then at the story created from the state shifts. Repeated practice builds flexibility in making transitions between states, and as your client experiences more flexible state shifts, their story about safety also changes.

EXERCISE
Using Imagery to Explore the Rhythm of Inhalation and Exhalation

The diaphragm contracts downward with each inhalation, making more space for the lungs, and relaxes upward with each exhalation, helping the lungs to empty. In the course of each breath cycle, the diaphragm changes shape from a "plate" to a "dome." To experiment with this, interlock your fingers to create the shape of a dome. On the inhalation, spread your elbows and flatten your hands, forming the shape of a plate. On the exhalation, lower your elbows and return your hands to the shape of the dome. Move through several breath cycles to get the feel of this rhythm.

Along with the contraction and relaxation of the diaphragm, each breath cycle is also a gentle exercising of the vagal brake. During inhalation the vagal brake relaxes and there is a slight increase in heart rate as more sympathetic influence is allowed. Relaxation of the vagal brake without total release maintains regulation so that the full expression of the sympathetic nervous system and the sense of being alone, cut off from others, is not activated. Exhalation brings reengagement of the vagal brake, a slower heart rate and increased parasympathetic influence supporting social engagement and connection.

This exercise invites clients to use the breath cycle to imagine the subtle flavor of moving inward into independent experience with each inhalation and outward into partnership with others on each exhalation. As the vagal brake efficiently manages the rhythm of breath, clients can experiment with the sense of moving between the solitude of "me" and the interconnectedness of "we."

Clients have a wide range of experiences with this practice. When introducing the practice, bring attention to finding the right degree of neural challenge. The shifts between inside and out, between feeling singular and interconnected, are difficult for many clients, and this practice offers the opportunity to work with finding safety in each state and flexibility in transitioning between the states.

For some clients, inhalation and imagining moving into individual experience brings a story of abandonment and isolation. The sense of being "safely solo" is often unknown. Alone may be equated with lonely or alone may have become a place of protection. Help these clients create an image of being alone that doesn't activate their survival system. Adjust the length of the inhalation so that it can be used successfully as a small experiment in imagining separation as a place of renewal.

For other clients, feeling connected to others via the exhalation imagery may initially be too intense and bring with it a sense of mistrust, the danger of being in relationship, and the commonly told story of being a misfit. With these clients, experiment with the continuum of connection from one end where there is simple awareness that others are in proximity to the other end where there is a joyful mingling. Use the exhalation to explore the spaces between these two ends.

- On the inhalation, imagine the subtle influence of sympathetic energy inviting you to enter your individual experience. Feel the breath filling your body. Feel the slight increase in mobilization that comes when the lungs are filled and the diaphragm changes shape from a dome to a plate. Follow the inspiration inside and explore the solitary experience. Feel the gentleness of the in-breath as it brings you into a moment of being "safely solo." Find the boundary between solitude and loneliness, the place where you feel the stirring of a familiar protection of separation, where your neuroception turns from safety to danger. Acknowledge this place and rest at the edges of safety.

- On the exhalation, as your ventral vagal system increases its influence, sense the move out of "me" into a flavor of "we," of being safely joined with others. On the exhalation, can you picture your breath moving in synchrony with others? You may imagine your breath moving to the edge of connection, not quite linking, staying just out of reach. You may feel an intertwining with one other breath or weaving into connection with many breaths. Explore the edges of feeling safe in this experience. Ride your exhalation only as far as your neuroception continues to be one of safety. On each out-breath, test the boundaries and honor your own placement along the continuum of connection.

- Continue the cycle of breath. Inhale moving into internal connection and synchrony with self. Exhale transitioning into connection with the world outside yourself and into harmony with others. Inhale into individual experience. Exhale into shared experience. Explore the ways these transitions happen several times each minute.

It is the goal that over time, attending to the rhythm of the breath will begin to feel safe and soothing and bring with it increased ease in making transitions and moving between "me and we." With this practice, clients are breathing the beginnings of a new story.

More Ways to Engage the Breath

- Drawing a breath: Four-square breathing, or box breathing, is a simple breath practice commonly taught to clients as a resource to manage anxiety. Combine breath and imagery as you imagine sketching a square, the first side being drawn with an in-breath, the next on the out-breath, taking two breath cycles to complete the square. Inhale to a count of 4, exhale to a count of 4. Extend the count as you build capacity. This practice combines the vagal benefits of slow respiration and balanced breathing. Change the shape from a box to a rectangle, and experiment with increased ventral vagal influence through longer exhalation or increased sympathetic influence through longer inhalation.
- Bubble blowing: A deep inhalation and a long, slow exhalation is necessary to successfully blow a stream of bubbles. Blow bubbles with others and add play to the experience.
- Playing a breath-powered instrument builds vagal tone. Kazoos are inexpensive and are fun and easy to use!
- Breathing into activation: Sometimes the autonomic need is for increased energy. Breath practices can be used to mindfully release the vagal brake and bring in more energy. There are many stimulating breaths including the breath of fire and the breath of joy.

Breath personifies a client's autonomic state. "How are you breathing?" is directly connected to "Where are you on your autonomic map?" Breath is a direct, easily accessible, and rapid way to shape the state of the nervous system. With an understanding of the basic concepts underlying breath as a portal to autonomic regulation, you can be creative in the ways you bring breathing practices into the therapy session and the ways you invite your clients to attend to breath practices between sessions. The way we breathe says a lot about the state of our body and the story we are living.

TONING THE NERVOUS SYSTEM THROUGH THE RECEIVING AND SENDING OF SOUND

The world is never quiet.

—ALBERT CAMUS

Sound is one of the ways the autonomic nervous system eavesdrops on the environment. Our ancestors survived in part because they could hear and respond to threats they could not see. Throughout the evolution of the autonomic nervous system, ancient sound memories remain.

Sound carries survival information, prompting us to approach or withdraw. Babies hear in utero, and a baby comes into the world already knowing their mother's voice. Because the autonomic nervous system responds to different qualities of sound, the sound environment we inhabit fosters restoration or triggers survival reactions. Our autonomic longing is for a diverse soundscape that brings the Social Engagement System alive.

In the famous line from the Brothers Grimm fairy tale, Little Red Riding Hood says, "What big ears you have." And the wolf replies, "The better to hear you with, my dear." It is not however the size of the ear that allows us to hear sounds of friendship and danger; rather, the muscles in the middle ear allow mammals to hear these sounds. Looking back at our evolutionary history, vertebrates evolved into mammals, and as the jawbone first formed a double joint, the three bones that make up the mammalian ear (birds and reptiles only have one) detached from the jawbone (Anthwal, Joshi, & Tucker, 2013). Mammals could now hear new sounds, and, importantly, the sound of the human voice is within the frequency bands created by this evolution of the middle ear (Porges, 2011a).

Through sound, we receive cues of safety and danger. We respond through hardwired neural pathways and through pathways patterned by experience. Sound frequencies and variations in pitch evoke different autonomic states and emotional experiences (Porges, 2010). The autonomic nervous system responds to low-frequency sounds (such as thunder or the rumbles of trucks) as sounds of a predator and to high-frequency sounds (such as a shrill scream or a baby's cry) as signals of pain and danger. In response to these types of sounds, the neuroception of safety is lost, and the autonomic nervous system activates a survival response.

Hearing safety and seeing safety are not totally separated experiences. The neural pathway that controls the eyelid and the pathway controlling the middle ear muscle that allows us to hear human voice is a shared pathway (Porges, 2011a). In relationships, including the therapy relationship, a high value is placed on eye contact, and we often assign positive meaning to sustained eye contact and make a negative interpretation of interrupted eye contact. Through a polyvagal perspective, maintaining and breaking eye contact is a story of state regulation as we try to find the "just right" place on our autonomic map. Sometimes the auditory pathway is the perfect portal of connection when eye gaze is too much. One of my clients who uses my eyes and the sound of my voice to feel safe knows she can look away and my voice will stay with her until she is ready to see my eyes again. She says my voice follows her into her disconnection, offering her a way back. Teach your clients about the intuitive wisdom of their autonomic nervous system in adjusting levels of connection, and then track with them their experiences of regulating through sight and sound.

The Sound of Safety

Speech is the mirror of the soul.

—PUBLILIUS SYRUS

According to a 2014 Gallup poll, texting is the most common form of communication for Americans under age 50. In the *Time* magazine mobility poll (a 2012 survey of close to 5,000 people of all age groups and income levels in eight countries—the United States, United Kingdom, China, India, South Korea, South Africa, Indonesia, and Brazil), 32% of all respondents said they would rather communicate by text than phone, even with people they know very well. Our cell phones help keep us connected but often do so through nonvocal communication.

Talking exercises elements of the Social Engagement System: the ventral vagus through the need for breath control, the larynx to make sound, the auditory pathways as we hear the sound of voice, cranial nerve V (trigeminal nerve) as the mouth moves to make sound, and cranial nerve VII (facial nerve) as our face expresses what we are saying. As we shift more toward e-mail and text, it is important to remember to talk. Most of us have an ongoing experience of inner speech throughout the day that is rich in auditory content (Scott, Yeung, Gick, & Werker, 2013), and it's not uncommon for us to talk out loud to ourselves. Talking to ourselves exercises the cranial nerves involved in speech, allows us to hear the auditory qualities of our voice, and to play with pitch and prosody.

Conversation adds the experience of reciprocity to talking. We exercise our vagal brake with patterns of listening and responding. Conversations have implicit turn-taking rules so speakers and listeners can avoid gaps and overlaps and find the timing that creates the flow of conversation (Filippi, 2016).

The vagal brake releases as we bring energy to our talking and engages as we move into quiet to listen. When the pattern is out of sync, the result is often a moment of biological rudeness—a violation of a neural expectancy and a move out of connection (Porges, 2017a). When the back-and-forth flow of conversation is interrupted, the move between internal and external states is uneven, and we experience autonomic misattunement.

Many clients live isolated lives, missing regular opportunities to talk with other people. Lack of social connections not only is a risk for loneliness and autonomic distress but also results in limited opportunities for conversation. For these clients, there are few chances to experience the neural exercises involved in having a conversation: exercising the vagal brake, tracking moments of biological rudeness and making a repair, the back-and-forth rhythm of reciprocity. Bringing conversational reciprocity into the therapy hour offers clients opportunities to practice and predictable experiences of language creating safe connection.

How can therapists work with clients to explore the ways they make and take in sound? Through Polyvagal Theory, we recognize the importance of prosody—the music of the voice. The pitch of your voice effectively conveys your emotional state (Belyk & Brown, 2016). A monotone voice, or a voice that is too shrill or too deep, alerts the nervous system to possible danger, while a voice with appropriate patterns of rhythm and sound invites the listener into safe connection. Prosody communicates what is beneath the words, the intent of the speaker. Autonomic knowing, hearing cues of danger underneath the words while being told that what you feel is not what is happening, is a common experience for many clients. In fact, humans reliably recognize a broad range of vocally expressed emotions, even when the spoken words are out of sync with the emotion (Belyk & Brown, 2016).

EXERCISE
Playing with Prosody

- With your clients, create a list of words that activates their three autonomic states and then experiment with speaking the words in different tones of voice. Track the nuance of response to each. Does the autonomic response change? Does the psychological story change if the state shifts?

- Next, experiment with speaking statements in different tones of voices. "I'm fine" or "It doesn't matter to me" are commonly spoken sentences that are easy test statements. Ask your clients to identify others that are familiar in their everyday experiences. Speak them to your clients with a variety of tones of voice and have them track how prosody effects their trust in the statement. What is the autonomic message they receive? Have your clients speak the statements to you in different tones of voice. What is their autonomic response to their own changes in prosody?

- With your clients, identify common words that predictably activate autonomic survival states—their language triggers. Clients often identify a specific word that brings sympathetic or dorsal vagal activation. These are words that have been linked through experience to danger or life-threat and now predictably bring a move into autonomic protection. It's helpful for clients to get to know their language triggers. For example, one of my clients identified an immediate dorsal vagal response to the word *leaving* but a ventral vagal response to the phrase *taking a break*. Ask your clients to share triggering words with important people in their lives and find alternative words to use in their everyday conversations.

- Create a list of words with your clients that bring their ventral vagal energy alive. These words become autonomic resources for your clients to use outside of sessions to either help them return to a ventral vagal state or to bring active appreciation to the presence of a ventral vagal state. The words can be said silently or spoken out loud. Use your client's ventral vagal word list in sessions to support transitions between states. At the end of a session, the reciprocity of sharing a ventral vagal word, speaking and receiving the word from client to therapist and therapist to client, creates an autonomically attuned ending.

EXERCISE
Connecting through Vocal Bursts

The voice communicates a wealth of information. Vocal bursts are the common sounds that populate our speech and convey emotion without words. Involuntary groans and sighs and voluntary expressions such as "ahhh," "mmm," "ohhhhh," and "humph" are examples of vocal bursts. Research shows that when hearing a vocal burst, the listener picks up the speaker's emotion correctly with a high degree of accuracy (Schröder, 2003; Simon-Thomas, Keltner, Sauter, Sinicropi-Yao, & Abramson, 2009) and that vocal bursts are understood across languages (Laukka et al., as cited in Belyk & Brown, 2016) and across species (Farago et al. as cited in Belyk & Brown, 2016). Simon-Thomas et al. (2009) looked at a group of studies and concluded that there are at least 14 emotional states that the human voice can communicate without words. It is not uncommon for therapists to have moments of not knowing what to say or to worry they will say the wrong thing. If, when at a loss for words, you offer a vocal burst, it is highly likely that your client will receive your emotional intention.

Vocal bursts are common in our everyday speech, communicating both autonomic and emotional tone. Bring attention to these nonlanguage cues of safety and danger that are automatically received and can be intentionally sent.

- Invite your clients to experiment with sending and receiving vocal bursts. Help them notice the experience on both ends of the sound. What is their autonomic response? What is their story?
- Make sure to have your clients experiment with a full range of vocal bursts; sounds that send a message of connection and sounds that send a message of protection.
- Have your client try this without eye contact so sound is the only cue and then again with eye contact to add the visual cues to the sound. What changes?
- Track during a session. Stop and notice when a vocal burst is expressed. What is the emotion carried in the sound? How does the autonomic state change in response to the sound?

Other Sounds

Hum comes from the Latin root *humus* meaning "earth" and "ground." It seems everyone can hum, and although there is no research on humming, the world is filled with people who say they feel happy when they hum. Even people who can't sing will hum without embarrassment. Humming increases ventral vagal tone. I've found that inviting clients to hum as an autonomic exercise usually brings a smile and a positive response.

For many people, singing is a more challenging experience. Singing is a form of guided breathing that exercises the larynx, lungs, heart, and facial muscles and requires breath control and changes of posture, all of which tone the ventral vagal system. Singing in a group adds the experience of reciprocity. The synchronized respiration that happens when a group sings together has been shown to increase heart rate variability, a marker of vagal tone (Vickhoff et al., 2013).

Chanting (intoning a single note with multiple syllables) combines sound, breath, and rhythm. Chanting increases breath control and includes extended exhalation. Studies have shown that chanting reduces anxiety and depression, blocks the release of stress hormones, and increases immune function. Kalyani and colleagues (2011) found that when chanting "OM" (as opposed to chanting "ssss"), the limbic region deactivation observed was similar to that in studies using vagal nerve stimulation and concluded it is likely the sensation of vibration around the ears in the chanting of "OM" activates the vagus through the auricular pathways.

As a result of the evolution of the mammalian middle ear millions of year ago, we are able to connect to the world through a rich and diverse sound environment. Sound is all around us signaling danger and inviting connection. The autonomic nervous system is wired to hear certain frequencies sending sounds of safety and other frequencies sounding an alarm. Experiences of safety, danger, and life threat are powerfully shaped by our autonomic responses to sound.

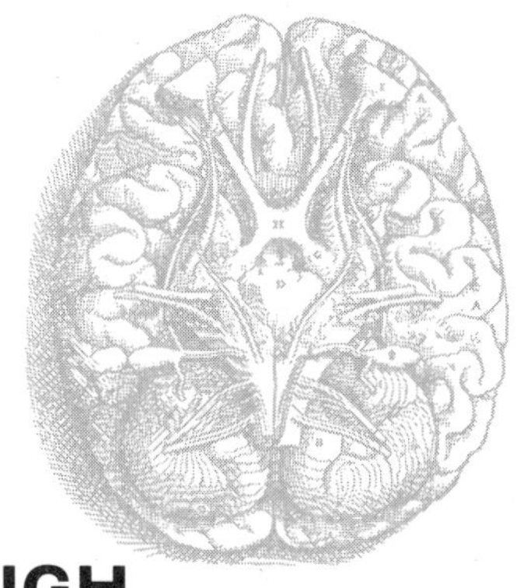

CHAPTER 12

REGULATING THROUGH THE BODY

While Leonardo da Vinci was painting the *Mona Lisa* and Copernicus was putting the sun at the center of the universe, Descartes, embracing the ancient Greek philosophers who believed in the separation of mind and matter, was defining dualism. Out of this enduring legacy, Cartesian dualism has resulted in doctors who treat the body and therapists who work with the mind. This biomedical model brought a wealth of medical knowledge and technologies to treat illness and has at the same time limited our understanding of the role of the mind in the experience of health (Mehta, 2011). Until recently, psychotherapy has focused on the mind with the body being an afterthought. van der Kolk (2014) points out that although the mind–body connection has in the past been dismissed by Western science, it is understanding of the mind–body connection that is now unquestionably changing the way therapists treat trauma. Therapists are coming to appreciate that effective therapy is body-oriented therapy. Body-oriented psychotherapies are based on the belief that the client's relationship with self, engagement with others, and movement in the world is inherently a mind–body experience (Bloch-Atefi & Smith, 2014). The full range of experience, from trauma to joy, shows up in the body, and the autonomic nervous system tells this story.

TOUCH

To touch can be to give life.

—MICHELANGELO

From the early history of psychotherapy forward, there has been disagreement about the use of touch. Freud first embraced and then banned touch. Ferenczi and Reich, contemporaries of Freud, considered the body an integral part of psychological healing and were proponents of touch. Today, touch as a therapeutic intervention is not commonly taught and is, in fact, often warned against (McRae, 2009). Although touch can be used to heal, for many clients past experiences with touch have been harmful, and nonsexual touch may be a missing experience. For both therapists and clients, the use of interpersonal touch can be confusing.

Touch is one of the basic ways we communicate. Looking at touch through an evolutionary perspective, people who worked closely together survived and were successful, and it may be that physical contact promoted that closeness (McGlone as cited in Denworth, 2015). Touch is the first sense to emerge in utero and the most developed at birth. Skin is the largest human organ, and touch is integral to our growth and development. Early touch experiences shape adult experiences (Gallace & Spence, 2010).

The emerging science around the healing power of touch is undeniable. Touch elicits emotions, modulates emotions, and communicates emotions (Gallace & Spence, 2010). Sustained maternal touch during Tronick's "face-to-face still-face" paradigm has been found to lessen the physiological impact of the mother's facial unavailability (Feldman, Singer, & Zagoory, 2010). In a 2009 study, adult participants receiving moderate pressure massage experienced a shift from sympathetic nervous system to vagal activity, while light massage brought increased sympathetic nervous system response (Diego & Field, 2009). Touch stimulates the autonomic nervous system, and the vagal stimulation supports reduced depression, pain, and stress and increased immune function (Diego & Field, 2009).

Doidge talking about Feldenkrais wrote, "Touch was always important to him because he believed that when his nervous system connected with the other person's, they formed one system, 'a new ensemble . . . a new entity' " (Doidge, 2015, p. 183). The act of touching provides information to the person being touched (the client) about the state of the person who touches (the therapist). Touch can convey presence and empathy (Connor & Howett as cited in Papathanassoglou & Mpouzika, 2012). Many clients suffer from lack of interpersonal touch in what Tiffany Field, director of the Touch Research Institute at the University of Miami School of Medicine, calls "touch hunger." (Field, 2014) With the admonition against touch so prevalent in the practice of therapy, clients can feel untouchable. How might this affect a client's autonomic state and the accompanying story?

Talking and teaching about touch through a polyvagal perspective is a safe way to bring touch into the therapy process and help your clients explore the regulating capacities of friendly touch. Returning to their autonomic map, clients can identify what kind of touch brings ventral vagal warmth, sympathetic distress, and dorsal vagal numbing. By looking at autonomic responses to touch separately from the elements of story, the experience of touch can be explored as a physiological event and assessed along a continuum of distress to pleasure. Without the surrounding story, clients begin to build a new relationship to touch. They are able to identify the autonomic cues of safety and danger that surround their touch experiences. They can then look back at prior touch experiences and track their autonomic responses of connection or protection, and begin to rewrite their psychological story.

Around the world, people use physical connection as a greeting, including touching forehead to forehead, rubbing noses, kissing one or both cheeks, and handshakes. Handshaking is an age-old practice that can be seen on ancient Greek reliefs, is referenced in Homer's *Iliad* and *Odyssey*, and is pictured on Roman coins. With a handshake, we enter into a reciprocal relationship. A handshake to begin a social interaction has been shown to increase people's perceptions of trust, activate their positive evaluation of competence and trustworthiness, and reduce their avoidance behaviors (Dolcos, Sung, Argo, Flor-Henry, & Dolcos, 2012).

Greeting clients with a handshake can send cues of safety to their nervous systems and create a ventral vagal readiness to enter into the therapeutic alliance. Ending the session with a handshake can be an affirmation of the therapeutic connection. The everyday way of expressing connection and intent through a handshake activates an autonomic response and offers an open and uncomplicated way to talk with your clients about touch and help them track their autonomic response. By bringing mindful attention to the touch experience, tracking reactions through the autonomic response hierarchy, and engaging in explicit conversation, touch can be brought out of the implicit experience of neuroception into explicit awareness.

If a therapist is uncomfortable with touch, they can't effectively bring touch into their work with clients. Talking about touch is something many therapists and many clients shy away from, and yet engaging in that conversation normalizes the experience of interpersonal friendly touch. Not having a conversation about touch says as much to your clients as having a conversation about touch. Creating a touch agreement is a rich process that unfolds as therapy progresses.

Looking at touch through the autonomic lens, and keeping that frame when using touch, brings safety into the powerful experience of connection created through physical contact.

With the autonomic map as a guide, therapists and clients can create autonomically informed touch agreements. The experience of creating a touch agreement is an opportunity to look at responses to touch, separate the physiological experience from the psychological story, and try small experiments with different kinds of interpersonal touch. By the time a touch agreement has been fully explored, therapists and clients will together have identified the co-regulating qualities of different kinds of touch and determined when to offer and when to avoid touch. Touch is an effective mode of communication when it is designed to deliver a specific message and used regularly between people who understand both the mode and the meaning (Bezemer & Kress, 2014). With these elements in mind, talk with your clients about touch and create a shared understanding of if, when, and how to use touch as a co-regulating resource. What kind of touch is an effective regulator? What kind of touch predictably dysregulates? When might regulation through touch be helpful during the therapy session? The answers to these questions will be different for each client. One client may tell you they want to be touched on the shoulder, while another only wants to be touched on the hand. Some clients want touch as they begin to feel a dorsal vagal move toward dissociation. Many clients in a sympathetically activated state only want to know you are there at a distance. Besides offering a hand or touching the arm, knee, or shoulder, another touch practice is to place a hand in the middle of a client's back. This often activates ventral vagal energy and, notably, is also where the back aspect of the heart *chakra* is. By naming what you are doing—"I'm putting my hand on the middle of your back to invite your ventral vagus into more activity: Feel the beginning return of that regulating energy"—you bring your client's attention to the regulating capacities of the ventral vagal system, reminding them of the inherent resource they embody. In addition to feeling the safe touch of your hand and an increase in regulating energy, the proximity of sitting next to your client adds the warmth of sitting side by side, which is often felt by clients as a safe interpersonal touch experience.

As both an alternative to touch when interpersonal touch is not available or desired, and as an addition to interpersonal touch, your client's self-touch and mirroring of your client's self-touch are two effective options. The following gestures can be made by your client with you echoing them when desired. Naming the intended autonomic outcome reminds the client that their nervous system is a biological resource ready to activate in service of regulation.

- Place a hand or hands over your heart where the vagal brake does its job.
- Place one hand on the side of your face and one hand on your heart, reminding your system of the power of the face–heart connection.
- Place a hand or hands at the base of your skull where your vagus nerve originates or a hand at the base of your skull and a hand on your heart or side of your face, connecting your vagal roots to the larger ventral vagal system.
- "Cup" the eyes (as described in Doidge, 2015) with fingers on the forehead, palms over the eyes but not touching them, and bring parasympathetic energy. Feel the warmth around the eyes and the enlivening of your Social Engagement System.

- And finally, experiences of touch are stored as tactile memories that we can consciously recall (Charité–Universitätsmedizin Berlin, 2011). Help your clients find their positive touch memories. Remembered touch brings touch to life as a resource.

MOVEMENT

I too dance the rhythm of this moving world.

—RUMI

Even before birth, when we are still safe inside the womb, movement is essential to life. We are already experiencing ourselves as moving beings, an experience that continues throughout our lifetime. The autonomic nervous system reacts to body movement and to shifts in posture in order to maintain a stable internal environment and support interactions with the outside world. Baroreceptors, which are sensors located in blood vessels, respond quickly to changes in body position, increasing or decreasing heart rate via the action of the vagal brake. Intentionally changing posture is a way to influence autonomic state. Shifting of posture brings a sense of activation as the vagal brake is relaxed, followed by a sense of calm as the vagal brake reengages (Porges & Carter, 2017). Changing posture (including lying down, sitting, standing, turning, rocking, leaning) changes autonomic tone.

One way to use movement to shape the autonomic nervous system is to use a therapy ball. Sitting on a therapy ball requires constant micro-movements. For clients who tend toward collapse, making the small, ongoing body adjustments necessary to avoid falling off the therapy ball keeps enough energy moving in their system to stay out of dorsal vagal shutdown, and consequently they are more able to stay present. For clients who tend toward sympathetic activity, the need to adjust the intensity of movement to stay seated on the ball is a natural way to engage the actions of the vagal brake.

In a University of Rochester School of Nursing study, nursing home residents with dementia showed positive responses to use of a rocking chair, including fewer medication requests, improved balance, and fewer expressions of anxiety, depression, and stress (Watson, Wells, & Cox, 1998). These outcomes rely on a regulated autonomic nervous system. Polyvagal Theory gives a rational for these results, reminding us that "rocking provides an efficient and direct influence on the vagus" (Porges, 2011a, p. 190). A rocking chair in your office is a way to help clients "move" into regulation.

Exploring the Edges

Approach movements and receptive hand gestures create a positive attitude toward others (Koch as cited in Fuchs & Koch, 2014). Through an autonomic lens, we might see this as activating a ventral vagal openness to connection. Movements with smooth transitions create receptivity toward the environment (Fuchs & Koch, 2014), again corresponding to a ventral vagal response. People sitting in a slumped posture remember more negative events, and those sitting in an upright posture remember more positive events (Riskind as cited in Fuchs & Koch, 2014). Perhaps this is due in part to autonomic tone. And when movement is inhibited, which through an autonomic lens commonly brings sympathetic or dorsal vagal activation, the experience and processing of emotions is impaired as well (Fuchs & Koch, 2014).

The autonomic nervous system is a system of motion. In the Three Movements exercise, clients use "inward, outward, and center" movements to explore the boundaries between states and exercise the actions of the vagal brake.

EXERCISE
Three Movements

- Begin in "center." Ask your client to find the posture that brings them a sense of being anchored in ventral vagal regulation. Then have your client begin to slowly move inward by lowering their head, bending forward and pulling in their arms and legs, while closely tracking their autonomic state. Moving from center inward, there are nuances of quiet, deep relaxation, and peaceful stillness shaped by an active vagal brake. Ask your client to track the subtle shifts and describe their experience to you with each change. In its extreme, this movement becomes the fetal position, which is often linked to dorsal vagal collapse. Have your client come just to the edge of safety, the place at which the state turns from nourishing to depleting. This is the moment when the vagal brake can no longer work effectively. At that point, have your client begin slowly unfolding, coming back to center noticing the slight shifts that accompany the posture changes.
- Invite your client to reconnect with their ventral vagal anchor and rest in center again.
- Next ask your client to slowly transition outward, stretching their arms up and out, lifting their chin looking up toward the sky, and arching their back while closely tracking their autonomic state. In its extreme, this movement brings the unsafety of vulnerability with the chest and throat exposed, but before reaching that state, the extension brings a sense of enlivenment, determination, and joy. Ask your client to track these subtle shifts and describe the experience, again stopping just

as they reach the edge of safety. Here is where the vagal brake can no longer hold the system in regulation and the state changes from energizing to overwhelming. At that point, have your client begin the slow return from extension back toward center again, reporting the subtle shifts that accompany each small movement.

Moving between the center, inward, and outward postures is a natural way to exercise the vagal brake. Clients can move through the full sequence or choose to either bend or extend tracking the moment-to-moment shifts and connecting to the range of ventral vagal experiences that are found "between the edges." As a practice, these movements offer your clients a direct way to come into connection with the restorative powers of ventral vagal calm and the expansive powers of the ventral vagal zest for life.

EXPERIMENTING WITH ELEMENTS OF THE SOCIAL ENGAGEMENT SYSTEM

> *Each contact with a human being is so rare, so precious, we should preserve it.*
>
> —ANAÏS NIN

Facial expression, eye gaze, tone of voice, and tilting the head are all signals of safety, whereas absence of these signs is a cue of danger triggering autonomic states of protection. One experience brings the feeling of being in the company of a friend eliciting stories of safety and connection, while the other gives rise to stories of danger and isolation and a sense of being near a stranger or even an enemy. It is the Social Engagement System, made up of cranial nerves V, VII, IX, X, and XI, that orchestrates this autonomic experience.

EXERCISE
The Sunglasses Experiment

Understanding emotions from facial expressions is a part of social reciprocity, and people pay the most attention to eyes when processing facial features (Chelnokova et al., 2016; Domes, Steiner, Porges, & Heinrichs, 2012). This experience uses sunglasses to mask the cues the muscles around the eyes (the orbicularis oculi) send, and the eyes search for, in our quest for connection. The exercise uses elements of the Social Engagement System—eye gaze, facial expression, head turn and tilt, and vocalization—to experiment with cues of safety and danger. During each step of the sequence, actively track autonomic responses. Take time after each step to talk about the autonomic experience, and, at the end of the exercise, make sure there is a full return to co-regulation and connection.

While seemingly a simple exercise, the Sunglasses Experiment brings powerful autonomic responses. This exercise highlights the power of neuroception to create stories of fear, anxiety, and mistrust. Even within a long-standing attuned relationship, when the eyes are hidden a sense of unsafety quickly arises along with an autonomic story that the environment is now dangerous. The exercise also speaks to the power of the Social Engagement System to restore safety and connection. As the eyes are revealed and sounds are added back in, the autonomic nervous system relaxes, and reconnection happens.

This exercise is appropriate for individual, couple, family, and group experiences. In a setting larger than the therapist–client dyad, the therapist moves from participant to facilitator.

- The therapist and client each put on a pair of sunglasses with dark lenses that mask their eyes and look at each other with an expressionless face, an unmoving head, and without vocalization. This effectively restricts the cues of safety sent from the Social Engagement System.

- The client removes their sunglasses while the therapist continues to wear theirs. The therapist first keeps an expressionless face, unmoving head, and remains silent before shifting into facial expression, allowing their head to turn and tilt, and offering connecting sounds through vocal bursts ("ahhh," "mmmm," "ohhhhh").
- Then the client wears sunglasses while the therapist removes theirs and they repeat the sequence, first inhibiting the Social Engagement System and then activating the Social Engagement System.
- Finally the client and therapist both take off their sunglasses and connect through eye gaze, smiling, a natural tilt of the head, and vocal bursts. This brings a palpable sense of relief, often with a laugh, and a move into closer proximity. With the return of co-regulation, the sense of ventral vagal safety is restored.

Heart Warming

With an active Social Engagement System, you reach out and your client experiences your warmth. Perceived warmth is the single most important quality people use in deciding how to respond to others, and those decisions are made in fractions of seconds (Fiske, Cuddy, & Glick, 2006). People who are perceived as warm send autonomic cues of safety, inviting approach and connection.

Brain and body systems that process social warmth and physical warmth share common pathways (Inagaki & Eisenberger, 2013). Physical temperature affects how we perceive and interact with others; physical warmth promotes interpersonal warmth (Williams & Bargh, 2008). When social warmth is missing, we unconsciously try to self-regulate through physical warmth. Skin temperature actually changes in response to experiences of connection or exclusion (Ijzerman et al., 2012), and the manipulation of temperature, adding physical warmth when social warmth is missing, can change the experience. Warm environments, hot showers or baths, holding hot drinks, or holding hot packs changes people's impressions of others and brings a positive shift toward connection (Williams & Bargh, 2008).

The reaction to physical warmth and to substituting physical warmth for social warmth is not a conscious choice. Bringing these implicit responses into explicit awareness and then exploring with clients the possibilities for moments of physical warmth can add options for self-regulation. Physical warmth cannot take the place of social warmth but can lessen the intensity of an experience. The simple act of holding a cup of hot tea increases the physical sensation of warmth, which then increases the psychological experience of warmth. A hot shower or bath can reduce feelings of social exclusion. Wrapping up in a warm blanket can moderate the sense of isolation. Heartwarming is both a physical and psychological experience.

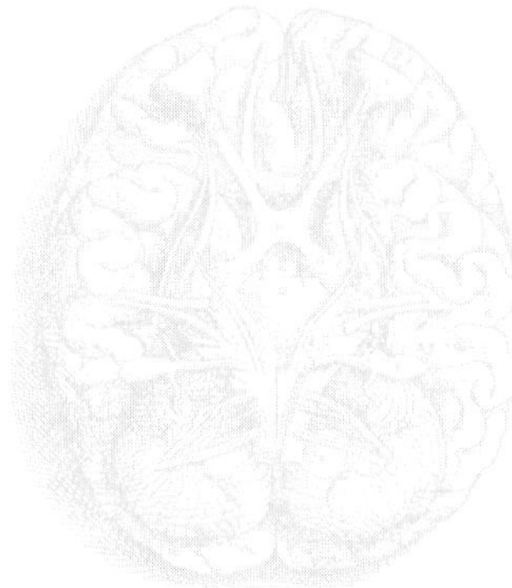

CHAPTER 13

VAGAL REGULATION WITH THE BRAIN IN MIND

Imagine a busy highway with four lanes going north and one lane going south. This is the vagus at work: four lanes of sensory information carrying messages from the body to the brain, and one lane of motor response sending information from the brain to the body (Schwarz, 2018). Eighty percent of the vagal fibers are afferent (body to brain), channeling a flow of "bottom-up" information. The remaining 20% are efferent fibers (brain to body) that originate in the cortex and end in the nuclei of the Social Engagement System. It is these pathways that create opportunities for top-down regulation and through which we can engage in neural exercises to increase vagal tone.

THE ART OF SAVORING

> *Thy memory be as a dwelling-place for all sweet sounds and harmonies.*
>
> —WILLIAM WORDSWORTH

Savoring is the practice of bringing to life a positive moment from the past and intentionally appreciating the individual elements of the experience in order to generate and amplify its positive affect. Rick Hanson's (2009) Taking in the Good practice is a lovely example of this. Through an autonomic lens, savoring energizes the ventral vagal system. The savoring experience is the result of a savoring process (a sequence that transforms a positive event into positive feelings) and savoring beliefs (a person's perception of their ability to enjoy positive experiences) (Bryant, Chadwick, & Kluwe, 2011).

Savoring is associated with regulating emotions (Carl et al. as cited in Speer, Bhanji, & Delgado, 2014). We naturally reminisce, our history pulling us back into moments of happiness. Intentionally bringing positive memories to life is a proactive way of maintaining and deepening a ventral vagal state. Remembering positive autobiographical memories helps people manage negative affect (Carl et al. as cited in Speer et al., 2014), and savoring may be important in regulating and maintaining positive emotions, which in turn promotes well-being (Speer et al., 2014). Savoring however can also regulate through an inhibiting action that dampens the intensity or shortens the duration of the positive experience (Bryant et al., 2011). Some clients' savoring beliefs don't support strengthening a positive experience and instead work to inhibit the experience. "I can't let myself enjoy this because then I'll want more" and "Good things never last" are common examples of regulating through inhibiting.

Bryant and Veroff (as cited in Jose, Lim, & Bryant, 2012) identify several ways to increase and prolong the savoring experience. Two of the strategies identified as increasing the value of savoring are especially relevant when looking through a polyvagal lens: verbally sharing the experience with others, which adds reciprocity to the skill; and focusing on the physical sensations of the experience, which keeps the focus on the ventral vagal experience and the Social Engagement System. For people who experience only occasional positive daily experiences, momentary savoring helps them sense the glimmers. People who consistently engage in the use of savoring are likely to maintain a positive mood even in the absence of positive life events (Jose et al., 2012).

Engaging in moments of savoring is a neural exercise. We can enter into the savoring skill by noticing an experience happening in the moment or through intentional reminiscence. We can savor the state or savor the experience. Savoring the state limits attention to the sensations of embodied ventral vagal activity and uses physiology to frame the act of enjoyment. For many clients, savoring the state is the starting point—the right amount of neural challenge for a successful experience. Savoring in this way separates the state from any elements of story, allowing a client to notice and name and simply be with their autonomic state as a physiological event. Once clients are able to savor their state, savoring the experience brings in the images, feelings, and thoughts that make up the ventral vagal moment, adding appreciation of the ways their physiological and their psychological systems are connected.

In clinical work, therapists can be on the lookout for a moment to savor. These are the glimmers that happen regularly even with the most complicated cases and are often unnoticed. Using the frame of savoring, looking for ventral vagal moments and stopping to take time to notice them conveys to your clients the importance of recognizing moments of regulation. This is not to discount or minimize a client's suffering, but rather is an intentional act of remembering and engaging their inherent biological resource. In the midst of trauma-saturated lives, there are micro-moments of ventral vagal safety and connection worthy of savoring. Once clients understand the science of savoring and become accustomed to stopping and savoring, they begin to look for moments to savor on their own.

EXERCISE
Savoring the State

- Bring attention to a moment of ventral vagal regulation.
- Stay present to the physical sense of this state (e.g., breath, heartbeat, warmth, energy moving, a sense of internal space).
- Imagine your vagal brake working effortlessly, smoothly, keeping the flow of ventral vagal energy moving.
- Bring your attention to fully savoring this state. Stay in the savoring experience for 20–30 seconds.

If sympathetic or dorsal vagal responses begin to intrude, bring your client's attention to engaging the vagal brake to preserve the savoring moment. You can invite your client to feel the energy of their vagal brake safely regulating the moment of savoring. Before entering into a savoring practice, it can be helpful to first help your client create an image of their vagal brake relaxing and reengaging. Then, when needed, you can use the image to help your client sustain the savoring experience. Common images clients have created for the vagal brake include the brakes on a bicycle, and a bridge or a door opening and closing.

EXERCISE
Savoring the Experience

- Bring attention to a moment of ventral vagal regulation.
- Sense the moment in your body and then invite in the images, feelings, and thoughts that accompany the moment.
- Actively receive the fullness of the experience: sight, sound,

emotion, belief, and body. Invite physiology and story to move together.

- Bring your attention fully to the experience for 20–30 seconds.

If sympathetic or dorsal vagal responses begin to intrude when savoring the experience, ask your client to share with you the individual elements of their experience. Often, saying the pieces of the savoring experience out loud is enough to bring clients back into the ventral vagal experience.

Although savoring for 20–30 seconds sounds easy, for some clients 20 seconds, even with support, is too great a challenge for the capacity of their vagal brake. If savoring turns from a deepening experience to an inhibiting one, the benefits of savoring are lost. Help your clients experiment with savoring honoring their own autonomic timeline. With practice, the capacity of the vagal brake increases and clients are able to sustain a longer savoring. For clients for whom the 30 seconds is simple and they could savor for much longer, stick to the 20- to 30-second time frame. These savoring exercises are meant to be quick moments of resourcing.

Sharing their story of savoring is a way for clients to strengthen the experience. The experience is changed when language is added and shared within a safe and attuned relationship. We relive in the retelling. When therapists invite their clients to share the savoring experience, clients commonly report a sense of the experience expanding and extending. Outside of sessions, your clients can share their experience with someone they can trust to respond with interest.

Encourage your clients to stop and savor whenever they notice a ventral vagal moment they want to mark. While adding reciprocity to the savoring process can increase and prolong the experience, the sequence of savoring without the component of sharing is also beneficial as an individual practice (Bryant & Verdoff as cited in Jose et al., 2012).

EXERCISE
SIFTing as a Resource

Dan Siegel (2010) uses the SIFT acronym to bring awareness to sensations, images, feelings, and thoughts in a practice of identifying activities of the mind and moving into a process of discernment. Discernment is a method of dis-identification, and SIFTing used in this way is a process of separating. SIFTing can also be used as a process of incorporating. Use of SIFTing to savor a ventral vagal experience brings sensation, image, feeling, and thought together, creating a resource that can be returned to as desired.

Pat Ogden (2015), in her Sensorimotor Psychotherapy model, uses the "Five Building Blocks of Present Moment Experience" (thoughts, emotions, movements, body sensations, five-sense perception) to bring mindfulness to a positive experience. This action of recall resources a ventral vagal moment in ways similar to the following SIFTing Exercise.

Creating a SIFT

In the SIFT exercise, the four elements of body sensation, image, emotional feeling, and thought are layered together to create an integrated physiological and psychological experience of ventral vagal engagement. There are two ways to find an experience for the SIFT exercise. One way is to listen for a story of safety and connection during the therapy session and choose that moment to SIFT. A second way is to decide to engage in the SIFT exercise and have your client actively retrieve a ventral vagal memory to use.

- Once the experience to SIFT has been agreed on, have your client tell the story of the memory and, together, listen for the element (sensation, image, feeling, thought) that feels most alive and accessible to begin the SIFT exercise. It doesn't matter where you begin the SIFTing process. When the starting point has been identified, begin the SIFT process by repeating your client's statement for that element. The remaining layers are then added one element at a time.

- As your client shares each element, repeat the description, offering your client's words back to them so they can receive the experience. As each successive element is added, build the layers of the SIFT, repeating the entire sequence each time. In this way, you are holding the SIFT with your client, voicing back to them their own rich description of each layer and building their ventral vagal experience.
- When the four layers are complete, narrate the full SIFT for your client, inviting them to rest in the completed SIFT and let it fill their body and mind.
- Ask your client to give their SIFT a title as a way of easily reconnecting with the new resource, and write the title and layers on a card for your client to take with them.

Beach

S: the feeling of warm sand under my feet

I: long stretch of beach with gentle waves

F: happy

T: I'm home

Safe

S: breathing space in my chest

I: standing in the sunshine

F: open

T: I'm okay

Once a SIFT has been created, the next step is to test it and strengthen its availability as a resource. Peter Levine (2010) developed the idea of using pendulation (oscillating between) as a way to safely and intentionally move between activation and ease. In strengthening the SIFT, use pendulation to exercise the vagal brake. Clients naturally tend to turn toward one of the elements of the SIFT, identifying it as the easiest pathway to engage. The first step in exploring the use of pendulation is to identify which of the four layers is the easiest for your client to activate as they begin to re-create the SIFT.

- Help your client bring the SIFT to life by narrating the four elements.
- Then ask your client to identify an experience that will bring a "neural challenge" to exercise their vagal brake. Your client may choose to tell you what the challenge is but it is not necessary. In this exercise, the autonomic challenge is only used as a way to exercise the vagal brake and increase ventral vagal flexibility. This first test should be a small challenge—just enough to bring a bit of autonomic dysregulation.
- Your client moves from the ventral vagal state of the SIFT into increased influence of their sympathetic or dorsal vagal system, putting attention on the identified challenge and telling you when they feel the autonomic state shift.
- As soon as your client identifies their state shift, help them engage their vagal brake and bring a return to ventral vagal regulation by recalling the SIFT. Begin by describing the element your client identified as the easiest pathway back, and then add the other layers until the full SIFT has been re-created and your client identifies a return to ventral vagal regulation.
- Repeat the pendulation process in a different test experience with either the same degree of neural challenge or a slightly stronger one depending on your client's response. It is important that your client doesn't move into a fully mobilized sympathetic state or dorsal vagal collapse. The goal is to successfully

release and reengage the vagal brake and build your client's confidence in their capacity to return to regulation.

- If your client has a hard time returning to the regulation of their SIFT, use your Social Engagement System to send stronger cues of safety (increased use of prosody, use of proximity, facial expression).
- At the end of the exercise, review the SIFT and pendulation experience, bringing explicit attention to your client's vagal braking capacities and their ability to successfully move between states.

While the SIFT is not used to resolve a challenging experience it can be used to explore bringing more ventral vagal regulation to an upcoming event that a client identifies as distressing. Clients can create many SIFTs over the course of therapy. By writing each on an index card, a client has a simple, accessible way to remember and reconnect to their SIFTing resources. My practice is to use fluorescent index cards, which have proved to be easy for my clients to keep track of and make a colorful stack over time. With attention to reciprocity, I write the SIFT for my clients and hand it to them, adding my own ventral vagal energy.

EXERCISE
Three New Ways

From a ventral vagal state, curiosity pulls us into exploration, engagement, and meaning making through a reflexive, bottom-up process. We also have access to top-down curiosity that can be used to intentionally explore new and challenging events (Kashdan, Sherma, Yarbro, & Funder, 2013). Curiosity comes when there is a belief that new information is available and that exploring the new information is manageable (Kashdan et al., 2013). Through an autonomic perspective, we can be curious when our neuroception is one of safety. For many clients, anything new is equated with being dangerous. The flexibility of response needed to support curiosity has been replaced by the rigidity of adaptive survival reactions. Exercises that invite clients to look for new information need to be titrated so the autonomic nervous system stays out of protective survival responses and maintains enough ventral vagal influence to bring curiosity to the process.

As clients begin to actively shape their autonomic response patterns, finding and feeling small shifts is an important part of the repatterning process. The way to shift thinking and shape behavior is with changes that are neither too extreme nor too similar (Berger, 2016). Following the Goldilocks principle, something perceived as too different activates fear; too similar and no need for change registers; just right and it feels safe enough to approach. When working with incremental change, emphasizing the small differences is essential (Berger, 2016). Without observation, clients often miss the moments of subtle change, attending instead to the familiar habitual responses. When dysregulation has been the customary response, clients need a way to safely look for micro-moments of autonomic regulation. Three New Ways is a daily practice that supports clients in this process.

The number 3 is important in making judgments and in prediction (Carlson & Shu, 2007). The "rule of three" indicates that the third repeated event is a pivotal point in perceiving an emerging pattern (Carlson & Shu, 2007). Because clients are entrained in habitual response patterns, perceiving a new pattern is both elusive and essential. Using the rule of three to guide the practice, ask your clients to take time at the end of the day to review their autonomic responses. Were there times when their reaction was not exactly the same as it has been? When they responded in a slightly different way? When their autonomic state felt not as intense? When the story changed just a bit? These are the important micro-moments that are interrupting old, familiar response patterns and indicate change is happening. Keeping a daily log of their "three new ways" gives clients a way to track shifts in their autonomic state and the accompanying stories. I often have my clients share their daily three new ways with me so we can track together. One client told me that while she still couldn't imagine what she called "upper case moments of JOY" she discovered she was now pretty predictably experiencing "lower case fun". Over time, clients are able to see new patterns stabilize and begin to trust that these are not aberrations but are now their routine responses.

EXERCISE
Continuums

To be or not to be.

—WILLIAM SHAKESPEARE

We think in categories and continuums. Using categorical thinking, we assign people and things to categories at opposite ends of an extreme, shaping how we perceive feelings and engage with others (Satpute et al., 2016). Continuous thinking, in contrast, brings attention to nuances and a sense that movement along a gradation of response is possible (Master, Markman, & Dweck, 2012). Trauma often creates categorical, all-or-nothing thinking. There is no middle ground. Creating continuums (template p. 255) is a way for clients to identify endpoints and explore the gradual transitions that happen between two distinct extremes. Using endpoints of regulation and dysregulation, clients can explore what is often the unfamiliar territory of regulation and the space between connection and protection.

- Help your client choose a habitual experience or belief to focus on and have them name the familiar end of the continuum and then consider what word might describe the opposite end. The words for the opposite ends of a continuum are personal to each client and are often unexpected (shattered-engaged, desolate-connected, devastation-peace).

- Once the continuum has been created, invite your client to begin to explore the space between the ends. What happens when they think about moving back and forth along the continuum? How does their autonomic state shift? How does their story change? What gets in the way of transitions?
- Help your client name places along the continuum and add those words to the drawing. Start at one end and move slowly toward the other end. Invite your client to rest in each place, feel the autonomic experience, and share the story.

EXERCISE
Seeing through States

A single experience, when seen through each of the autonomic states, generates three different versions of the event. Individual states color feelings, permit and restrict behaviors, and create their own characteristic stories. The ventral vagal story will include elements of safety and care. The sympathetic nervous system will write a story of anxiety, anger, and action. The dorsal vagal description will be one of collapse and a loss of hope. Seeing through each of the autonomic states helps clients more deeply understand the ways state creates story.

- Choose an experience.
- Create a simple statement to describe the experience.
- Say the statement as if you were speaking from each state. The same words will sound very different and convey different meanings when spoken from each state.

- Notice the sound, feeling, and story, and compare the three experiences.

Experiences of disconnection and connection are common occurrences, making them good choices for experimenting. As an example, for an experience of disconnection, the simple statement might be "I'm done." From a dorsal vagal state, it sounds colorless, might feel like withdrawing in defeat, and may bring up a story about never finding connection again. From a sympathetic state, the words sound edgy and harsh, might feel rejecting, and may create a story about walking away in anger. From a ventral vagal state, the words carry the sound of kindness, the feeling might be one of compassion, and the story may be one of graceful ending.

A statement for connection might be "I agree." From a dorsal vagal state, the statement sounds lifeless, might feel like submission, and may bring with it a story of going along because it doesn't matter anyway. From a sympathetic state, the words sound strident, might feel aggressive, and may carry a story about an unwilling concession. From a ventral vagal state, the sound is one of joining, with a feeling of joy, and a story of connection.

ON BEING BETWEEN

> *The path you took to get here has washed out; The way forward is still concealed from you.*
>
> —JOHN O'DONOHUE

The experience of actively repatterning the nervous system is one of transition. Before no longer feels true, but after has not quite made itself known. Clients recognize that their new autonomic state doesn't fit with their old story. This state–story mismatch sets in motion an experience of feeling untethered, ungrounded, unsure of how to engage with others and move through daily living experiences. As clients shape their nervous systems toward more ventral vagal regulation, it is as if each is a trapeze artist in midflight. Having let go of the first trapeze and flying toward the next brings a moment of doubt. Will the bar appear? Will I be ready to grab it? Therapists accompany clients in making that leap of faith. Working through an autonomic lens, therapists support their clients in tolerating "being between" and help to resource the new states while giving their clients' new stories time and space to take shape.

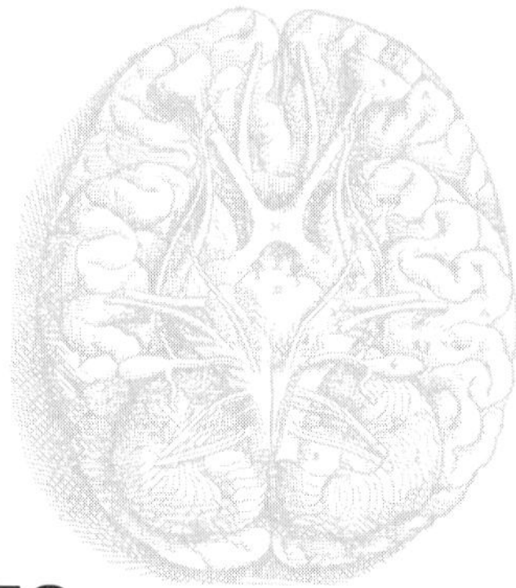

CHAPTER 14

INTERTWINED STATES

Guided by the three circuits of the autonomic nervous system, we move through moments of connection and protection in a search for safety. While most autonomic responses are understood through ventral vagal connection, sympathetic mobilization, or dorsal vagal immobilization, there are also experiences that involve complex interactions of more than one autonomic state. For many clients, the experiences that require cooperation between states bring an intensity that is too great a challenge for their nervous system to meet. When the autonomic ability to blend states is limited, our clients miss the richness of play, the tenderness of intimacy, and the inspiration of awe and elevation.

THE MAGIC OF PLAY

It is a happy talent to know how to play.

—RALPH WALDO EMERSON

Play has been called the universal language of childhood. For many clients, it is a lost language. We are born with the instinct to play but, "Play only occurs when one is safe, secure and feeling good, which makes play an exceptionally sensitive measure for all things bad" (Panksepp & Biven, 2012, p. 355). Play is universally recognized as an important contributor to a child's health and well-being and is included by the United Nations Convention on the Rights of a Child as a right of every child. Children who are deprived of opportunities to play are less resilient, struggle in friendships, and have difficulty with autonomic and emotional regulation (Milteer & Ginsberg, 2012). The pull toward play doesn't end with childhood. Play continues to shape our brains and bodies. Adults missing play opportunities are less curious, less imaginative, and lose a sense of joyful engagement in daily living (Brown & Vaughn, 2009).

Play is a neural exercise that strengthens the ability to flexibly transition between activity and calm (Porges, 2015b). For many people, however, opportunities for play bring the dysregulating energies of a survival response rather than ventral vagal anticipation. Play evokes responses along the continuum of connection to protection, sometimes enlivening the Social Engagement System and sometimes triggering a protective response. Autonomic responses to play are shaped by personal play histories. For trauma survivors, experiences that are unpredictable and unexpected bring cues of danger, and because play is both spontaneous and flexible (Panksepp & Biven, 2012), play challenges a trauma survivor's ability to maintain autonomic regulation, engage in reciprocal experiences, and stay safely connected. Many clients avoid play, and, when they do decide to give play a try, the experience can quickly turn from fun to fear. Play is a blend of two autonomic states made possible when ventral vagal social engagement and sympathetic mobilization work together (Porges, 2009b). The vagal brake relaxes, allowing the sympathetic mobilization of play, and then reengages before the mobilization turns from play into protection. Imagine these two systems metaphorically holding hands: if that connection is lost, the liveliness of play quickly turns from safety to danger.

Polyvagal play requires "reciprocal and synchronous interactions using the social engagement system as a 'regulator' of mobilization behavior" (Porges, 2015b, p.5). From a polyvagal perspective, play is a face-to-face, present-moment experience during which the autonomic nervous system moves between increased sympathetic nervous system influence and active inhibition via the vagal brake. The phrase "doesn't play well with others" describes a client whose neuroception brings cues of danger that overwhelm the capacities of their vagal brake when attempting to engage in the experiences of co-regulation that are inherent in interactive play.

The Practice of Play

Safe, interactive play opportunities tone the nervous system. Through repeated experiences, the capacity of the Social Engagement System to regulate reactions is strengthened. Clients become more autonomically regulated and resilient in the face of stress. Play is often a neglected component of adult therapy, and yet, knowing the ways interactive play positively shapes the nervous system, the value that play adds to a client's quality of life is undeniable.

EXERCISE

Exploring a Play History

The National Institute for Play (www.nifplay.org) identifies seven patterns of play. While each pattern of play can be enacted in a reciprocal, synchronous way, only attunement and social play are necessarily interactive and thus predictably create a polyvagal play experience.

- Attunement play (the first play experience with infant–mother gaze, ongoing experiences of gaze-to-gaze resonance)
- Body and movement play (play in motion)
- Object play (early experience with manipulating objects, common adolescent or adult experiences of engaging with technology)
- Social or interactive play (two or more people with involvement of the Social Engagement System)
- Imaginative or pretend play (creating a different sense of story and place)
- Storytelling or narrative play (hearing and telling personal stories)
- Creative or fantasy play (transcending ordinary reality; using fantasy to shape and reshape ideas)

Using the Patterns of Play Worksheet (template p. 257), explore with your client their experiences with each pattern of play. What play patterns are present and absent in their history and in present time? What themes are evident?

EXERCISE
Create a Personal Play Profile

What are your client's play preferences? What are the cues of safety and danger that accompany specific opportunities for play? What beliefs are built on their autonomic experiences with play? The Personal Play Profile spells out the general "play rules" a client identifies as necessary to be able to mobilize sympathetic energy while also using their Social Engagement System to maintain an attitude of play. With practice, the client becomes more skillful in regulating the movement between activation and calm, and the play rules will change. Invite your client to revisit their play profile periodically to track changes and update their play rules.

Using the Personal Play Profile Worksheet (template p. 259), help your clients identify the cues of safety and danger for each of the play categories. Include both environmental and relational cues. What are their play preferences? What elements bring the right degree of neural challenge to a play experience?

Experimenting with Play

The play history and profile bring awareness to a client's response to play. With this information, clients can begin to safely experiment with moments of play. Imagining a polyvagal play experience is often a safe way to begin. Whether shared out loud or experienced internally, clients use their autonomic maps to track their response and adjust the imagery to stay within the right degree of neural challenge to maintain the attitude of play.

Bring a playful attitude into your therapy sessions. Experiment with gentle back-and-forth banter or find an experience that brings shared laughter. Moments of in-person play are often more activating than the imagined play experience. Because you are present and actively engaged in the interactive play, your client can push their limits and explore moving to the edge where play begins to turn from fun to danger. As your client tracks their autonomic state shifts, use your Social Engagement System to send cues of safety to help your client stay in play and out of protection.

Adding interactive play to the therapeutic process offers clients an effective neural exercise to tone the nervous system. Through repeated opportunities for polyvagal play, the Social Engagement System is strengthened, and your clients experience an increased capacity for quick, efficient down regulation of sympathetic mobilization. From infancy through the end of life, we long to play. We are nourished by play not with screens but in connection with others, one autonomic nervous system resonating with another.

THE TENDERNESS OF STILLNESS

With stillness comes the benediction of Peace.

—ECKHART TOLLE

We depend on each other for survival. We need to be able to disarm our defenses and come into a shared experience of safe immobilization, first to meet our early nurturing needs and then for ongoing moments of intimate connection. How do we move into stillness without stimulating shutdown? Through a polyvagal perspective, stillness is possible when the ancient dorsal vagal and new ventral vagal circuits work together. This blend of states allows the experience of immobilization without fear. Over the course of evolution, the immobilization system has been modified to support intimate needs (Porges, 2009b). The dorsal vagal circuit can be enlisted to support social behaviors that require stillness. When actions of immobilization are coupled with feelings of connection—feelings that don't trigger defense—then immobilization without fear is possible (Devereaux, 2017).

Experiences of immobilization without fear show up in many forms. The act of sitting in silence with someone without feeling the need to fill the space with words is a measure of feeling safe in stillness. The ability for self-reflection requires turning inward and becoming quiet. Every day, we are expected to move from action to quiet as we interact with larger systems. These experiences are difficult for people whose nervous systems send signals of danger when there is even a slight move toward immobilization. The challenge becomes greater when the immobilization-without-fear experience includes physical contact (holding hands, sharing an embrace, dancing in the arms of a partner, sexual intimacy). Even sleeping next to a loved one is a test of the ability to immobilize without fear. Coming safely into stillness requires the ventral vagus to restrain the escape movements of the sympathetic nervous system and join with the dorsal vagal system while inhibiting its movement into protective dissociation.

For many clients, the autonomic challenge of becoming safely still is too great. Without enough cues of safety from another Social Engagement System to co-regulate or the ability for individual regulation through a reliable vagal brake, the autonomic nervous system quickly moves out of connection into collapse and dissociation. Through autonomic experiments designed to create micro-moments of immobilization without fear, autonomic response patterns can be reshaped to support safety and trust in intimate connections.

EXERCISE

Exploring the Story of Stillness

Name It

Words offer a gentle entry into the autonomic experience. This top-down experience of stillness is often the safe starting point for clients.

- Experiment with different words that describe the experience of being safely immobile (e.g., still, quiet, inactive, at rest, embraced, held). For each word, have your client notice their autonomic response and the beliefs that accompany the state.

Help your client find a word that brings safety into their experience of stillness.

Observe It

Use of an observer state to consider an image is a way to titrate an experience of exploration.

- Ask your client to describe a picture of stillness. What does a safe moment of immobilization look like? Looking at the picture, can they hold onto their sense of safety? What are the words that can anchor the experience?

Imagine It

Guided imagery brings the experience alive through multiple senses and is a way to experiment with embodying a state of immobilization without fear.

- Have your client create richly detailed imagery of feeling safely immobilized. Guide them into an embodied experience of the imagery. In the beginning, inhabiting the image for a micro-moment might be the client's "just right" experience. Help your client engage in repeated micro-moments and explore adding further cues of safety to support the ability to prolong the experience of being safely still.

Experience It

Real-time experiments within the safety of the therapeutic relationship offer opportunities for clients to use co-regulation to enlist their dorsal vagal system in immobilizing without moving into protection.

- Have your client explore coming into physical stillness.

Sequence slowly from motion to rest while tracking autonomic state shifts. The autonomic shifts may be strong or subtle, so it is important to attend to moment-to-moment tracking. Ask your client to narrate the autonomic experience and follow it with them.

- Find moments to sit together in silence during the therapy session. Move into stillness through the linking of your own ventral and dorsal vagal circuits and then encourage your client to sense the cues of safety your stillness is sending. Support them in tracking their autonomic shifts. What specific cues help your client find silence connecting and not life-threatening? Play with subtle changes and track the state shifts and accompanying stories.
- If your practice includes handshakes or hand-holding, those experiences can be used to explore moments of immobilization without fear.

Experiment with It

Finding ways to explore moments of safe immobilization in everyday life takes the practice beyond the therapy hour, offering the "small and often" opportunities needed to reshape autonomic response patterns.

- Help your client create a list of small experiments to try between sessions. These may include identifying moments to practice stillness in social and work situations; creating a plan to engage in brief moments of self-reflection; allowing periods of silence in a conversation; practicing sitting quietly next to a person; and finding a safe person with whom to explore physical contact including holding hands and hugging.

The ability to immobilize without activating the fear response is dependent on the oldest and newest parts of the autonomic nervous system joining forces. Within the story of safety provided by the ventral vagus and the Social Engagement System, the dorsal vagus can bring its capacity for stillness.

AWE

> *Dwell on the beauty of life. Watch the stars, and see yourself running with them.*
>
> —MARCUS AURELIUS

Awe brings a sense of wonder. It lies "In the upper reaches of pleasure and on the boundaries of fear" (Keltner & Haidt, 2003, p. 297). We feel small and at the same time connected to something much larger than ourselves, and this sense of connection leads us into a willingness to share and care (Piff, Dietze, Feinberg, Stancato, & Keltner, 2015). Awe graces us not through material things or social interactions but rather through information-rich experiences like those found in nature, art, and music (Shiota, Keltner, & Mossman, 2009). We feel awe in response to mountains, storms, oceans, the repetition of waves, and the patterns of nature (Keltner & Haidt, 2003).

Awe challenges our ordinary ways of thinking. For a moment, we step out of ourselves and our usual ways of being in the world. Most experiences of awe are not ones of social engagement but rather are solitary and seem to promote a moment of stillness that makes time appear to slow down (Rudd, Vohs, & Aaker, 2012). The aftereffects of experiences of awe, however, move people into a state of curiosity and toward connecting and attuning with others. Physically, awe experiences have been found to predict lower levels of inflammatory responses (Stellar, Cohen,

Oveis, & Keltner, 2015), and daily, small moments of awe predict well-being in the future (Gordon as cited in Keltner, 2016). My daily awe practice is to go outside each morning and stand under the stars, feeling a part of something so big that I have no words. Then I look for the Big Dipper and imagine it pouring abundance over the world.

Awe is found in both extraordinary moments and in everyday experiences. Opportunities to experience small moments of awe are all around us, and yet awe is often missing from our lives. Because awe is often experienced in solitude, clients who have no predictable social support can connect with the resourcing experience of awe. People have a desire to return to the environment in which they experienced awe (Shiota, Keltner, & Mossman, 2009), so encouraging clients to reenter past awe-inspiring environments invites them to reexperience awe and encourages them to create a practice of opening to everyday awe. The positive effect of small moments of awe make adding a daily awe experience an interesting prescription for helping clients build their ventral vagal capacities.

Slowing down is usually a necessary prerequisite to recognizing awe, although sometimes an experience is so awe inspiring that it reaches into our busy lives and leaves us awestruck. Music and art are both predictable, accessible ways to encounter awe. Nature, in its vastness and repeating patterns, reliably brings people into feeling awe. Experiences of awe move us beyond the constraints of our daily experience of self. For clients, this broader perspective, the sense of being connected to something larger than oneself, is often reassuring.

EXERCISE
Connecting with Awe

Talk with your clients about the benefits of awe, and consider with them the variety of awe-inspiring moments that happen in both extraordinary and everyday experiences. Support them in looking for awe in their everyday experiences and building a personal daily awe practice.

- Make an intention to find one awe-inspiring moment each day.
- Connect with the natural world and look for tiny moments of awe in the patterns of nature. This can be done by being out in nature or through viewing images of the natural world.
- Make a practice of standing outdoors and taking in the experience of being one small human woven into the vastness of the planet.
- Experiment with music and find compositions that reliably bring wonder, amazement, or reverence.
- We are pulled to return to the places where we experienced awe, so keeping an awe journal is a way to remember those places. Where are your personal places of everyday awe that are easy to visit? Where are the places of extraordinary awe?

ELEVATION

My religion is kindness.

—DALAI LAMA XIV

Awe and elevation are part of the same family of emotions. Elevation was first described by Thomas Jefferson as the way observing of an act of charity brings a strong desire to engage in grateful and charitable acts (Algoe & Haidt, 2009). Haidt describes elevation as "a warm, uplifting feeling that people experience when they see unexpected acts of human goodness, kindness, courage, or compassion. It makes a person want to help others and to become a better person himself or herself" (Keltner & Haidt, 2003, p. 305). Elevation, with its social focus, has the potential to send ripples of kindness out into the world as the witness of good deeds becomes a doer of good deeds (Haidt, 2000). Autonomically, the experience of elevation dually activates sympathetic and ventral vagal circuits (Piper, Saslow, & Saturn, 2015) and is commonly felt as goosebumps, tears in the eyes, and warmth in the chest (Algoe & Haidt, 2009).

Listening to stories of acts of kindness and watching videos of altruistic acts are ways to generate elevation experiences. If as Jefferson proposed, elevation is a way to "exercise our virtuous dispositions, thereby making them stronger" (Jefferson as cited in Algoe & Haidt, 2009), then elevation experiences are a way for clients to tone their nervous systems.

The lives of clients are enriched by experiences of play, stillness, awe, and elevation. For many clients, one or more of these important experiences is too great a neural challenge for their systems, and, as a consequence, these nourishing connections are missing from their daily lives. Without the ability to play, to be safe in stillness, to experience everyday awe, and be inspired by elevation, some of the vibrancy of daily living is lost. These complex autonomic pathways are valuable both as ways to tone the nervous system and as essential parts of a life well lived and well loved.

SECTION IV **SUMMARY**

Happiness is not a matter of intensity but of balance and order and rhythm and harmony.

—THOMAS MERTON

The autonomic nervous system is a complex system capable of both co-regulation and self-regulation. Our first move is toward regulation through connection, but if those safe connections are either unavailable or unreliable, the autonomic nervous system then turns to self-regulation. Clients most often come to therapy with nervous systems that are shaped away from connection toward protection. For many clients, co-regulation is unfamiliar, frightening, and something to be avoided, and their self-regulating attempts are based in the survival responses of the sympathetic and dorsal vagal systems.

Guided by Polyvagal Theory, you can help your clients engage the active pathways of autonomic intervention to reshape these habitual responses. The chapters in Section IV offer both interactive and individual options to work with clients in repatterning their autonomic pathways. As clients begin to reshape their autonomic nervous systems, they will start to trust in their ability to co-regulate and begin to self-regulate from a ventral vagal state. An autonomic nervous system that co-regulates and self-regulates with ease creates the possibility for clients to move out of their past needs for protection and embody a system that finds joy in connection.

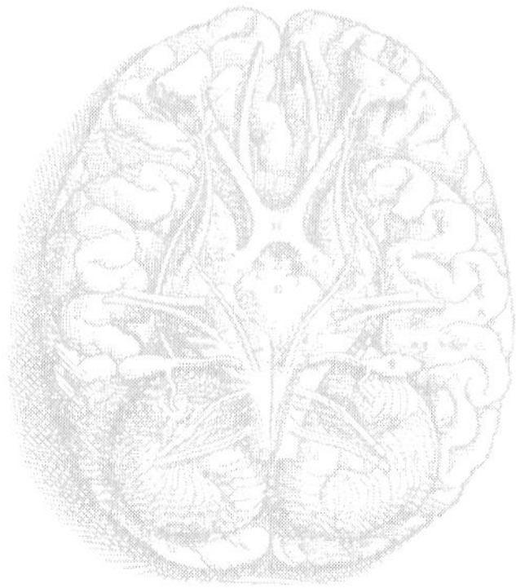

CONCLUSION

Most of the fundamental ideas of science are essentially simple, and may, as a rule, be expressed in a language comprehensible to everyone.

—ALBERT EINSTEIN

Shared language is the commonly understood set of references, visions, experiences, and interactions that provide a foundation for strong communications; the language that develops as partners work together (IGI Global dictionary). We are wired to want to be in connection, and one of the ways we come into connection is through communication. Using a shared language builds understanding and gives a frame of reference for interactions (Thomas & McDonagh, 2013). We feel the safety of "being on the same page." Polyvagal Theory is the language of the autonomic nervous system. By developing and nurturing this common language, we create a platform for communicating that cultivates connection.

Creating a shared language takes time and requires intention (Thomas & McDonagh, 2013). Making the decision to add an autonomic foundation to your therapy practice calls for an intention to become fluent in the language of Polyvagal Theory and a commitment to teaching your clients. You can learn "from the inside out" by first trying out the exercises in this book yourself and then taking the work into your clinical practice.

Polyvagal-informed therapy honors the role of the autonomic nervous system in shaping our physiological experiences and psychological stories and offers strategies to engage the rhythm of regulation in fostering change. Research is beginning to show that autonomic flexibility can be enhanced over time (Kok & Fredrickson, 2010) and that balancing the autonomic nervous system may be an effective way to regulate the release of neurotransmitters (Jerath, Crawford, Barnes, & Harden, 2015). An interesting study on "Loving Kindness Meditation" found that not only did the meditator's autonomic state change, but that another person in the room who was unaware they were being sent the four loving kindness thoughts also showed a shift toward parasympathetic regulation and reported an increased sense of well-being (Shaltout, Tooze, Rosenberger, & Kemper, 2012). Ventral vagal energy has the potential to create a powerful ripple effect.

Teaching Polyvagal Theory to your clients begins the process of creating a shared language and sets the stage for working from an autonomic foundation. The initial mapping sequence brings the language into action, and the additional maps and tracking skills offer a menu of options that can be tailored to your clients' preferences. Sharing the language of Polyvagal Theory changes the way we engage in therapy. By going deeper, we learn how to move up the autonomic ladder. Using the framework of the autonomic hierarchy, we help our clients "rise to the occasion."

The following brief clinical stories are shared to give a closer look at what Polyvagal Theory might look like in practice. The first, Ramona's Story, so named in this vignette for the ways the client is reminiscent of the spunky and spirited Ramona in Beverly Cleary's children's books, is a colleague's story of working with a child who found a way to be seen and understood through a creative mapping experience. The second, A Polyvagal Success Story, is another colleague's description of working with a client who had early experiences of unpredictable attachment and was struggling with high levels of reactivity that he was unable to understand or manage. This vignette offers a look at the ways the capacity for autonomic regulation is a powerful agent of change. The third, A Polyvagal Approach to Complex Trauma, is the story of my own work with a client with a complex trauma history who had tried many other ways of working without success.

RAMONA'S STORY

Ramona is a 9-year-old client in my practice. One of the reasons Ramona is in counseling is because she struggles with seemingly random outbursts of anger and frustration. Much of this is directed physically and verbally toward her younger sibling, and she is challenged at school and in social situations with peers as well. These experiences often leave Ramona collapsed in a heap on the floor. She has been unable to talk about why they happen or name what is upsetting her during or after these episodes of autonomic dysregulation.

In my office, Ramona took to IFS (Internal Family Systems) like a duck to water. She sculpted her "parts" from clay, drew them, and created stories with them in the sand tray. Ramona told me that understanding what's going on with her parts really helped her feel better and feel less angry. Yet she continued to collapse into angry, tearful outbursts in family and social situations and was still unable to speak either with her mother or with me about what was happening.

I introduced Ramona to Polyvagal Theory by drawing a ladder on my whiteboard with a black dry-erase pen and describing the three states of the autonomic nervous system. She understood immediately. I asked her if she wanted to make her own ladder, and she took the whiteboard from me, erased the ladder I had made, and began to use the colored dry-erase markers to draw her own. It was green at the top, red in the middle, blue at the bottom, and beautifully wobbly. She instinctively used color to create the sections of her ladder. She was curious about the transitions between states and blended crayons on scrap paper to create just the right shade to illustrate what it looked like between the states.

Next, we made a map of her day from an autonomic perspective. She divided the whiteboard into zones and wrote the times of her day she wanted to track. She used colored foam blocks to track different moments that occurred throughout her day. I watched her deep concentration as she very carefully chose, arranged, and rearranged the red, blue, and green blocks many times until she knew she had the sequence just right. An important moment was when Ramona illustrated how she went from ventral vagal, to sympathetic, to dorsal vagal, back to sympathetic, and then back to dorsal vagal at one specific point during her school day.

I waited until she had completed tracking her entire day to notice aloud the blocks of red (sympathetic) and blue (dorsal vagal) in her mostly green (ventral vagal) day. I asked her if she could tell me what had happened in the section of her map that showed so many state shifts, and for the first time, Ramona was able to talk about one of the dysregulated autonomic collapses her mother had described to me. By using the sequence of colored blocks to guide her, Ramona was able to find the language to tell me the series of events that had occurred and what had been happening inside her at that time. This allowed me, for the first time, to be able to be there with her in what had been up until that point an indescribable, frightening, and lonely experience.

By using Polyvagal Theory to help Ramona track her autonomic reactions to noises, to peers, and to many other stimuli in this way, I now can be with her, see her, feel her, and hear her in what had been previously isolating autonomic experiences.

A POLYVAGAL SUCCESS STORY

When I asked my client what brought him to therapy, he said he wanted to be less reactive. Because I had just finished a training in Polyvagal Theory and found it to be incredibly useful in helping people make shifts in their lives quickly, I decided to use Polyvagal Theory as the foundation for treatment. I taught my client the basics of the theory, and we began mapping. We filled in the Personal Profile map and used examples from the past week at work, at home, with his partner, and with his 6-year-old child to identify his placement on the ladder. In a matter of just a few weeks, he could easily identify his autonomic state. He quickly learned how to recognize when he was dysregulated in either his experience of collapse or mobilization and became interested in identifying what triggered those experiences. We completed the Triggers and Glimmers Map and, along with the triggers, he began noticing glimmers at home in interactions with his partner and child. Filling out the Regulating Resources Map was an ongoing interactive experience during our sessions, and my client was excited to have a list of ways to shift his state. I kept a blank ladder map out in our sessions, and each week we explored experiences through the autonomic lens, a lens he has adopted as the way he sees his daily interactions. Naming his experiences as states and staying out of the stories allowed him to play with a variety of ways to come back into regulation. Through his autonomic nervous system, he could recognize the shifts and trust the physiological cues. The question "Where does that belief belong on your ladder?" became important.

When my client was in particularly stuck places, it was helpful to return to his early history and review the lack of opportunities he had for co-regulation and how that shaped his patterns of connection and protection. There was often a persistent sympathetic–dorsal vagal looping, and he was able to identify the stories that kept that loop activated. We worked to safely explore the dorsal vagal experience and learn what his view was from the bottom of the ladder. Without the story, he found he could regulate up the hierarchy quickly. Once he knew he could do that, then together we returned to hear the story from his dorsal vagal collapse and how the story shifted as he moved into sympathetic mobilization and again as he regulated up to ventral vagal.

My client consistently reported less reactivity and savored this way of interacting with the people in his world. He reached his initial treatment goal in under 8 months and moved to less frequent sessions aimed at supporting his ability to maintain autonomic regulation. Most striking was his amazement that he was able to shift his day-to-day experience so profoundly in such a short amount of time. Just as my client delighted in the efficiency of this work, it was an opportunity to use Polyvagal Theory as my primary modality, and I equally delighted in its effectiveness.

A POLYVAGAL APPROACH TO COMPLEX TRAUMA

What progress, you ask, have I made? I have begun to be a friend to myself.

—HECATO

This is the story of the initial 4 years of my work with a client with a complex trauma history. My client came to me after engaging in therapy with many other providers and trying many therapeutic modalities, all of which had left her feeling she was "more challenged than anyone else" and wondering why she couldn't recover. She described living between feeling profound hopelessness and fear and anxiety. She told me no treatment had helped her with that struggle. She had lots of language to talk about it but no abilities to find relief from it. Medication and therapy only escalated her experiences, compounded her shame, and increased her despair. Even the slightest attempt to explore her trauma history left her "diving head first into reexperiencing." Stabilization was a place she longed for but could never find. She couldn't find it with others, by herself, or in her body. Safety in everyday life didn't exist. When I introduced Polyvagal Theory, my client met the idea with some resistance, anticipating another therapeutic disaster, but her tenacity about healing allowed us to move forward.

From the beginning of our work, my client found identifying "what didn't happen" to be an important part of the process. Using the science of connection to explore her early missing experiences of co-regulation, I offered facts about how experiences shape the nervous system that allowed her to feel some self-compassion. She discovered that it wasn't easy for her to regulate because she never had opportunities to learn how. Polyvagal Theory showed her that although she would ideally have learned to co-regulate and then self-regulate in her childhood, her nervous system was still able to be patterned, and she could learn now.

We used the therapeutic relationship to actively experiment with co-regulation. My client understood that her early missing experiences needed to be replaced by present-time opportunities to be in connection with a reliably well-regulated person. Consistency and continuity were two qualities she identified as most important, and after many months of meeting my client with predictable, stable, ventral vagal co-regulating opportunities, her once highly reactive nervous system began to quiet during our sessions, and curiosity emerged. Along the way, I had my own unavoidable times of autonomic dysregulation, and naming those for my client was important. She told me that tracking my own nervous system and naming my own moments of dysregulation helped her trust that what she was feeling, her neuroception, was right and trust that I was safe.

Another important aspect of what didn't happen was that working autonomically didn't challenge her stories. With a polyvagal perspective, we took another route. She learned to separate her autonomic response from her stories about herself. She practiced the skills of noticing, naming, and turning toward her reactions. She learned to respect that "going off the deep end," as she described it, was an adaptive survival response and not a fundamental character flaw. She found there was no shame when she went off the deep end again and again. Without the layers of shame, she realized how much those responses were once needed for survival and appreciated how they now made living so overwhelmingly difficult.

My client, like many trauma survivors, had a system that she said was "allergic to hope." She liked that Polyvagal Theory didn't rely on hope, that it was based on science. Learning the basics of Polyvagal Theory taught her to appreciate the autonomic hierarchy and that her system had a built-in bias toward moving up the ladder toward regulation. Her childhood trauma created a different trajectory, and the traumatic events in her adult life solidified patterns of protection, but she was willing to believe the science that proposed her autonomic nervous system, if given a chance, could learn to work in new ways.

She described our work as a "steady diet of glimmers" that she was able to feel knitting together. Savoring the glimmer experiences began to subtly shift her stories because her micro-moments of ventral vagal safety were a mismatch to her old survival stories. She began experiencing the possibility of safety and the delicate beginning of new stories. She identified that her messy moments were less daunting and more acceptable and that thinking about living with the common experiences of autonomic state shifting was very different from thinking that she was intrinsically defective.

With an ability to map and track her autonomic states, reach for and find regulation (both interactive and individual), my client finally felt moments of embodied safety. Recently, she told me trust is no longer a language of neediness and dependency, it is now a language of resilience. She likes that Polyvagal Theory has given her verifiable skills in tracking her levels of regulation, that it is not about doing it right or wrong, not a contest between survival and hope.

My client describes herself as a work in progress. Her once recurrent suicidality is no longer present, and she talks instead about her increasingly frequent experiences of embodied safety. Learning to track her autonomic state shifts doesn't promise unending ease but, as she says, "provides a reliable way to endure the dysregulation. I can live in my intense moments, notice and name, and have confidence that my system will regulate."

My client recently reflected on her past therapy experiences. She talked about how over and over she sought therapy and that many therapists and modalities might have been effective but, without a polyvagal foundation, her ability to heal was doomed to fail. My client and I now have a platform to safely bring in other therapies to work with her unresolved trauma. Even as we add in other modalities, we continue to rely on a polyvagal foundation attending to autonomic states, finding the right degree of neural challenge for the session, and following her autonomic wisdom. Relying on her knowledge of the autonomic nervous system in concert with predictable opportunities for co-regulation and reliable self-regulating skills has created a neuroception of safety that supports the difficult work of trauma processing.

THROUGH A POLYVAGAL LENS

I dwell in possibility.

—EMILY DICKINSON

Clinical work with trauma from a polyvagal perspective begins with befriending. Clients often feel like they are at war with their autonomic nervous systems and feel betrayed by their patterns of dysregulation. Looking beyond clinical diagnosis invites clients to see their behaviors and beliefs as adaptive responses in service of survival. At its heart, a polyvagal approach helps clients release the burden of shame they carry.

Through mapping, clients become aware of the commonly experienced responses shared across human autonomic systems and discover the unique patterns that personalize their systems. Rather than a perpetual feeling of being "too much" (e.g., needy, emotional, volatile, anxious, unstable), clients can redefine themselves as having an internal surveillance system that is sensitive to cues of danger. Noticing, naming, and turning toward their reactions without shame begins the process of learning to navigate in new ways. As our clients' internal worlds reorganize, their state shifts become more nuanced. They recognize new ways of regulating and begin to manage autonomic triggers with a measure of flexibility.

We are defined by our need, and our ability, to co-regulate. "Polyvagal Theory . . . forces an attention away from the individual to the individual within context" (Porges, 2016, p. 5). Polyvagal Theory in therapy acknowledges that co-regulation is a necessary prerequisite for self-regulation and that a trauma history is embedded with missing experiences of safe and predictable co-regulation. We recognize that co-regulation doesn't create dependence but rather builds a foundation for our clients' self-regulation and resilience, and with this in mind, we use the therapeutic relationship to offer frequent, predictable opportunities to co-regulate.

Neuroception delivers a constant stream of information. Do cues of safety make it safe to connect or do cues of danger bring the need to disconnect? Long before we can consider a response, our autonomic nervous system has reacted, and these repeated individual reactions form habitual patterns of response. Through a polyvagal lens, we understand that these physiological states create psychological stories. Clients' stories about themselves, about others, and about their relationships are anchored in their autonomic states. It is in states of regulation that clients can have thoughts that are bolder, more expansive, creative, and perhaps even spiritual (Porges, 2016).

The promise of Polyvagal Theory to help clients move through their trauma histories and into a life of well-being is grounded in the science of the autonomic nervous system. The art of bringing Polyvagal Theory into therapy is in honoring the innate wisdom of the autonomic nervous system and finding ways to bring the right degree of challenge to reshape patterns of protection and resource patterns of connection.

Knowing that the ventral vagal state of safety and connection is the state that supports change, our first responsibility as therapists is to embody that state and then help our clients enter into that place of safety. Underneath our clients' patterns of protection are patterns of connection waiting to be nurtured. The question, "What does the autonomic nervous system need in this moment to climb the ladder to safety?" is the question that guides our work.

When my clients talk about their ongoing moments of messiness, I remind them we can add "yet" and invite the autonomic nervous system to continue on its path toward regulation. "I can't find safety in connection . . . yet. I'm not able to regulate well . . .

yet. I haven't found a reliable co-regulating relationship . . . yet." *Yet* is powerful ventral vagal word. It is a harbinger of change.

This book presents many pathways to map, navigate, and shape the autonomic nervous system and is also an invitation to creativity. Once Polyvagal Theory shifts from cognitive comprehension to an embodied understanding, the possibilities for engaging the rhythm of regulation are infinite.

APPENDIX: AUTONOMIC MEDITATIONS

The meditations follow the list of their descriptions.

Old Vagus: This meditation is an "eyes open" meditation using an image of the vagus as a focal point. Focusing on the image with the invitation to feel the embodiment of the vagal pathways offers a safe way for the listener to come into connection with their autonomic nervous system.

Honoring the Vagal Brake: This meditation brings awareness to the role of the vagal brake. The meditation brings the listener into the ebb and flow of experience that accompanies the release and reengagement of the vagal brake and creates an experience of savoring the capacities of the vagal brake.

An Integrated System: This meditation takes the listener on a tour of the autonomic nervous system in homeostasis. The meditation highlights the role of each of the three branches of the autonomic nervous system in their nonreactive roles that enhance well-being and brings awareness to the sense of an integrated system.

Autonomic Navigation: This meditation creates the experience of "planting your flag in Ventral Vagal land" and using that anchor in an active ventral vagal state to safely connect with the states of sympathetic mobilization and dorsal vagal collapse.

Feeling the Face–Heart Connection: This meditation brings the face–heart connection to life with touch and image.

Map, Track, Honor, Nourish: This meditation invites the listener to bring their autonomic map alive and travel the "shape" of their day.

Safely Still: This meditation travels the pathways of the vagus as its branches join to bring safety to stillness, inviting the listener into the experience of quiet and safely coming to rest.

Benevolence: This meditation brings awareness to the use of active, sustained ventral vagal energy in service of healing.

OLD VAGUS

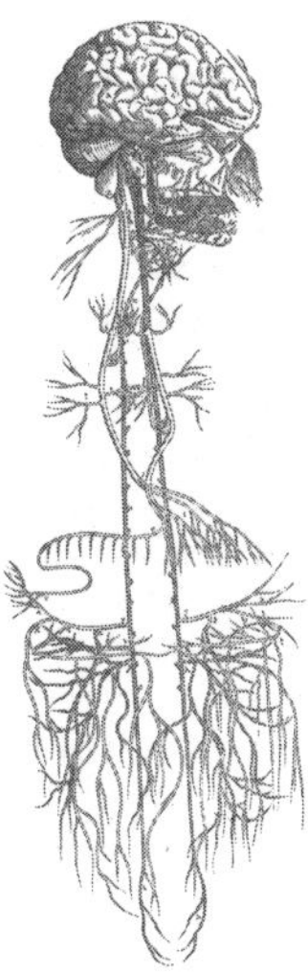

Rest your gaze on the image of the vagus, cranial nerve X, the longest cranial nerve, aptly named the wanderer . . .

Follow the vagal pathways from the base of your skull down to their roots deep in your viscera . . .

Sense into the branches of these fibers . . .

Feel the flow of energy up and down the vagal highway . . .

Savor the familiarity of this embodied home . . .

HONORING THE VAGAL BRAKE

Close your eyes if that feels comfortable or soften your gaze to connect inward. Begin to explore the actions of the vagal brake as it works to support your capacity for connection. Imagine your vagal brake working like the brakes on a bicycle, releasing to allow more speed and reengaging to slow your momentum. Play with that image for a moment. Feel the speeding up and slowing down . . . speeding up and slowing down . . .

Your vagal brake is guiding the ebb and flow of energy and experience. Breathe in and feel the hint of speeding up. Breathe out and feel the slowing down and spaciousness. Breathe in and feel the increase of energy. Breathe out and feel the return of ease.

Imagine your vagal brake relaxing and releasing. Experience the rise of joy, excitement, passion, alertness, interest, active engagement . . . let that energy fill you.

Now imagine your vagal brake reengaging. Move into the experience of calm, ease, relaxation, and the simple happiness that brings.

Explore on your own for a bit. Feel the rise and fall of energy being guided by your vagal brake. Visualize the action of your vagal brake . . . relaxation and return, release and reengagement. Let the experience fill you.

As you prepare to move back into outward connection, take a last moment to appreciate the actions of your vagal brake . . .

AN INTEGRATED SYSTEM

Begin by making the turn from outward awareness to inner experience. Close your eyes if that feels comfortable or simply soften your gaze. Allow yourself to disconnect from the world around you and connect inside as you begin your exploration of the qualities of an integrated autonomic nervous system. This is the system in balance, where the three streams of autonomic experience join their energies to work in cooperation, bringing health, growth, and restoration. Move into connection with these regulating energies . . .

Begin in the ancient dorsal vagal branch . . . the part of your autonomic nervous system that lies below the diaphragm. Envision your diaphragm, the muscle at the bottom of your ribs separating your chest from your abdomen. Then begin to move slowly downward following your digestive tract. Feel into your stomach, your intestines . . . sense the process of digestion that brings nutrients to nourish you. This is the realm of the dorsal vagus . . . slow, deliberate, steady. Take a moment to feel this ancient beat . . .

Now travel upward to the sympathetic branch and find movement and energy. Feel your spinal cord and then sense into the middle of your back. Feel your sympathetic nervous system circulating your blood, influencing your heartbeat, making moment-to-moment adjustments to your body temperature. The rhythm here awakens you. Sense the stirring of energy. Soak in this invitation toward movement . . .

And now to find the newest branch, the ventral vagus, return to your diaphragm and move up to your heart, to your lungs, to your throat. This is the system of breath, beat, and sound. Sense a sigh of relief. Feel the rhythm of your heart . . . the vibration in your throat. Continue upward to your face, eyes, and ears. Find the energy of engagement . . . the pull toward connection. Allow that energy to build and fill you.

From this place, tune in to the gentle ways the ventral vagus watches over your system, bringing regulating energy allowing the sympathetic and dorsal vagal branches to do their work. Bathe in this experience of homeostasis . . .

AUTONOMIC NAVIGATION

Just as explorers claim new land by planting a flag, "plant your flag" in the territory of your ventral vagal state. Feel yourself rooted in the energy of safety this system offers. Your breath is full. Each exhalation moves you along the pathway that supports safety and connection. There is a rhythm to your heart rate. The beat brings well-being. You're held in the autonomic safety circuit. Your body-to-brain pathway sends messages of stability, and the returning brain-to-body pathway creates the story of safety. From this foundation of safety, with the sense of your flag firmly planted in your ventral vagal system, you can begin the journey to explore your sympathetic and dorsal vagal responses.

Reach into the mobilized energy of your sympathetic nervous system. Your breath changes. Your heart rate speeds up. You want to move. Your thoughts begin to swirl. Imagine the sympathetic sea and the energy that moves here mobilizing your system toward action. Perhaps you can feel the wind blowing, disturbing the sea, and sense the waves—rolling breakers, crashing surf. Notice you can safely navigate this sympathetic storm. You are tethered to your safety circuit. Remember your flag is firmly planted, your anchor is deeply dug into the firm ground of ventral vagal regulation.

Return to the place where your flag is planted. Feel into the regulating energies of breath and heart rate. Feel a flow of warmth in your chest. Sense the solid ground beneath you, your ventral vagal system sending signals of safety.

Now gently begin the descent into the dorsal vagal state. This is not the dorsal dive that can take you out of present-time awareness into numbness. This is an experimental dipping of your toe into the feeling of disconnection. Energy begins to drain from your body, and everything starts to slow down. You feel a restriction of movement. Titrate this experience bringing active remembrance of your connection to your ventral vagal state—the place you first planted your flag. Feel those regulating energies controlling the depth and the speed of your dorsal vagal descent. You are moving along a slope, not plummeting into space. Your flag is secure, holding your place in ventral vagal regulation, allowing you to safely explore the dorsal vagal experience.

Come back to where you started in ventral vagal regulation. Return once more to where you planted your flag. Savor the ways you can befriend your sympathetic nervous system and dorsal vagal responses when guided by your autonomic safety circuit.

FEELING THE FACE–HEART CONNECTION

Close your eyes if that feels safe or simply soften your gaze. Place your hands at the base of your skull. Here in the brain stem is the evolutionary origin of your Social Engagement System. Focus your attention on the place where your brain stem meets your spinal cord, the space where five cranial nerves come together to form the pathways of your face–heart connection. This is the hub of your Social Engagement System. Rest here for a moment. Sense the beginnings of your quest for connection.

Now, move your hands placing one hand on the side of your face and the other over your heart. Feel the flow of energy moving between your hands, traveling from your face to your heart and your heart to your face. Follow this pathway in both directions.

Explore the ways your face–heart connection searches for contact and signals safety. Sense this system reaching out into the world, listening for sounds of welcome, looking for friendly faces, turning and tilting your head seeking safety. Feel your heart joining in the search.

And now feel this system broadcasting signals of safety . . . your eyes, your voice, your head movements inviting others into connection. Your heart sending its own welcome.

Move between the two experiences of sending and searching. Broadcasting and receiving.

Take time to savor the pathways of your face–heart connection.

MAP, TRACK, HONOR, NOURISH

Close your eyes or simply soften your gaze, and settle into comfortable awareness of your autonomic nervous system. Bring your autonomic map to life. See your map in your mind's eye, and find your place on it.

Explore the terrain. Where has your autonomic journey taken you today? Retrace the path you've traveled. See individual moments marked along the way.

Take a moment to reflect on those experiences. Notice the shape of your route . . . the directions your autonomic pathway has taken you.

See large-scale state changes illustrated in steep angles.

Notice the nuanced shifts found in soft curves.

Appreciate the path your nervous system has taken in service of your safety. The path you have traveled to this moment in time—to this particular place on your map.

Take a moment to listen to the autonomic story your map is telling.

SAFELY STILL

Close your eyes or soften your gaze, whichever feels right for you in this moment. As you begin to move inside, make the intention to explore the feeling of quiet and experience a moment of being safely still.

Come into connection with your vagus nerve. Feel the ancient energy of immobilization and the new energy of connection moving together, two branches of one nerve joining to create an experience of stillness without fear.

Sense the fibers of these two vagal pathways traveling together as you begin to move from action to quiet. Feel your wise social vagus reassuring your ancient protective vagus that, in this moment, it is safe to become still. Sense your system begin to enter into stillness without fear.

Pause in the stillness for a moment or a micro-moment. Feel the blend of your two vagal circuits. Within the ventral vagal story of safety, your dorsal vagus is bringing stillness. And from this state where is it safe to be still, you are open to reflection, ready to sit in silence and savor intimate connection.

BENEVOLENCE

Close your eyes or simply soften your gaze. Find the place inside your body where you sense the stirring of ventral vagal energy. This may be your heart, your chest, your face, behind your eyes, or somewhere else unique to your system. Feel the place where your energy of kindness is born. Settle into that space for a moment.

Join in the flow of ventral vagal energy as it moves throughout your body. Maybe there is a sense of warmth spreading. Perhaps your heart feels as if it is expanding or your chest feels full. There might be a tingling in your eyes or a tightness in your throat. Take a moment to get to know your own personal experience of this ventral vagal flow. Stop and savor this state.

Now imagine actively using this energy in the service of healing. Feel the power of this state to hold another person, another system in care and compassion.

Visualize the many ways you can actively use this state to shape the world.

Maybe you are holding a loved one in your stream of ventral vagal energy to ease their suffering.

Or perhaps you are the person with an enlivened ventral vagal system in the midst of dysregulation.

Take a moment to recognize the people in your life and the places in your world that are in need of your ventral vagal presence. Imagine moving into those connections from your state of ventral vagal abundance.

Through the active, ongoing, intentional offering of ventral vagal energy, you are a beacon of kindness, generosity, goodness, compassion, friendship, and common humanity.

Create an intention to beam benevolence.

WORKSHEETS

You can find the following worksheets online at
https://www.rhythmofregulation.com/worksheets

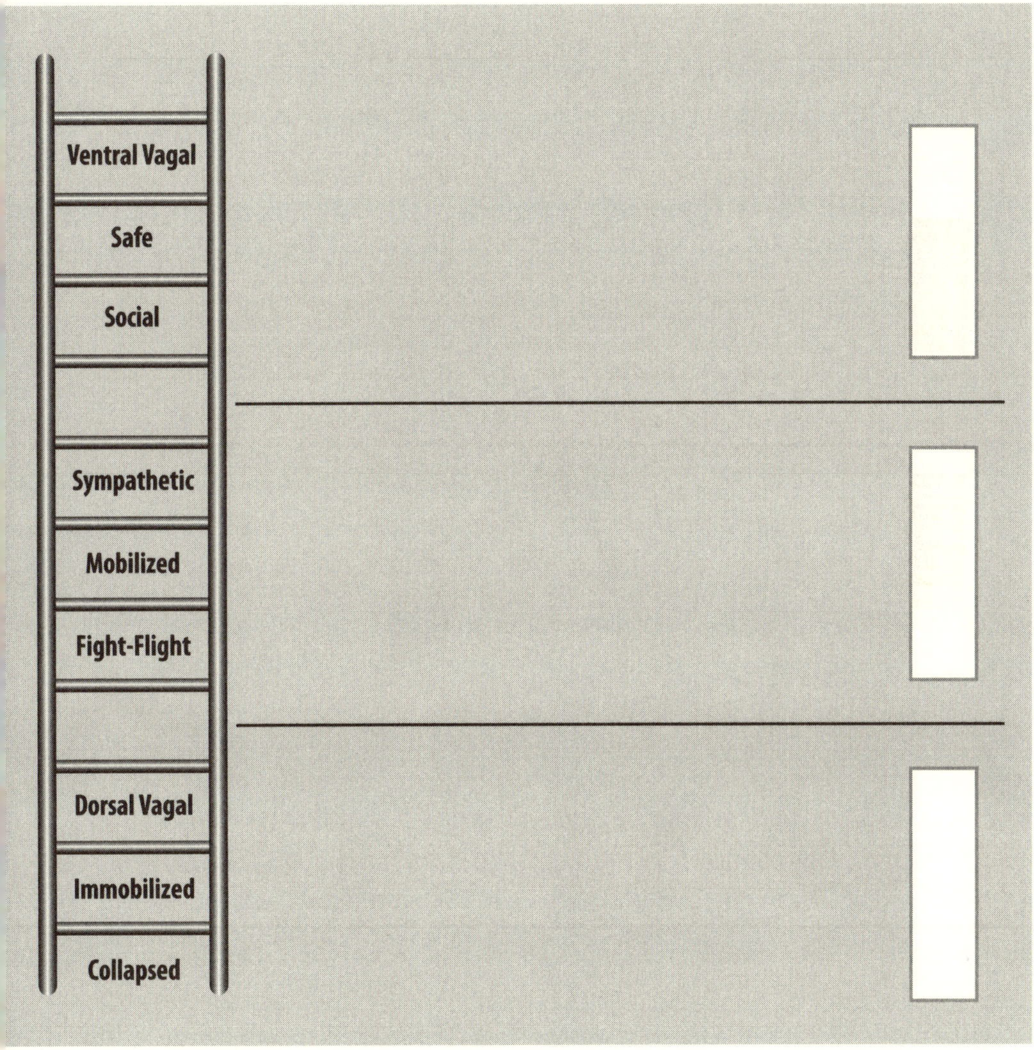

PERSONAL PROFILE MAP

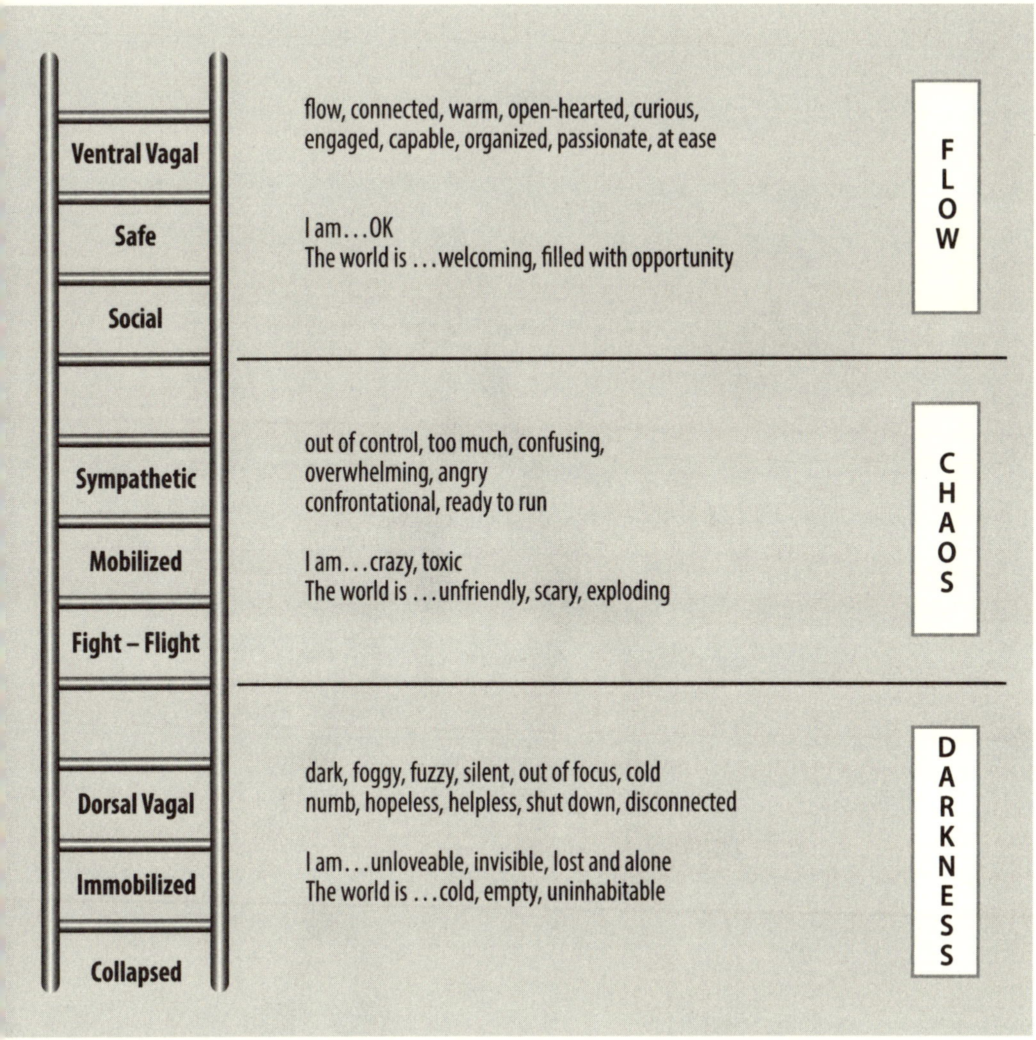

Personal Profile Map Example

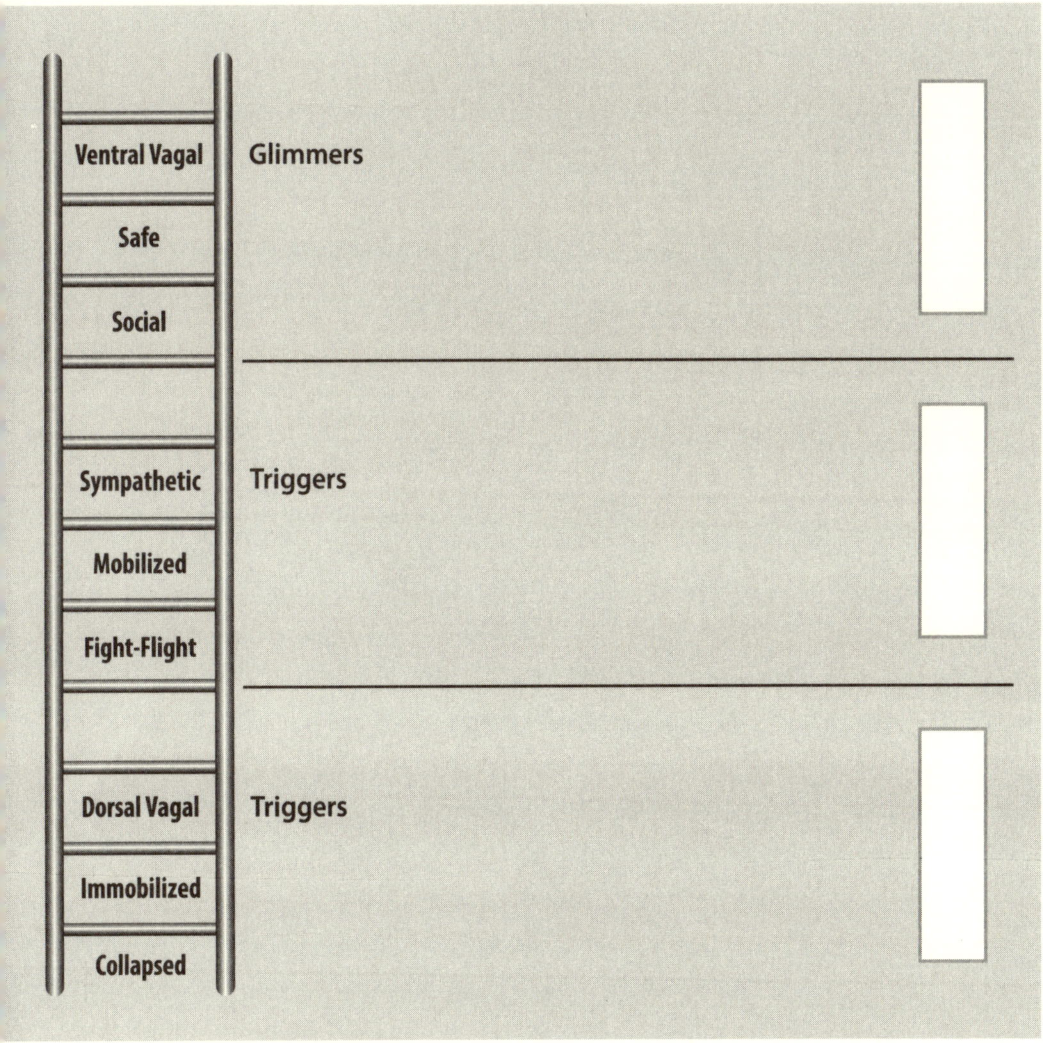

Triggers and Glimmers Map

Glimmers

a smile, emails with friends, feeling the sun on my face, coffee with a friend, songs on the radio, watching a favorite tv show with my partner, dinner with friends, driving by the beach, early morning quiet time, playtime with the kids, my dog, my cat

CONNECTED

Triggers

raised voices, deadlines, Facebook posts, arguing with my partner, bills I can't pay, having to co-parent with my ex, the morning commute, not being listened to, my to-do list, noisy co-workers, long lines

AGITATED

Triggers

constant demands I can't meet, being ignored, feeling powerless to make a difference, watching the news, chronic pain, illness, losing a friend, being left out of conversations

NUMB

Triggers and Glimmers Map Example

Things I can do on my own:	Things I can do with others:
What helps me stay here?	What helps me stay here?
What moves me out of here?	What moves me out of here?
What moves me out of here?	What moves me out of here?

Regulating Resources Map

Things I can do on my own:	Things I can do with others:	
What helps me stay here? go for a walk feel the sun on my face go to the beach take a drive time alone in the morning coffee sitting in the sunshine listen to music garden cook intentional breath	**What helps me stay here?** walk with a friend meet a friend for coffee giving or getting a hug Skype with family and friends a night out with my partner dinner with family game night	LIGHT
What moves me out of here? clean de-clutter dance in the kitchen sing along to loud music scream and swear out loud to myself exercise – go for a walk or a run organize closets create to-do lists take a shower	**What moves me out of here?** rant to a friend talk or text go for a walk/run with a friend go to a class at the gym go to a yoga class ask someone to listen to me without needing to "fix it"	FRENETIC
What moves me out of here? sleep prayer cry nature remember moments in the past when I felt ok imagine being around someone I feel safe with turn on the radio/tv meditation hot tea hot bath/shower	**What moves me out of here?** accept a hug let someone sit with me text/email with a friend go for a walk without talking go sit in a place where there is activity and people	BLANK

Regulating Resources Map Example

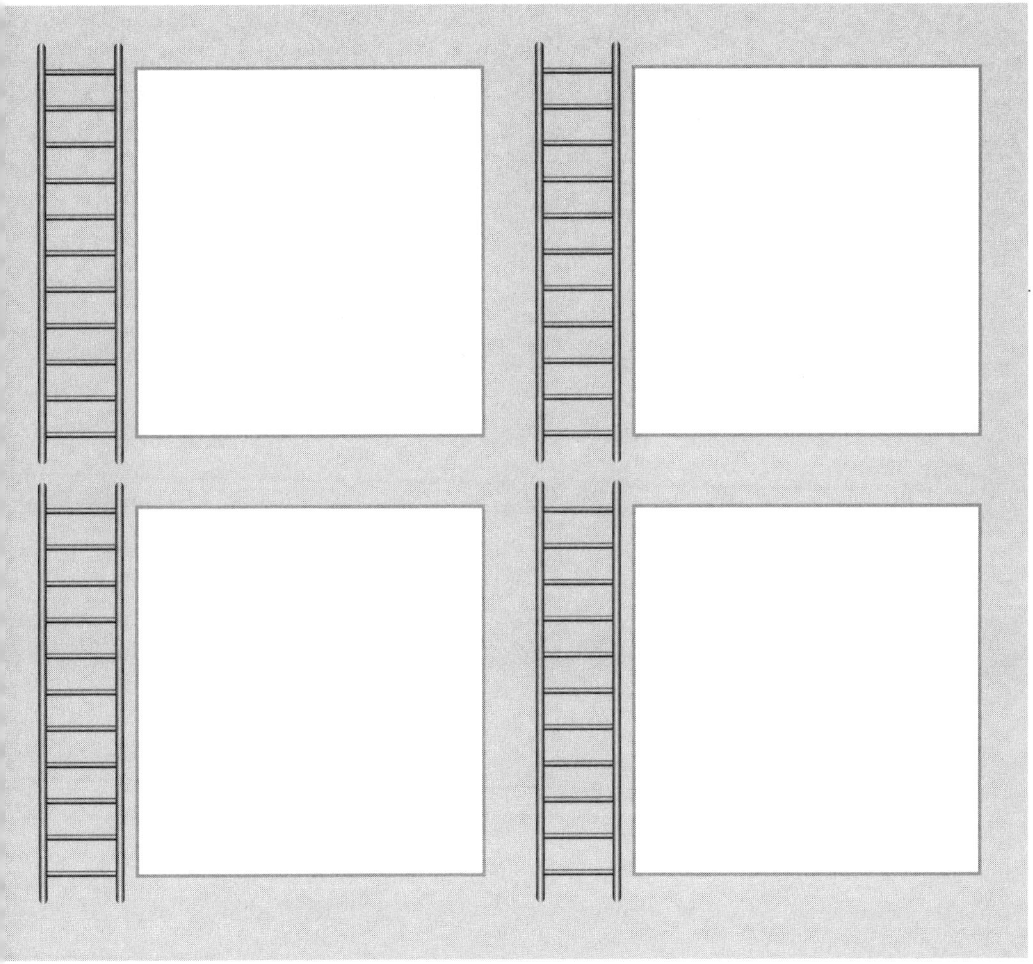

Four Map Tracking

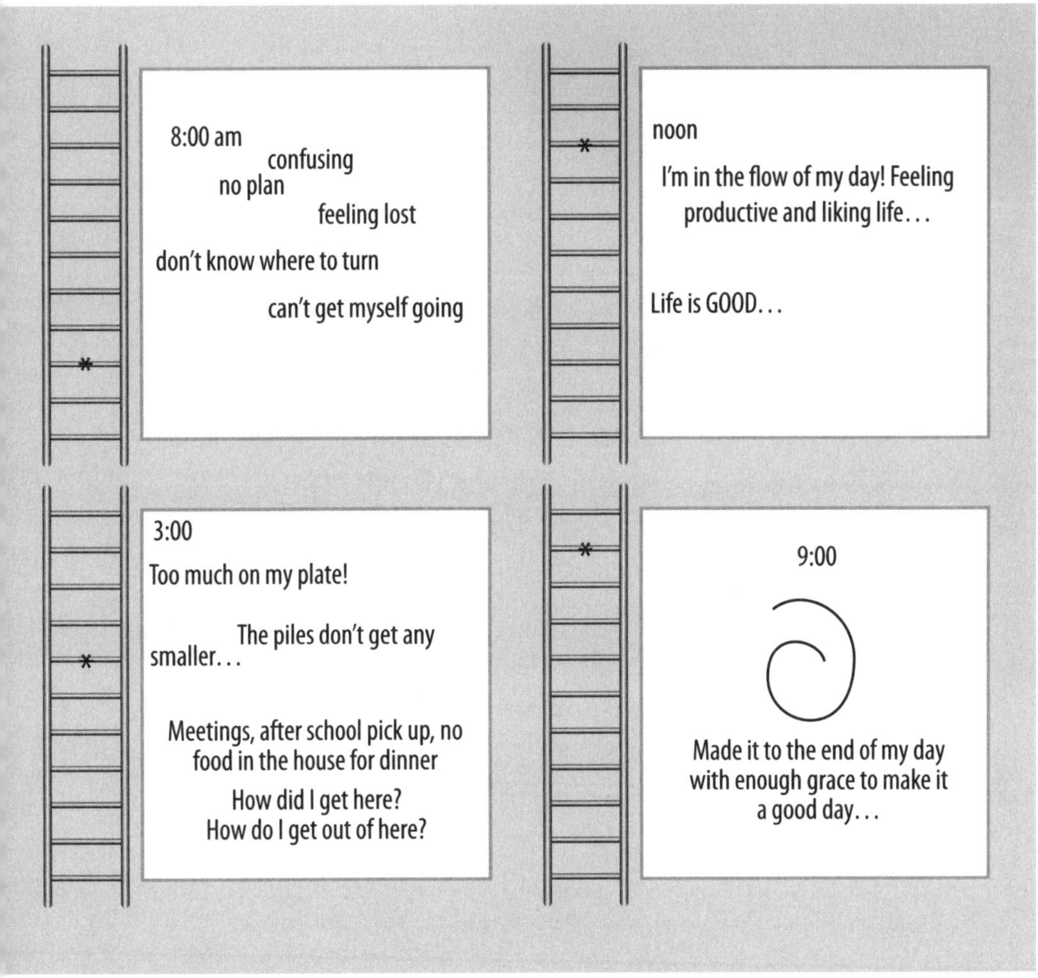

FOUR MAP TRACKING EXAMPLE

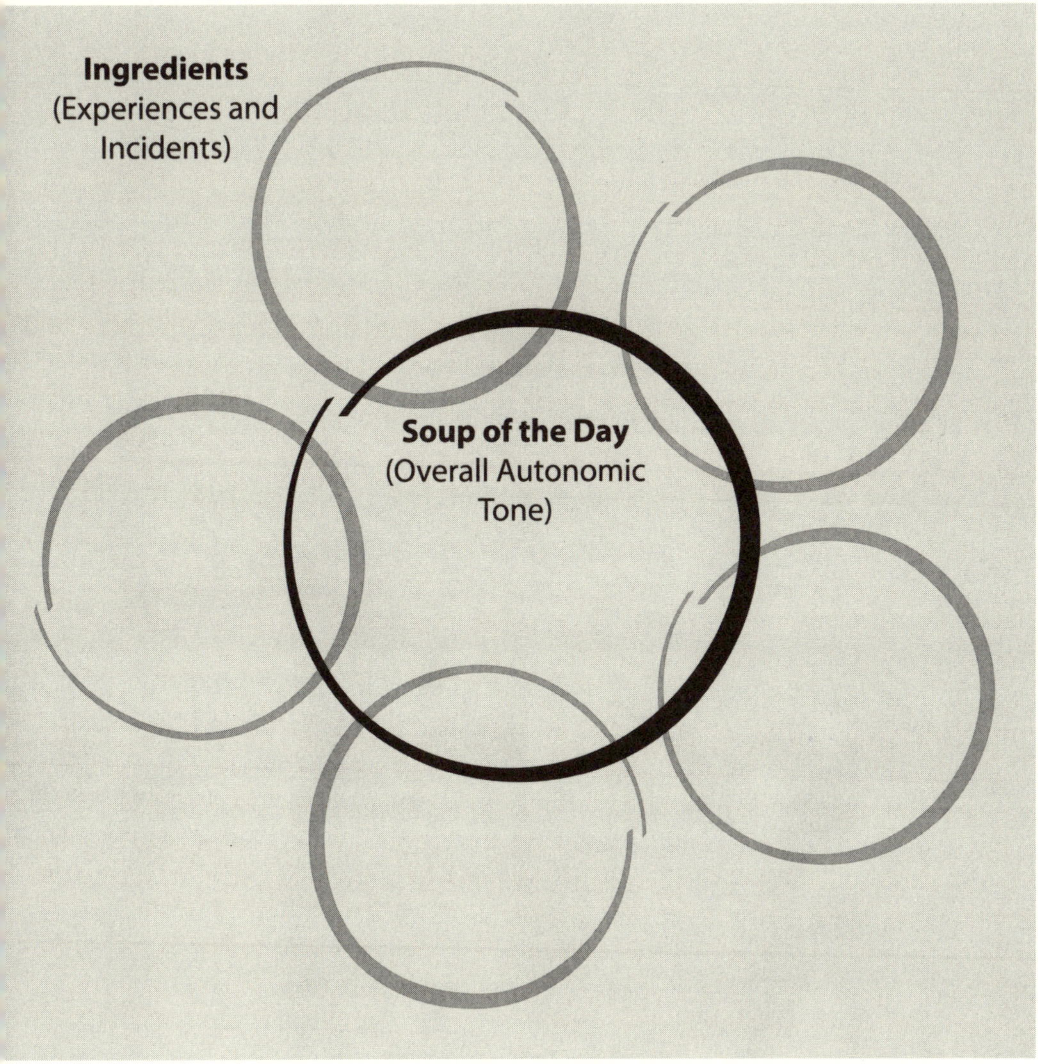

Soup of the Day

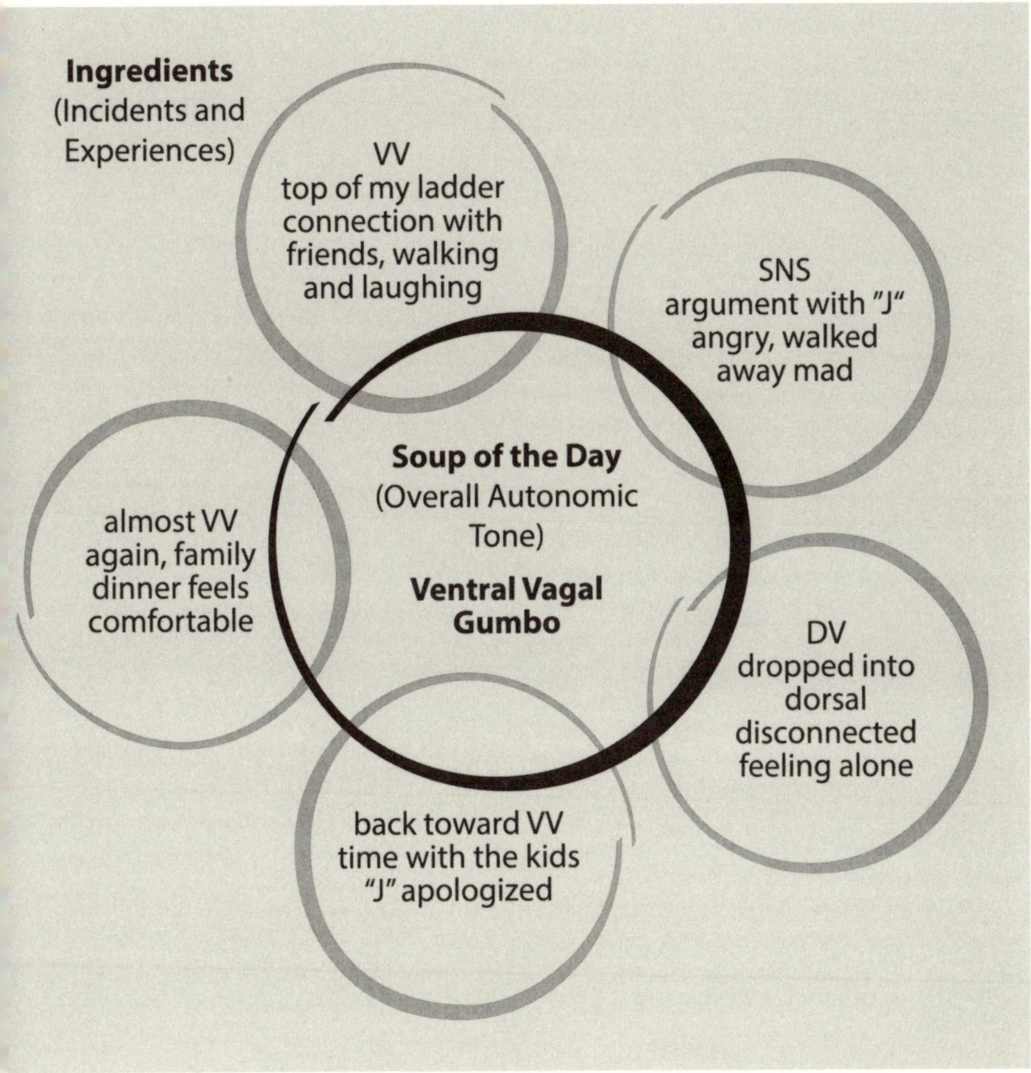

Soup of the Day Example

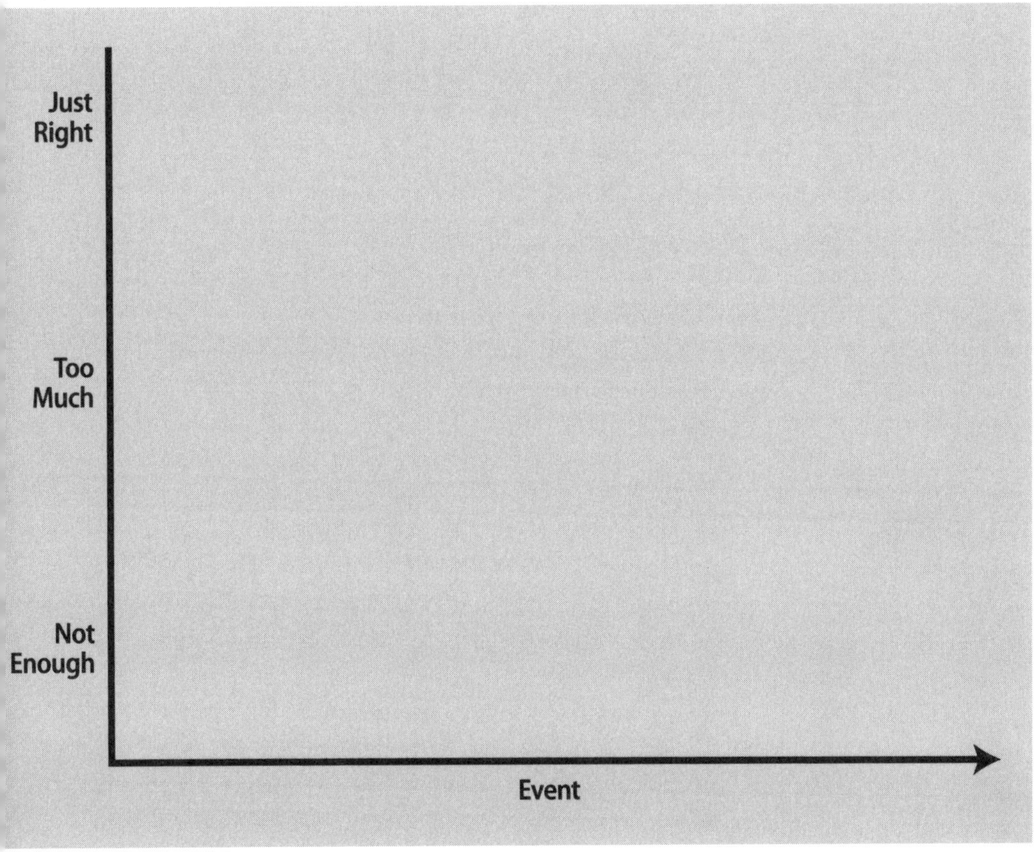

Goldilocks Graph

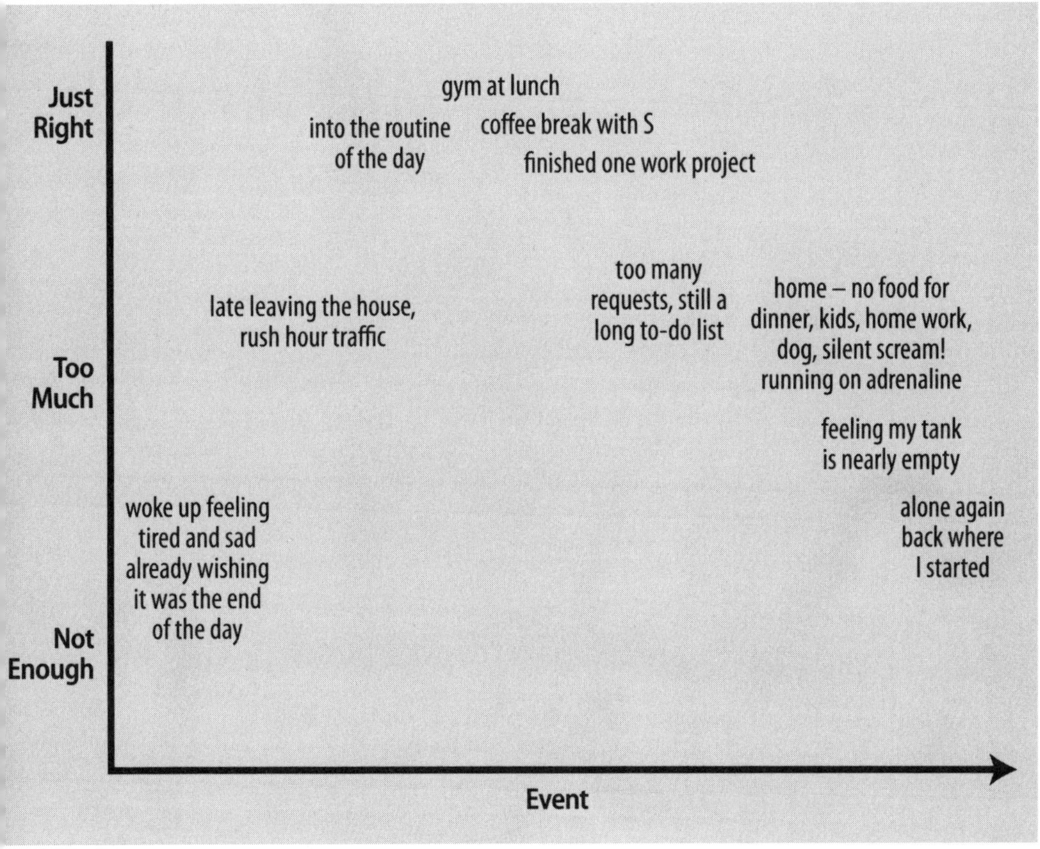

Goldilocks Graph Example

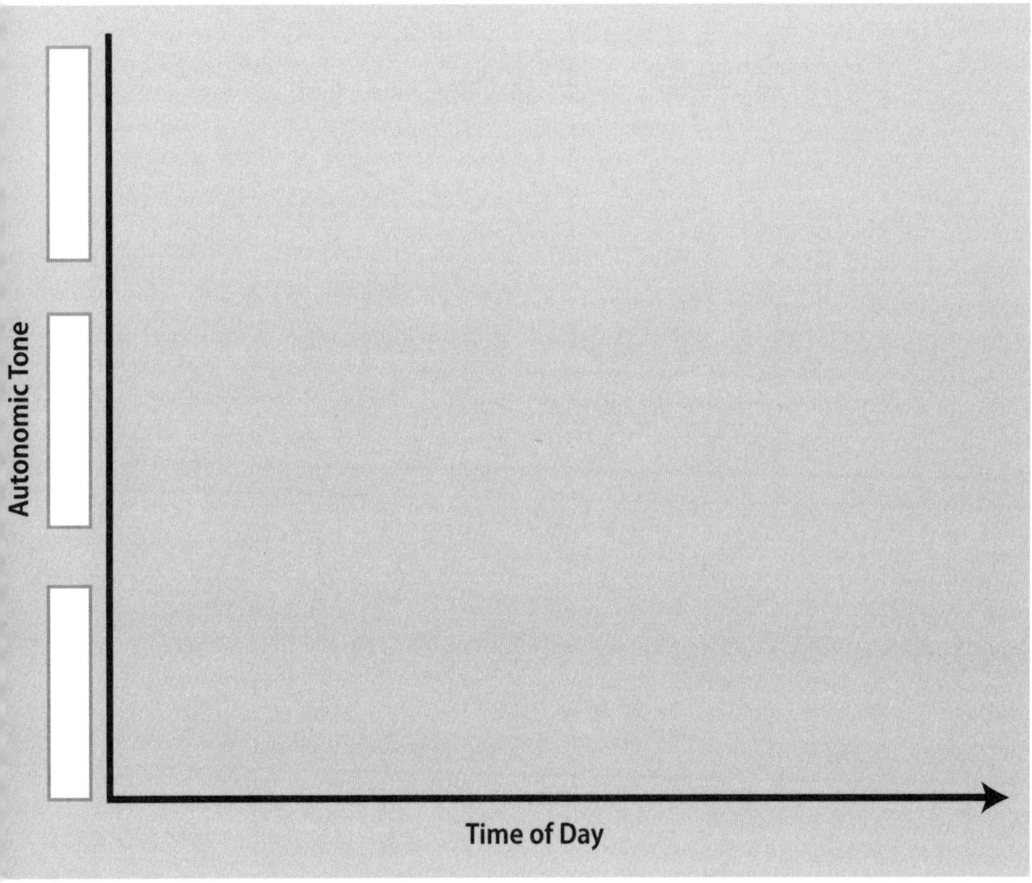

Time and Tone Graph

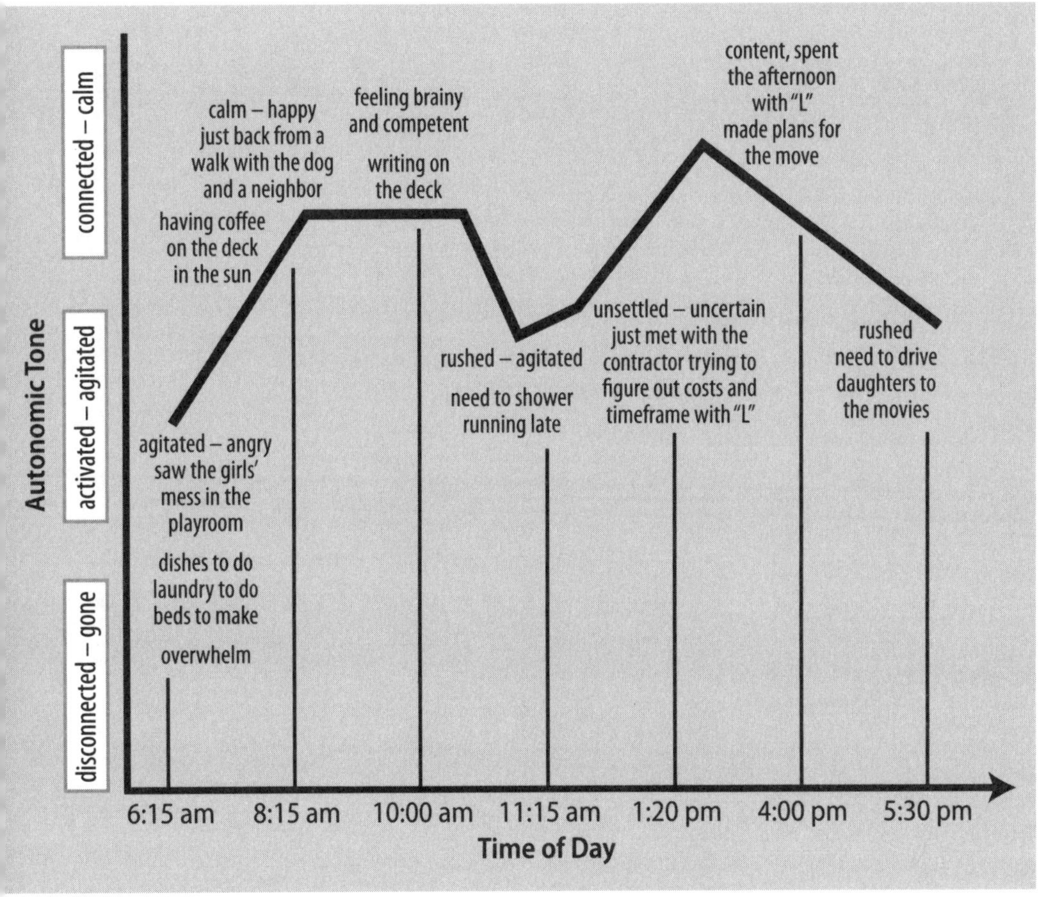

Time and Tone Graph Example

What happened?
Briefly describe the experience. Incudes details of the event and your autonomic responses.

Notice and name the cues of DANGER.
What were the cues of danger in the environment? In your body? Sensed through your Social Engagement System?

Notice and name the cues of SAFETY.
What were the cues of safety in the environment? In your body? Sensed through your Social Engagement System?

Cue Sheet pg 1

How might you **resolve** cues of danger? (environment, body, Social Engagement System)

How could you **invite in** cues of safety? (environment, body, Social Engagement System)

CUE SHEET PG 2

What happened?
Briefly describe the experience. Incudes details of the event and your autonomic responses.

Seeing someone for the first time after a long estrangement. Running into each other without being prepared for the experience.

I felt a slight separation in my body – a sense of beginning dissociation.
I noticed a heaviness in my chest, shallow breathing, and feeling hot.

Notice and name the cues of DANGER.
What were the cues of danger in the environment? In your body? Sensed through your Social Engagement System?

Returning to a place that has lots of memories – everywhere I go there is something that triggers a memory.
Unexpectedly seeing this person and being unprepared for it.

Intense body reaction – flight before I dissociate.

It felt dangerous to see her eyes and hear her voice.
It felt scary to be in the same room with her.

Notice and name the cues of SAFETY.
What were the cues of safety in the environment? In your body? Sensed through your Social Engagement System?

Hearing and seeing the ocean always calms me. This place is surrounded by water, it's all around me. I need to remember to notice it.

I now have skills to track beginning dissociation and interrupt the process.
Keeping my body moving keeps me present.
My breath keeps me out of collapse.

When I look back, there were other people around – there were safe faces to look at and the sound of friends talking and laughing.

Cue Sheet Example pg 1

How might you **resolve** cues of danger? (environment, body, Social Engagement System)

Stay away from the most triggering places.
Be in spaces that let me keep moving – always with an exit nearby.
Plan ahead – try to control contact so that I can predict it and limit it.

Track my autonomic responses in the moment so I know where I am on the ladder and know which resources to use.
Disconnect without dissociating by keeping a safe physical distance.
Pay attention to my breath.

Practice what I could do and say – try it out with a trusted friend.
Make sure I'm with other people who I feel safe with.

How could you **invite in** cues of safety? (environment, body, Social Engagement System)

Stay connected to the sight, sound, and smell of the ocean. I take it for granted since it's all around and remembering to actively soak it in will keep me feeling present. When I'm connected to the ocean I feel grateful and strong.
Carry a striped beach stone as my talisman.
Create a concrete "wheels up" plan. Write it down and carry it in my pocket.

Remain connected to my breath. Breathing has become a predictable way for me to regulate. Trust my autonomic nervous system to let me know what is safe, when to move, when to connect.

Look around the room to find friendly faces – I know in this group there are always kind eyes. Watch for glimmers and take a moment to savor them.
Remember my sisters are always there for me – I can call them whenever I want.

Cue Sheet Example pg 2

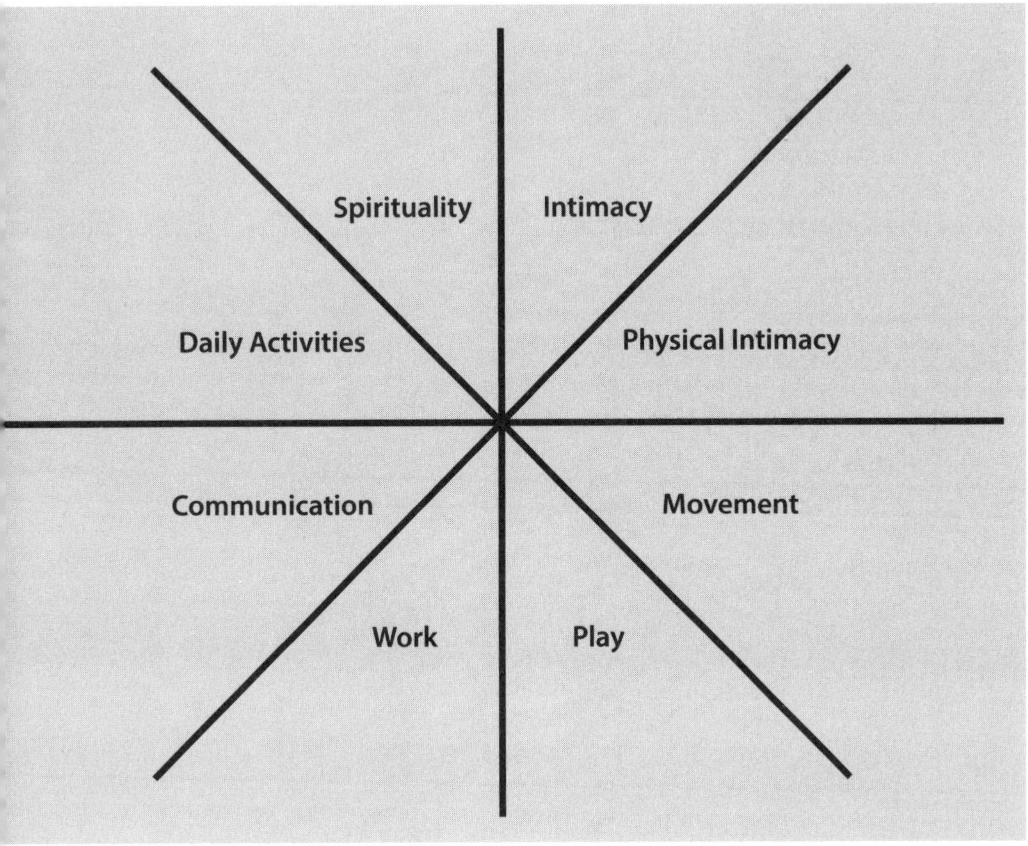

Patterns and Tempo

Identify the two ends of the continuum. Use the boxes to label them. Then move incrementally between the two identifying the "in between" places. Use the space underneath the continuum to write a short comment about each newly identified place.

Continuum

Dorsal Vagal
TIME

Ventral Vagal
NOURISHING
SELF

1. 2. 3. 4. 5. 6. 7. 8. 9.

1. Depleted, void
2. Need to get from one chaotic moment to the next. In a Tasmanian spin!
3. Breathe. "I'm here now." Vagal brake releasing to let me be here for the moment.
4. Back into the chaos as I need to race to the next moment. SNS charge!
5. Feeling depleted again. Too much left undone. Overwhelming to see. Dipping back into DV.
6. Slow down and breathe. Vagal brake releasing so I can see some options. Feeling VV energy.
7. Looking for cues of safety.
8. Ventral vagal energy to help me recognize and regulate. Asking myself, "What matters?"
9. Feeling the light that keeps me regulated. VV nourishment.

Continuum Example

	Attunement	Body Movement	Object	Social Interactive	Imaginative Pretend	Storytelling	Creative Fantasy
Present							
Past							

Patterns of Play: In each category list the ways you played. Identify your past play and present play experiences.

Patterns of Play

	Attunement	Body Movement	Object	Social Interactive	Imaginative Pretend	Storytelling	Creative Fantasy
Present	trouble finding a close friend fear being left behind again	yoga – inverted poses because I love being upside down... reminds me of the joy and freedom I felt diving	my childhood blanket (great memories) a necklace made from three stones found in special places with special people I don't ever take it off, would feel lost without it	being a part of "WOW" (Women On the Water)	I like to imagine a different ending when things get too difficult It's fun to pretend I'm someone else "try it on for size" and see what it feels like	checking people out through telling funny personal stories I need friends who can laugh with me in the difficult times	traveling to offbeat places thinking about living and working far away from here I still use fantasy to escape
Past	I had a best friend until fifth grade... then she found a new one	roller skating swimming and diving I loved to be at the pool all day	my doll "Fizzy" the blanket my godmother made me	out in the neighborhood with my friends out of the house and away from my family going to a friend's house and being part of a "normal" family for an afternoon	my imaginary friend "Mrs. Oh" she was safe and reliable	I lived in stories I told funny stories about myself and my family to keep people out - so they wouldn't look deeper	I dreamed of being a famous athlete traveling around the world my fantasies always included getting away from family and home

Patterns of Play: In each category list the ways you played.
Identify both your past play and present play experiences.

Patterns of Play Example

Personal Play Profile

Attunement	
Body Movement	
Object	
Social Interactive	
Imaginative Pretend	
Storytelling	
Creative Fantasy	

What are your "rules of play"? In each category identify what cues of danger shut down play, what cues of safety support an experience of play, and what beliefs are associated with each category.

Personal Play Profile

Personal Play Profile

Attunement	**Danger:** an unpredictable person, signals that are confusing, a space that is loud, an unexpected mismatch **Belief:** I'm too much, too intense for this person. **Safety:** shared humor, someone who listens **Belief:** I'm fun loving and can bring that into this relationship.
Body Movement	**Danger:** being out of tune with my body, ignoring my limits, feeling pain **Belief:** I'm not disciplined. **Safety:** feeling a flow, no self-consciousness, moving in sync with another person **Belief:** I can trust the way my body moves.
Object	**Danger:** worrying about losing the things I love to play with **Belief:** I can't keep track of things. **Safety:** tangible things I can hold onto that make me smile, things with special memories attached to them **Belief:** I don't need special things to have fun. I like having them but would be ok without them.
Social Interactive	**Danger:** feeling tired, stuck, can't relax, too many people, too much going on in the room **Belief:** I don't know how to do this anymore. I've forgotten how to have fun. **Safety:** being around people who are fun, feeling silly/playful **Belief:** I bring joy to the people I am with. I can initiate play and invite others to join me.

PERSONAL PLAY PROFILE PG 1

Imaginative Pretend	**Danger:** feeling tired, anxious, can't relax and be playful, people who are concrete thinkers **Belief:** I don't know how to do this anymore. **Safety:** feeling playful, other people who are playful **Belief:** Anything is possible.
Storytelling	**Danger:** my stories feel rehearsed, not authentic, people who are somber, always serious **Belief:** I'm telling a story to try and get you to do something or to not take responsibility for something I've done. **Safety:** feeling expansive, creative, being around people who can laugh at themselves **Belief:** I know how to tell a good story that will bring a smile to other people.
Creative Fantasy	**Danger:** comparing myself to others and feel boring and uninspired, being around people who are unimaginative **Belief:** I'll never be able to make a dream come true so why dream. **Safety:** time to daydream, someone to dream with **Belief:** Anything is possible.

What are your "rules of play"? In each category identify what cues of danger shut down play, what cues of safety support an experience of play, and what beliefs are associated with each category.

Personal Play Profile Example pg 2

REFERENCES

Algoe, S. B., & Haidt, J. (2009). Witnessing excellence in action: The "other-praising" emotions of elevation, gratitude, and admiration. *Journal of Positive Psychology, 4*(2), 105–127. doi:10.1080/17439760802650519

Al horr, Y., Arif, M., Katafygiotou, M., Mazroei, A., Kaushik, A., & Elsarrag, E. (2016). Impact of indoor environmental quality on occupant well-being and comfort: A review of the literature. *International Journal of Sustainable Built Environment, 5*(1), 1–11. https://doi.org/10.1016/j.ijsbe.2016.03.006

Anthwal, N., Joshi, L., & Tucker, A. (2013). Evolution of the mammalian middle ear and jaw: Adaptations and novel structures. *Journal of Anatomy, 222*(1), 147–160. doi:10.1111/j.1469-7580.2012.01526.x

Apicella, F., Chericoni, N., Costanzo, V., Baldini, S., Billeci, L., Cohen, D., & Muratori, F. (2013). Reciprocity in interaction: A window on the first year of life in autism. *Autism Research and Treatment, 2013*, 705895. doi:10.1155/2013/705895

Beetz, A., Uvnäs-Moberg, K., Julius, H., & Kotrschal, K. (2012). Psychosocial and psychophysiological effects of human-animal interactions: The possible role of oxytocin. *Frontiers in Psychology, 3*, 234. http://doi.org/10.3389/fpsyg.2012.00234

Belyk, M., & Brown, S. (2016). Pitch underlies activation of the vocal system during affective vocalization. *Social Cognitive and Affective Neuroscience, 11*(7), 1078–1088. doi:10.1093/scan/nsv074

Berger, J. (2016, July 7). The goldilocks theory of product success. *Harvard Business Review.* Retrieved from https://hbr.org/2016/07/the-goldilocks-theory-of-product-success

Bezemer, J., & Kress, G. (2014). Touch: A resource for meaning making. *Australian Journal of Language and Literacy,* 37(2), 77–85.

Blaut, J., Stea, D., Spencer, C., & Blades, M. (2003). Mapping as a cultural and cognitive universal. *Annals of the Association of American Geographers, 93*(1), 165–185.

Bloch-Atefi, A., & Smith, J. (2014). *The effectiveness of body-oriented psychotherapy: A review of the literature.* Melbourne, Australia: PACFA.

Bolwerk, A., Mack-Andrick, J., Lang, F. R., Dörfler, A., & Maihöfner, C. (2014). How art changes your brain: Differential effects of visual art production and cognitive art evaluation on functional brain connectivity. *PLOS ONE, 9*(7), e101035. doi:10.1371/journal.pone.0101035

Brown, R. P., & Gerbarg, P. L. (2005). Sudarshan kriya yogic breathing in the treatment of stress, anxiety, and depression: Part I—neurophysiologic model. *Journal of Alternative and Complementary Medicine, 11*(1), 189–201. doi:10.1089/acm.2005.11.189

Brown, S., & Vaughn, C. (2009). *Play: How it shapes the brain, opens the imagination, and shapes the soul.* New York, NY: Penguin Books.

Brown, D. K., Barton, J. L., & Gladwell, V. F. (2013). Viewing nature scenes positively affects recovery of autonomic function following acute-mental stress. *Environmental Science & Technology, 47*(11). doi:10.1021/es305019p

Bryant, F. B., Chadwick, E. D., & Kluwe, K. (2011). Understanding the processes that regulate positive emotional experience: Unsolved problems and future directions for theory and research on savoring. *International Journal of Wellbeing, 1*(1), 107–126. doi:10.5502/ijw.v1i1.18

Cacioppo, J. (2011, January 25). Psychologist John Cacioppo explains why loneliness is bad for your health. Retrieved from http://www.igsb.

org/news/psychologist-john-cacioppo-explains-why-loneliness-is-bad-for-your-health

Cacioppo, J. T., & Cacioppo, S. (2014). Social relationships and health: The toxic effects of perceived social isolation. *Social and Personality Psychology Compass, 8*(2), 58–72. http://doi.org/10.1111/spc3.12087

Carlson, K., & Shu, S. (2007). The rule of three: How the third event signals the emergence of a streak. *Organizational Behavior and Human Decision Processes, 104*(1), 113–121. https://doi.org/10.1016/j.obhdp.2007.03.004 doi:10.1111/eci.12256

Chanda, M. L., & Levitin, D. J. (2013). The neurochemistry of music. *Trends in Cognitive Sciences, 17*(4), 179–193. doi:10.1016/j.tics.2013.02.007

Charité–Universitätsmedizin Berlin. (2011, May 16). How a person remembers a touch. *ScienceDaily.* Retrieved from http://www.sciencedaily.com/releases/2011/05/110510101048.htm

Chelnokova, O., Laeng, B., Løseth, G., Eikemo, M., Willoch, F., & Leknes, S. (2016). The µ-opioid system promotes visual attention to faces and eyes. *Social Cognitive and Affective Neuroscience, 11*(12), 1902–1909. http://doi.org/10.1093/scan/nsw116

Chinagudi, S., Badami, S., Herur, A., Patil, S., Shashikala, G. V., & Annkad, R. (2014). Immediate effect of short duration of slow deep breathing on heart rate variability in healthy adults. *National Journal of Physiology, Pharmacy, & Pharmacology, 4*(3), 233–235. doi:10.5455/njppp.2014.4.060520141

Copland, A. (1998). *What to listen for in music.* New York, NY: McGraw-Hill.

Craig, A. D. (2009a). How do you feel—now? The anterior insula and human awareness. *Nature Reviews Neuroscience,* 10, 59–70. doi:10.1038/nrn2555

Craig, A. D. (2009b). Emotional moments across time: A possible neural basis for time perception in the anterior insula. *Philosophical Transactions of the Royal Society B: Biological Sciences, 364*(1525), 1933–1942. http://doi.org/10.1098/rstb.2009.0008

Damasio, A. (2005). *Descartes error: Emotion, reason and the human brain.* New York, NY: Penguin Books.

Delong, T. J. (2011). The comparing trap. *Harvard Business Review.* Retrieved from https://hbr.org/2011/06/the-comparing-trap.html

Denworth, L. (2015, July 1). The secret social power of touch. *Scientific American Mind.* Retrieved from https://www.scientificamerican.com/article/touch-s-social-significance-could-be-explained-by-unique-nerve-fibers/

Devereaux, C. (2017). An interview with Dr. Stephen W. Porges. *American Journal of Dance Therapy, 39*(27). doi:10.1007/s10465-017-9252-6

Diego, M., & Field, T. (2009). Moderate pressure massage elicits a parasympathetic nervous system response. *International Journal of Neuroscience, 119*(5), 630–638. doi:10.1080/00207450802329605

Doidge, N. (2015). *The brain's way of healing.* New York, NY: Penguin Books.

Dolcos, S., Sung, K., Argo, J. J., Flor-Henry, S., & Dolcos, F. (2012). The power of a handshake: Neural correlates of evaluative judgments in observed social interactions. *Journal of Cognitive Neuroscience, 24*(12), 2292–2305. doi:10.1162/jocn_a_00295

Domes, G., Steiner, A., Porges, S. W., & Heinrichs, M. (2012). Oxytocin differentially modulates eye gaze to naturalistic social signals of happiness and anger. *Psychoneuroendocrinology, 38*(7). doi:10.1016/j.psyneuen.2012.10.002

Dutton, D. (2010, February). A Darwinian theory of beauty [Video file]. Retrieved from https://www.ted.com/talks/denis_dutton_a_darwinian_theory_of_beauty?language=en

Eisenberger, N. I. (2012). The neural bases of social pain: Evidence for shared representations with physical pain. *Psychosomatic Medicine, 74*(2), 126–135. http://doi.org/10.1097/PSY.0b013e3182464dd1

Eisenberger, N. I., Lieberman, M. D., & Williams, K. D. (2003). Does rejection hurt? An fMRI study of social exclusion. *Science,* 302(5643), 290–292. doi:10.1126/science.1089134

Ewert, A., Klaunig, J., Wang, Z., & Chang, Y. (2016). Reducing levels of stress through natural environments: Take a park; not a pill. *International Journal of Health, Wellness, and Society,* 6(1). doi: 10.18848/2156-8960/CGP/v06i01/35-43

Feldman, R., Singer, M., & Zagoory, O. (2010). Touch attenuates infants' physiological reactivity to stress. *Developmental Science, 13*(2), 271–278. doi:10.1111/j.1467-7687.2009.00890.x

Festinger, L. (1954). A theory of social comparison processes. *Human Relations, 7*, 117–140.

Field, T. (2014). *Touch.* Cambridge, MA: MIT Press.

Filippi, P. (2016). Emotional and interactional prosody across animal communication systems: A comparative approach to the emergence of language. *Frontiers in Psychology, 7*, 1393. http://doi.org/10.3389/fpsyg.2016.01393

Fiske, S. T. (2010). Envy up, scorn down: How comparison divides us. *American Psychologist, 65*(8), 10.1037/0003–066X.65.8.698. http://doi.org/10.1037/0003-066X.65.8.698

Fiske, S. T., Cuddy, A. J. C., & Glick, P. (2007). Universal dimensions of social cognition: Warmth and competence. *Trends in Cognitive Sciences, 11*(2), 77–83. https://doi.org/10.1016/j.tics.2006.11.005

Fosha, D. (2001). The dyadic regulation of affect. *Journal of Clinical Psychology/In Session, 57*(2), 227-42. doi: 10.1002/1097-4679(200102)57:23.0.CO;2-1

Fuchs, T., & Koch, S. C. (2014). Embodied affectivity: On moving and being moved. *Frontiers in Psychology, 5*, 508. http://doi.org/10.3389/fpsyg.2014.00508

Gallace, A., & Spence, C. (2010). The science of interpersonal touch: An overview. *Neuroscience & Biobehavioral Reviews, 34*(2), 246–259. https://doi.org/10.1016/j.neubiorev.2008.10.004

Garland, E., Gaylord, S., & Park, J. (2009). The role of mindfulness in positive reappraisal. *Explore (New York, N.Y.), 5*(1), 37–44. http://doi.org/10.1016/j.explore.2008.10.001

Geller, S. M., & Porges, S. W. (2014). Therapeutic presence: Neurophysiological mechanisms mediating feeling safe in therapeutic relationships. *Journal of Psychotherapy Integration, 24*(3), 178–192. http://dx.doi.org/10.1037/a0037511

Gerbarg, P. L., & Brown, R. P. (2016, November 30). Neurobiology and neurophysiology of breath practices in psychiatric care. *Psychiatric Times.* Retrieved from http://www.psychiatrictimes.com/special-reports/neurobiology-and-neurophysiology-breath-practices-psychiatric-care

Golembiewski, J. (2017). Architecture, the urban environment and severe psychosis: Aetiology. *Journal of Urban Design and Mental Health,* 2(1). Retrieved from http://www.urbandesignmentalhealth.com/journal2-psychosis.html

Graham, L. T., Gosling, S. D., & Travis, C. K. (2015). The psychology of home environments: A call for research on residential space. *Perspectives on Psychological Science, 10*(3), 346–356. doi:10.1177/1745691615576761

Grinde, B., & Patil, G. G. (2009). Biophilia: Does visual contact with nature impact on health and well-being? *International Journal of Environmental Research and Public Health, 2009*(6), 2332–2343. doi:10.3390/ijerph6092332

Haidt, J. (2000). The positive emotion of elevation. *Prevention and Treatment, 3*(3). doi:10.1037/1522-3736.3.1.33c

Hall, S. E., Schubert, E., & Wilson, S. J. (2016). The role of trait and state absorption in the enjoyment of music. *PLOS ONE, 11*(11), e0164029. http://doi.org/10.1371/journal.pone.0164029

Hanson, Rick. (2009). *Buddha's brain: The practical neuroscience of happiness, love, & wisdom.* Oakland, CA: New Harbinger.

Hawkley, L., & Cacioppo, J. (2010). Loneliness matters: A theoretical and empirical review of consequences and mechanisms. *Annals of Behavioral Medicine, 40*(2), 218–227. doi:10.1007/s12160-010-9210-8

Hyde, M. (2013, July 5). The revolution is over: The rude phone users have won. *Guardian.* Retrieved from https://www.theguardian.com/commentisfree/2013/jul/05/revolutioin-rude-mobile-phone-users-won

Inagaki, T.K., & Eisenberger, N. I. (2013). Shared neural mechanisms underlying social warmth and physical warmth. *Psychological Science, 24*(11), 2272–2280. doi:10.1177/0956797613492773

Ijzerman, H., Gallucci, M., Pouw, W. T., Weißgerber, S. C., Van Doesum, N. J., & Williams, K. D. (2012). Cold-blooded loneliness: Social exclusion leads to lower skin temperatures. *Acta Psychologica, 140*(3), 283–238. doi:10.1016/j.actpsy.2012.05.002

Jamieson, J., Mendes, W., & Nock, M. (2012). Improving acute stress responses: The power of reappraisal. *Current Directions in Psychological Science,* 22(1), 51–56. doi:10.1177/0963721412461500

Jerath, R., Crawford, M. W., Barnes, V. A., & Harden, K. (2015). Self-regulation of breathing as a primary treatment for anxiety. *Applied Psychophysiology and Biofeedback, 40*(2), 107–115. doi:10.1007/s10484-015-9279-8

Jordan, A. H., Monin, B., Dweck, C. S., Lovett, B. J., John, O. P., & Gross, J. J. (2011). Misery has more company than people think: Underestimating the prevalence of others' negative emotions. *Personality & Social Psychology Bulletin, 37*(1), 120–135. http://doi.org/10.1177/0146167210390822

Jose, P. E., Lim, B. T., & Bryant, F. B. (2012). Does savoring increase happiness? A daily diary study. *Journal of Positive Psychology,* 7(3), 176–187. http://dx.doi.org/10.1080/17439760.2012.671345

Kahn, P. H., Severson, R. L., & Ruckert, J. H. (2009). The human relation with nature and technological nature. *Current Directions in Psychological Science, 18*(1). doi:10.1111/j.1467-8721.2009.01602.x

Kalyani, B. G., Venkatasubramanian, G., Arasappa, R., Rao, N. P., Kalmady, S. V., Behere, R. V., . . . Gangadhar, B. N. (2011). Neurohemodynamic correlates of "OM" chanting: A pilot functional magnetic resonance imaging study. *International Journal of Yoga, 4*(1), 3–6. http://doi.org/10.4103/0973-6131.78171

Kashdan, T. B., Sherman, R. A., Yarbro, J., & Funder, D. C. (2013). How are curious people viewed and how do they behave in social situations? From the perspectives of self, friends, parents, and unacquainted observers. *Journal of Personality, 81*(2), 142–154. http://doi.org/10.1111/j.1467-6494.2012.00796.x

Keltner, D. (2012, July 31). The compassionate species. Retrieved from http://greatergood.berkeley.edu/article/item/the_compassionate_species

Keltner, D. (2016, May 10). Why do we feel awe? Retrieved from http://greatergood.berkeley.edu/article/item/why_do_we_feel_awe

Keltner, D., & Haidt, J. (2003). Approaching awe, a moral, spiritual, and aesthetic emotion. *Cognition and Emotion, 17*(2), 297–314. doi:10.1080/02699930302297

Kidd, C., Piantadosi, S. T., & Aslin, R. N. (2012). The Goldilocks effect: Human infants allocate attention to visual sequences that are neither too simple nor too complex. *PLOS ONE, 7*(5), e36399. http://doi.org/10.1371/journal.pone.0036399

Kidd, C., Piantadosi, S. T., & Aslin, R. N. (2014). The Goldilocks effect in infant auditory attention. *Child Development, 85*(5), 1795–1804. http://doi.org/10.1111/cdev.12263

Klarer, M., Arnold, M., Günther, L., Winter, C., Langhans, W., & Meyer, U. (2014). Gut vagal afferents differentially modulate innate anxiety and learned fear. *Journal of Neuroscience, 34*(21), 7067–7076. doi:10.1523/JNEUROSCI.0252-14.2014

Kogan, A., Oveis, C., Carr, E. W., Gruber, J., Mauss, I. B., Shallcross, A., . . . Keltner, D. (2014). Vagal activity is quadratically related to prosocial traits, prosocial emotions, and observer perceptions of prosociality. *Journal of Personality and Social Psychology, 107*(6), 1051–1106. doi:10.1037/a0037509

Kok, B. E., & Fredrickson, B. L. (2010). Upward spirals of the heart: Autonomic flexibility, as indexed by vagal tone, reciprocally and prospectively predicts positive emotions and social connectedness. *Biological Psychology, 85*(3), 432–436. doi:10.1016/j.biopsycho.2010.09.005

Kok, B. E., Coffey, K. A., Cohn, M. A., Catalino, L. I., Vacharkulksemsuk, T., Algoe, S. B., . . . Fredrickson, B. L. (2013). How positive emotions build physical health: Perceived positive social connections account for the upward spiral between positive emotions and vagal tone. *Psychological Science, 24*(7), 1123–1132. doi:10.1177/0956797612470827

Krcmarova, J. (2009). E. O. Wilson's concept of biophilia and the environmental movement in the USA. *Klaudyan: Internet Journal of Historical Geography and Environmental History.* Retrieved from http://www.klaudyan.cz/dwnl/200901/01_Krcmarova_pdf.pdf

Levine, P. (2010). *In an unspoken voice: How the body releases trauma and restores goodness.* Berkeley, CA: North Atlantic Books.

Levitin, D. (2016, February 16). Our brains are programmed for music—but is solitary listening keeping us from some of its benefits? *Billboard.* Retrieved from http://www.billboard.com/articles/news/6867464/neuroscientist-daniel-levitin-sonos-listening-study-qa

Li, P., Janczewski, W. A., Yackle, K., Kam, K., Pagliardini, S., Krasnow, M. A., & Feldman, J. L. (2016). The peptidergic control circuit for sighing. *Nature, 530*(7590), 293–297. doi:10.1038/nature16964

Mason, H., Vandoni, M., deBarbieri, G., Codrons, E., Ugargol, V., & Bernardi, L. (2013). Cardiovascular and respiratory effect of yogic slow breathing in the yoga beginner: What is the best approach? *Evidence-Based Complementary and Alternative Medicine, 2013,* 743504. http://dx.doi.org/10.1155/2013/743504

Master, A., Markman, E. M., & Dweck, C. S. (2012). Thinking in categories or along a continuum: Consequences for children's social judgments. *Child Development, 83*(4), 1145–1163. doi:10.1111/j.1467-8624.2012.01774.x

McGarry, L. M. & Russo, F. A. (2011). Mirroring in dance/movement therapy: Potential mechanisms behind empathy enhancement. *Arts in Psychotherapy, 38*(3), 178–184. https://doi.org/10.1016/j.aip.2011.04.005

McRae, A. (2009). The continuing evolution of touch in psychotherapy. *USA Body Therapy Journal, 8*(2), 40–46.

Mehling, W. E., Wrubel, J., Daubenmier, J. J., Price, C. J., Kerr, C. E., Silow, T., . . . Stewart, A. L. (2011). Body awareness: A phenomenological inquiry into the common ground of mind body therapies. *Philosophy, Ethics, and Humanities in Medicine: PEHM, 6,* 6. http://doi.org/10.1186/1747-5341-6-6

Mehta, N. (2011). Mind-body dualism: A critique from a health perspective. *Mens Sana Monographs, 9*(1), 202–209. http://doi.org/10.4103/0973-1229.77436

Milteer, R. M., & Ginsberg, K. R. (2012). The importance of play in promoting healthy child development and maintaining strong parent-child bonds: Focus on children in poverty. *Pediatrics, 129*(1). doi:10.1542/peds.2011-2953

Nichols, W. J., & Cousteau, C. (2014). *Blue mind: The surprising science that shows how being near, in, or under water can make you happier, healthier, more connected, and better at what you do.* New York, NY: Little, Brown.

Nisbet, E., Zelenski, J., & Murphy, S. (2011). Happiness is in our nature: Exploring nature relatedness as a contributor to subjective well-being. *Journal of Happiness Studies,* 12(2):303-322. doi 10.1007/s10902-010-9197-7

Norris, C. J., Larsen, J. T., Crawford, L. E., & Cacioppo, J. T. (2011). Better (or worse) for some than others: Individual differences in the positivity offset and negativity bias. *Journal of Research in Personality, 45*(1), 100–111. https://doi.org/10.1016/j.jrp.2010.12.001

Ogden, P. & Fisher, J. (2015). *Sensorimotor psychotherapy: Interventions for trauma and attachment.* New York, NY: Norton.

Owen, N., Sparling, P. B., Healy, G. N., Dunstan, D. W., & Matthews, C. E. (2010). Sedentary behavior: Emerging evidence for a new health risk. *Mayo Clinic Proceedings, 85*(12), 1138–1141. http://doi.org/10.4065/mcp.2010.0444

Panksepp, J., & Biven, L. (2012). *The archeology of mind: Neuroevolutionary origins of human emotion.* New York, NY: Norton.

Papathanassoglou, E. D., & Mpouzika, M. D. (2012). Interpersonal touch: Physiological effects in critical care. *Biological Research for Nursing, 14*(4), 4310443. doi:10.1177/1099800412451312

Park, G., & Thayer, J. (2014). From the heart to the mind: Cardiac vagal tone modulates top-down and bottom-up visual perception and attention to emotional stimuli. *Frontiers in Psychology, 5*, 278. https://doi.org/10.3389/fpsyg.2014.00278

Payne, P., Levine, P. A., & Crane-Godreau, M. A. (2015). Somatic experiencing: Using interoception and proprioception as core elements of trauma therapy. *Frontiers in Psychology, 6*, 93. http://doi.org/10.3389/fpsyg.2015.00093

Piff, P. K., Dietze, P., Feinberg, M., Stancato, D. M., & Keltner, D. (2015). Awe, the small self, and prosocial behavior. *Journal of Personality and Social Psychology, 108*(6), 883–899. doi:10.1037/pspi0000018

Piper, W. T., Saslow, L. R., & Saturn, S. R. (2015). Autonomic and prefrontal events during moral elevation. *Biological Psychology, 108*, 51–55. https://doi.org/10.1016/j.biopsycho.2015.03.004

Porges, S. W. (n.d.). The polyvagal theory for treating trauma [Webinar]. Retrieved from http://stephenporges.com/images/stephen%20porges%20interview%20nicabm.pdf

Porges, S. W. (1997). Emotion: An evolutionary by-product of the neural regulation of the autonomic nervous system. *Annals of the New York Academy of Sciences, 807*, 62–77. doi:10.1111/j.1749-6632.1997.tb51913.x

Porges, S. W. (2003). The polyvagal theory: Phylogenetic contributions to social behavior. *Physiology & Behavior, 79*, 503–513.

Porges, S. W. (2004, May). Neuroception: A subconscious system for detecting threats and safety. *Washington, DC: Zero to Three.*

Porges, S. W. (2006). How your nervous system sabotages your ability to relate (Ravi Dykema, Interviewer) [Transcript]. Retrieved from http://acusticusneurinom.dk/wp-content/uploads/2015/10/polyvagal_interview_porges.pdf

Porges, S. W. (2009a). The polyvagal theory: New insights into adaptive reactions of the autonomic nervous system. *Cleveland Clinic Journal of Medicine, 76*(Suppl 2), S86–S90. http://doi.org/10.3949/ccjm.76.s2.17

Porges, S. W. (2009b). Reciprocal influences between body and brain in the perception and expression of affect: A polyvagal perspective. In D. Fosha, D. J. Siegel, & M. F. Solomon (Eds.), *The power of emotion: Affective neuroscience, development & clinical practice.* (pp. 27-54) New York, NY: Norton.

Porges, S. W. (2010). Music therapy and trauma: Insights from the polyvagal theory. In K. Stewart (Ed.), *Music therapy and trauma: Bridging theory and clinical practice.* (pp. 3-15) New York, NY: Satchnote Press.

Porges, S. W. (2011a). *The polyvagal theory: Neurophysiological foundations of emotions, attachment, communication, self-regulation.* New York, NY: Norton.

Porges, S. W. (2011b, November). Somatic perspectives on psychotherapy (S. Prengel, Interviewer) [Transcript]. Retrieved from http://stephenporges.com/images/somatic%20perspectives%20interview.pdf

Porges, S. W. (2012). Polyvagal theory: Why this changes everything [Webinar]. In NICABM Trauma Therapy Series. retrieved from: http://www.docucu-archive.com/view/f955e7b912128531339b01a319b1d936/Polyvagal-Theory%3A-Why-This-Changes-Everything.pdf

Porges, S. W. (2013). Beyond the brain: How the vagal system holds the secret to treating trauma [Webinar]. Retrieved from http://stephenporges.com/images/nicabm2.pdf

Porges, S. W. (2015a). Making the world safe for our children: Down-regulating defence and up-regulating social engagement to "optimise" the human experience. *Children Australia, 40*(2), 114–123. doi:10.1017/cha.2015.12

Porges, S. W. (2015b). Play as a neural exercise: Insights from the polyvagal theory. In D. Pearce-McCall (Ed.), *The power of play for mind brain health* (pp. 3–7). Retrieved from http://mindgains.org/

Porges, S. W. (2016, September). Mindfulness and co-regulation [Podcast]. Retrieved from http://activepause.com/porges-mindfulness-regulation/

Porges, S. W. (2017a). *The pocket guide to the polyvagal theory: The transformative power of feeling safe.* New York, NY: Norton

Porges, S. W. (2017b). Vagal pathways: Portals to compassion. In E. M. Seppala, E. Simon-Thomas, S. L. Brown, M. C. Worline, C. D. Cameron, & J. R. Doty (Eds.), *Oxford handbook of compassion science.* (pp. 189-202). New York, NY: Oxford University Press.

Porges S.W, & Carter C. S. (2011). Neurobiology and evolution: Mechanisms, mediators, and adaptive consequences of caregiving. In S. L.

Brown, R. M. Brown, and L. A. Penner (Eds.) *Self interest and beyond: Toward a new understanding of human caregiving* (pp. 53-71). New York: Oxford University Press.

Porges, S. W., & Carter, C. S. (2017). Polyvagal theory and the social engagement system: Neurophysiological bridge between connectedness and health. In P. L. Gerbarg, P. R. Muskin, & R. P. Brown (Eds.), *Complementary and integrative treatments in psychiatric practice.* (pp. 221-240). Arlington, VA: American Psychiatric Association Publishing.

Porges, S. W., & Furman, S. A. (2011). The early development of the autonomic nervous system provides a neural platform for social behaviour: A polyvagal perspective. *Infant and Child Development, 20*(1), 106–118. doi:10.1002/icd.688

Rim, S. Y., Hansen, J., & Trope, Y. (2013). What happens why? Psychological distance and focusing on causes versus consequences of events. *Journal of Personality and Social Psychology,* 104(3), 457–472. doi:10.1037/a0031024

Rudd, M., Vohs, K. D., & Aaker, J. (2012). Awe expands people's perception of time, alters decision making, and enhances well-being. *Psychological Science, 23*(10), 1130–1136. doi:10.1177/0956797612438731

Safran, J. D., Muran, J. C., Samstag, L. W., & Stevens, C. (2001). Repairing alliance ruptures. *Psychotherapy,* 38(4), 406–412. doi: 10.1037/a0022140

Satpute, A. J., Nook, E. C., Narayanan, S., Shu, J., Weber, J., & Ochsner, K. (2016). Emotions in "black and white" or shades of gray? How we think about emotion shapes our perception and neural representation of emotion. *Psychological Science,* 27(11), 1428–1442 doi:10.1177/0956797616661555

Scott, M., Yeung, H. H., Gick, B., & Werker, J. F. (2013). Inner speech captures the perception of external speech. *Journal of the Acoustical Society of America, 133*(4), EL286–292. doi:10.1121/1.4794932

Schäfer, T., Sedlmeier, P., Städtler, C., & Huron, D. (2013). The psychological functions of music listening. *Frontiers in Psychology, 4,* 511. http://doi.org/10.3389/fpsyg.2013.00511

Schröder, M. (2003). Experimental study of affect bursts. *Speech Communication, 40*(1–2), 99–116. https://doi.org/10.1016/S0167-6393(02)00078-X

Schwarz, R. (2018). Energy psychology, polyvagal theory, and the treatment of trauma. In S.W. Porges & D. Dana (Eds.), *Clinical applications of the polyvagal theory: The emergence of polyvagal-informed therapies.* New York, NY: Norton.

Seppala, E., Rossomando, T., & Doty, J. (2013). Social connection and compassion: Important predictors of health and well-being. *Social Research, 80*(2), 411–430. doi:10.1353/sor.2013.0027

Shaltout, H. A., Tooze, J. A., Rosenberger, E., & Kemper, K. J. (2012). Time, touch, and compassion: Effects on autonomic nervous system and well-being. *Explore, 8*(3), 177–184. doi:10.1016/j.explore.2012.02.001

Shiota, M. N., Keltner, D., & Mossman, A. (2009). The nature of awe: Elicitors, appraisals, and effects on self-concept. *Cognition and Emotion, 21*(5). doi:10.1080/02699930600923668

Siegel, D. (2010). *Mindsight: The new science of personal transformation.* New York, NY: Bantam Books.

Simon-Thomas, E. R., Keltner, D. J., Sauter, D., Sinicropi-Yao, L., & Abramson, A. (2009). The voice conveys specific emotions: Evidence from vocal bursts. *Emotion, 9*(6), 838–846. doi:10.1037/a0017810

Slavich, G. M., & Cole, S. W. (2013). The emerging field of human social genomics. *Clinical Psychological Science, 1*(3), 331–348.

Speer, M. E., Bhanji, J. P., & Delgado, M. R. (2014). Savoring the past: Positive memories evoke value representations in the striatum. *Neuron, 84*(4), 847–856. doi:http://dx.doi.org/10.1016/j.neuron.2014.09.028

Stellar, J. E., Cohen, A., Oveis, C., & Keltner, D. (2015). Affective and physiological responses to the suffering of others: Compassion and vagal activity. *Journal of Personality and Social Psychology, 108*(4). doi:10.1037/pspi0000010

Stillman, T. F., Baumeister, R. F., Lambert, N. M., Crescioni, A. W., DeWall, C. N., & Fincham, F. D. (2009). Alone and without purpose: Life loses meaning following social exclusion. *Journal of Experimental Social Psychology, 45*(4), 686–694. http://doi.org/10.1016/j.jesp.2009.03.007

Sumner, T. (2016, April 30). Thinking outside the Goldilocks zone. *Science News.* retrieved from: https://www.sciencenews.org/article/how-alien-can-planet-be-and-still-support-life. doi:10.1017/S0954579416000456

Thomas, J., & McDonagh, D. (2013). Shared language: Towards more effective communication. *Australian Medical Journal, 6*(1), 46–54. http//dx.doi.org/10.4066/AMJ.2013.1596

Tronick, E. Z. (1989). Emotions and emotional communication in infants. *American Psychologist, 44*(2), 112–119.

Tronick, E., & Reck, C. (2009). Infants of depressed mothers. *Harvard Review of Psychiatry, 17*(2), 147–156. doi:10.1080/10673220902899714

Turkle, S. (2015). *Reclaiming the power of conversation: The power of talk in a digital age.* New York, NY: Penguin Press.

van der Kolk, B. (2014). *The body keeps the score: Brain, mind, and body in the healing of trauma.* New York, NY: Penguin Books.

Vickhoff, B., Malmgren, H., Åström, R., Nyberg, G., Ekström, S.R., Engwall, M., . . . Jörnsten, R. (2013). Music structure determines heart rate variability of singers. *Frontiers in Psychology, 4*, 334. http://doi.org/10.3389/fpsyg.2013.00334

Vlemincx, E., Van Diest, I., & Van der Bergh, O. (2012). A sigh following sustained attention and mental stress: Effects on respiratory variability. *Physiology and Behavior, 107*(1), 1–6. https://doi.org/10.1016/j.physbeh.2012.05.013

Vlemincx, E., Taelman, J., Van Diest, I., & Van der Bergh, O. (2010). Take a deep breath: The relief effect of spontaneous and instructed sighs. *Physiology and Behavior, 101*(1), 67–73. https://doi.org/10.1016/j.physbeh.2010.04.015

Watson, N., Wells, T., & Cox, C. (1998). Rocking chair therapy for dementia patients: Its effect in psychosocial well-being and balance. *American Journal of Alzheimer's Disease,* 13, 296-308.

White, M., Smith, A., Humphryes, K., Pahl, S., Snelling, D., & Depledge, M. (2010). Blue space: The importance of water for preference, affect, and restorativeness ratings of natural and built scenes. *Journal of Environmental Psychology, 30*(4), 482–493. https://doi.org/10.1016/j.jenvp.2010.04.004

Williams, L. E., & Bargh, J. A. (2008). Experiencing physical warmth promotes interpersonal warmth. *Science, 322*(5901), 606–607. http://doi.org/10.1126/science.1162548

Williamson, J. B., Porges, E. C., Lamb, D. G., & Porges, S. W. (2015). Maladaptive autonomic regulation in PTSD accelerates physiological aging. *Frontiers in Psychology, 5*, 1571. http://doi.org/10.3389/fpsyg.2014.01571

Yerkes R. M., Dodson J. D. (1908). The relation of strength of stimulus to rapidity of habit-formation. *Journal of Comparative Neurology and Psychology*. 18: 459–482. doi:10.1002/cne.920180503

Yoto, A., Katsuura, T., Iwanaga, K., & Shimomura, Y. (2007). Effects of object color stimuli on human brain activities in perception and attention referred to EEG alpha band response. *Journal of Physiological Anthropology, 26*(3), 373–379. doi:10.2114/jpa2.26.373

INDEX